Fantasy

Fantasy

How It Works

BRIAN ATTEBERY

OXFORD
UNIVERSITY PRESS

OXFORD
UNIVERSITY PRESS

Great Clarendon Street, Oxford, OX2 6DP,
United Kingdom

Oxford University Press is a department of the University of Oxford.
It furthers the University's objective of excellence in research, scholarship,
and education by publishing worldwide. Oxford is a registered trade mark of
Oxford University Press in the UK and in certain other countries

Published in the United States of America by Oxford University Press
198 Madison Avenue, New York, NY 10016, United States of America

British Library Cataloguing in Publication Data
Data available

Library of Congress Control Number: 2021944922

ISBN 978-0-19-285623-4

DOI: 10.1093/oso/9780192856234.001.0001

Printed and bound in the UK by
TJ Books Limited

Acknowledgments

Thanks to Sylvia Kelso and Salvatore Proietti for permission to include quotations from correspondence.

Chapter 5 is based on a talk titled "James Tiptree Jr. Book Club; or, A Mitochondrial Theory of Literature," given at the 2016 Tiptree Symposium at the University of Oregon, which honored Ursula K. Le Guin. My thanks to Linda Long for organizing the symposium and to Andrea Hairston, Salvatore Proietti, and Ellen Klages for their helpful suggestions. An earlier version was published online at Tor.com on December 12, 2016: www.tor.com/2016/12/12/the-james-tiptree-jr-book-club-or-a-mitochondrial-theory-of-literature/

Contents

Introduction

Speaking of Fantasy

The nature of fantasy literature keeps changing. New voices come into the field, new traditions are drawn upon, innovations from other genres cross over, markets shift, social and philosophical concerns are different. A comprehensive survey from a decade or two ago now feels like a threadbare blanket covering some spots but leaving others exposed. And theories of fantasy developed to fit the eras of George MacDonald and William Morris or, more recently, Diana Wynne Jones and Terry Pratchett must be reformulated to fit Marlon James, Ken Liu, Aliette de Bodard, and Nnedi Okorafor. Yet the newer writers are also responding to their predecessors; there is continuity as well as change. This book is a snapshot of the current moment but it is also an attempt to read the present through the past and the past in the present.

Fantasy in any era presents some of the same challenges: to go outside conventional notions of the real, to trace connections that evade commonsense thought, and to tell lies that ring true. The answers keep shifting but the questions are pretty much inescapable. I believe that they all come down to variations on two central lines of inquiry. First, how does fantasy mean? How can a form of storytelling based on altering physical laws and denying facts about the past be at the same time a source of insight into human nature and the workings of the world? Second, what does fantasy do? What kind of social, political, cultural, intellectual work does it perform in the world—the world of the reader, that is, not that of the characters?

Each chapter of this book addresses these questions by focusing on a particular aspect of fantastic world-building and storytelling. It is impossible to separate those two activities because fantasy creates story-worlds: narrated spaces in which causality and character and consequence are inextricably entwined. This notion of a world that is also a set of narrative practices and possibilities is very close to Mikhail Bakhtin's concept of chronotope or time-space. Story-worlds are different from settings as perceived in realistic fiction—though not completely different. Real-world settings and plots are always more conventional, more genre-driven than they appear. It's just that the setting of a non-fantastic story can be assimilated into and extended by our knowledge of mundane history, geography, and society. Dickens's London is adjacent to, though not identical to, the Victorian London reconstructed by historians. Looking at realism from the standpoint of fantasy can make us more aware of the choices that go into the illusion that any stories adequately represent or reproduce reality. In realism, a lot of work goes into concealing the constructedness of the situation and the mechanisms of the plot. The subgenre of children's literature known as the family story is a good example of this willed invisibility. It is also a test case for the idea that fiction cannot be both realistic and fantastic at once. My first two chapters are thus mirror images of one another. The first asks how fantasy is true, the second looks at the artifice that underlies one variety of realism.

Chapter three is about the mythic sources of fantasy: something I have previously devoted an entire book to. This time around I'm looking at the way contemporary fantasies address the clash between mythic systems. In the modern world, particularly in urban environments, groups who might once have lived in isolation from one another and thus never faced serious challenges to their world views or the sacred stories through which those world views are passed on, now live beside and interact with people with radically different cultural narratives. The integrative structure that fantasy inherits from fairy tale offers glimpses of reconciliation between competing stories and the people whose understanding is based on those stories. Helene Wecker's *The Golem and the Jinni* (2013), for example, depicts diverse groups of immigrants in early 20th-century New York City and imagines that they have brought with them not only their foodways and family structures but also their supernatural beings. If a single neighborhood can house both a Jewish homunculus and an Arabic fire spirit, then interactions will extend from shop and street corner to the realms of the Platonic ideal and the divine. Neighbors nod to one another and universes collide, perhaps to find some sort of detente. Fantasy offers ways to situate conflicting beliefs within alternate narrative frameworks—alternate in the sense of both "other" and "alternating."

Chapter four focuses on the dynamics of story: the mechanism that impels the narrative and engages the reader. This narrative mainspring is usually described in terms of conflict, and yet conflict is only one form of resistance to the characters' desires, one hurdle between them and a happy ending. Most uses of the word are metaphorical: the "conflict" between humans and nature, for instance, is something else entirely. Fantasy offers other ways to engage us, to keep us in suspense, to reward our anxieties. By doing so, it offers alternative scripts for interaction, ways to bypass rather than engender conflict. A major example here is Patricia McKillip's *The Bards of Bone Plain* (2010), which frustrates attempts to read it in terms of an overreaching conflict but richly rewards analysis of its multiple forms of illusion and misperception.

In chapter five, I propose a way to look at the interconnectedness of literature. Source and influence studies, theories of intertexuality and met-afiction, and the very notion of genre are all attempts to explain how works of literature talk with one another. Like human beings, they assemble selves out of bits of other subjectivities and echoes of other voices. My proposal focuses on one particular branch of the fantastic, science fiction, and yokes together two metaphors. In the first, literature is a book club, a social structure built around shared experiences and an exchange of insights. In the second, texts are cells deriving their energy from other organisms that they have taken in and incorporated into their metabolisms: mitochondria. The latter metaphor is fetched pretty far and undoubtedly dependent on my imperfect understanding of the science involved. But what could be more appropriate for an exploration of science fiction, which does glorious things with imperfectly understood science?

With chapter six, the emphasis shifts from the semiotics of fantasy to its social functions. Part of the cultural work of the fantastic is to tell us that things need not be the way they are. The world could be, if not better, at least run on different principles. We generally separate this function off into a separate genre—utopia, accompanied by its evil twin dystopia. Yet the utopian impulse runs through many forms of the fantastic, from arcadian romance to science fiction. In this chapter, I look at the young adult dystopia, which became a publishing fad in the early years of this century in the wake of Suzanne Collins's wildly popular Hunger Games trilogy. Taking cues from Tom Moylan's notion of the critical utopia and Ursula K. Le Guin's sorting out of yin and yang utopias, I suggest we look for the glimpse of hope in the darkest dystopias and seek out stories that offer more positive social visions even for teenagers, who, as my friend Mike Levy used to say, love dystopias because they live in dystopia.

Chapter seven moves to fairy tales, and specifically to fairy-tale retellings by male writers. The impact of fairy tales on girls and women has been reported extensively and studied intensively by cultural critics, folklorists, and scholars and producers of literature. Important examples include Kay

Stone's 1975 essay "Things Walt Disney Never Told Us," Jack Zipes's anthology *Don't Bet on the Prince* (1987), and Angela Carter's subversive takes on Perrault's tales in her collection *The Bloody Chamber* (1979). It wasn't until I was teaching a course in gender and fantasy at Hollins University, and one of my students asked where were the fairy tales for abused boys, that I began to realize how little had attention had been paid to uses of fantasy for exploring and revising models of masculinity. In this chapter I look at stories by Neil Gaiman, Michael Cunningham, Hans Christian Andersen, and other men who have employed fairy-tale motifs in exposing damaging patterns of masculine behavior and attempting to construct more eutopian models of gender.

Chapter eight comes back to fantasy proper and asks what is political about the form itself. Is fantasy an inherently reactionary genre, as many (especially those who contrast it with science fiction) claim, or do its disruptions and revisions of the world offer something politically progressive or even radical? The trial run for this chapter was an address from a couple of decades ago that I titled "The Politics (if any) of Fantasy." In the meantime, both the political landscape and the genre have changed. I have dropped the parenthetical quibble and written a new analysis that, though tacitly in dialogue with the original speech, brings in a number of new examples and a new framework based on the idea of fantasy's particular affordances. Considering fantasy as a tool, what is it good for, and why, with regard to political analysis and activism?

Chapter nine is about what fantasy has to offer in the way of addressing fear. It may not be obvious that the impetus for this chapter, too, was political. Increasingly, fear and suspicion are roused by politicians and media conglomerates to attract supporters and subscribers and to keep them in line. If you can make strangers look like enemies and enemies look like monsters, you can justify any form of abuse—and make people pay for their own oppression. Fear turns off rational thought and alters perceptions; it can also be exciting and even addictive. There are works of fantasy that resort to pushing these sorts of emotional buttons, but the genre also offers ways to turn mindless fear into something else. Anyone who works through the fantasies of Tolkien, Le Guin, or their peers—or rather, anyone who lets those fantasies work through them—will find new resources to deal with fears great and small, even *timor mortis*, the dread of death.

These chapters represent my usual working method. I'll notice a loose thread in the fabric of literature, start tugging at it, see where the seams come apart, and ask what that tells us about the original garment. If I'm lucky, some sort of thesis emerges along the way, but it's never something I started out to prove, nor do I begin with a particular theory that I want to demonstrate. This method doesn't make it easy to extract the core ideas for application elsewhere. Accordingly, I have added a short final chapter summarizing discoveries, as plainly stated and as logically organized as I can make them, my very modest version of a Wittgensteinian *tractatus*. I would not recommend skipping ahead to this chapter for the good stuff: the fun is in the unfolding, at least for me in writing, and, in my experience, for audiences as well. The summary may be most useful for people who want to raise objections, since I make all my claims there as baldly as possible.

And I know that some will disagree, since I have tried all these ideas out on audiences. The title of this introduction is literal. Each chapter is based on a public talk about something related to what John Clute calls fantastika, meaning the larger territory of the fantastic, which extends from fairy tale to utopian science fiction. I have been fortunate enough to have many chances to think out loud, in public, about the literature of the unreal. That means I have watched audiences respond with varying mixtures of amusement, boredom, surprise, confusion, and enlightenment. When invited to speak on the same subject more than once, I've had the chance to try out different formulations, to throw out obvious clangers, and to update references. I have also had to listen to myself repeatedly. Since no one is easier to bore than oneself, I have been motivated to be more succinct, more concrete, more entertaining. I've grown conscious of habits of speech and thought, but also noticed lines of inquiry I didn't realize I was pursuing. Two of those emerged over time to become the core questions of this entire project: how fantasy means and what it does.

The first question echoes a title by John Ciardi: *How Does a Poem Mean?* (1959). Ciardi, a practical critic in the tradition of I. A. Richards, rightly shifted the emphasis from *what* poetry means to *how*, since any poem worth the breath it takes to utter it means both too many things to reckon, and nothing but itself. "Meanings" as we usually assign to them to poetry, are interpretations, and thus translations of the poem into more expository, less powerful language. Despite the well-known Italian saying about translation as betrayal—*traduttore, traditore*—some interpretations are not so much traitorous as illuminating, never replacing the poem itself but embellishing and enhancing our readings of it, like illuminations in a medieval manuscript. With fantasy, the problem is less with interpretation than with application. A mode that begins by denying its own veracity is hard to pin down to any truth. How can an unreal world represent real experience?

What do elves and dragons have to do with the price of eggs or the value of friendship?

Since a problem is also an opportunity, I take fantasy's apparent disavowal of reference, relevance, and realism as an invitation to think laterally, symbolically, and structurally. In the chapters that follow, I am deeply indebted to the insights of fantasy writers such as J. R. R. Tolkien, George MacDonald, and Ursula K. Le Guin, as well as to fellow readers and scholars of the fantastic. I have been speaking of fantasy—and listening to others speak about it—for pretty much my entire academic life. Each of these chapters is an extension of a conversation begun in a classroom or at a gathering such as the International Conference on the Fantastic in the Arts. Each is full of borrowings from and unconscious echoes of my students, friends, and colleagues. Many of them were in the audiences I was speaking to as I developed impressions into more formal arguments. They didn't hesitate to pin me down or correct my worst mistakes. I am grateful to have had the opportunity to look people in the eye as I made statements about fantasy's capacity for meaning, statements that often felt outrageous or banal or both at once when I wrote them, but which sometimes seemed to strike a chord in listeners.

If my first question is indebted to Ciardi, my second is an outright theft from Jane Tompkins, whose book *Sensational Designs: The Cultural Work of American Fiction, 1790–1850* (1986) introduced me to the idea that literature might actually *do* something other than just sit there and look pretty. The word "work" might make literature sound earnest and drab, but if we think of fiction not as performing good works like a charitable Victorian but as working *on* us, changing us, challenging us, and enabling us to remake the world, then Tompkins's notion of cultural work becomes a powerful tool for investigating power and pretense and injustice and ignorance through the reading of literature. And, yes, fantasy too performs work in the world, though perhaps not in ways as obvious as Tompkins's core example *Uncle Tom's Cabin*, which made it impossible to claim that slavery was anything but evil. Fantasy tends to work indirectly, just as it means obliquely. And its work is bound up in its playfulness: to read fantasy attentively and seriously is to value its capacity for fun and games. It often works—that is, does its work—by undercutting the solemnity with which we approach love, or authority, or the gods.

So I have been going around saying to audiences that fantasy does this or that, and I can attest that it does those things for at least some of the people who listened and questioned and reacted. Their nods and frowns and laughter have shaped this book. Criticism is conversation, as Kenneth Burke reminded us with his parable about learning to write critically: the beginning critic has just entered a room where a lively discussion has been going on for some time and must listen, gradually venture a comment or two, and adapt to the tone and temper of the room. With some literary topics, that conversation is pretty obscure, owned by a few cognoscenti and couched in insider language. But with fantasy, the conversation sprawls from classrooms to coffee shops to basements where a lively game of Dungeons and Dragons has been going on for years. People read fantasy for pleasure, and they talk about it online and IRL. That is both a challenge and a boon to the academic critic—which is to say, to me. When I write about fantasy, I know I am making claims about something people care about and something about which my listeners might have exhaustive knowledge. If those people matter, then fantasy matters.

Earlier work on fantasy—and not just mine—tended toward the apologetic. Going back at least to Tolkien and Lewis, commentators on the fantastic could assume a skeptical reception from the literary establishment. Hence the need to establish a pedigree for modern fantasy: this is the stuff Homer sang and Shakespeare's troupe played; modern fantasy deserves respect as the true heir to medieval romance and surrealism and contemporary magical realism! All that is still true but it's less necessary: the battle has been won in all but a few snobbish magazines and classrooms where aging professors lecture from yellowing notes. Fantasy pervades modern culture, and not just print culture. Now it seems to me that a more urgent defense is needed to justify studying stories at all. The humanities, including the once respected English major, are under attack from politicians and career counselors and bean-counting administrators. Never mind how many studies show the career benefits—even in the business world—of studying history and philosophy and languages and literatures. There may be a political motivation behind this attack: people who read well and carefully are harder to fool. They are likely to think for themselves, and to empathize with the Other who is being so carefully set up as a scapegoat.

So how does fantasy fit into this new battle plan? No longer outcast within elite culture, it may well be the humanities' new champion. Its pervasiveness might well be the strongest argument for the value of making up and studying stories. One of Ursula K. Le Guin's short stories, "Ether, OR," (1995, about a little Oregon town that wanders from mountains to desert to seacoast), is dedicated "To the Narrative Americans." We are all Narrative Americans, or Africans, or Australians; we are all descended from storytelling ancestors with whom we might or might not share blood or genes. It behooves us to know ourselves and our cultural DNA. One of the oldest strands of that DNA is visionary storytelling, which is to say, fantasy. By speaking of fantasy, we pass it on and maybe give it a boost along the way.

Even if I had room to thank everyone with whom I've had instructive and encouraging conversations over the years, I would be sure to forget someone important, so I won't try to list them all. I owe special thanks, however, to those who made it possible for me to spend half of 2019 as Leverhulme Visiting Professor at the University of Glasgow, with frequent excursions to other parts of the UK and France. A majority of these chapters were tested on audiences during that stay. Rob Maslen wrote the proposal which the Leverhulme Trust funded; Head of School Alice Jenkins was tremendously supportive. Farah Mendlesohn, Maria Nikolajeva, Andrew Butler, and Marek Oziewicz offered invaluable assistance and advice. Students, faculty, and staff at the School of Critical Studies were amazing, as were my hosts everywhere I went. I have had wonderful conversations closer to home with my graduate students and assistants on the *Journal of the Fantastic in the Arts*: Monty Vierra, Kristi Austin, Tiffany Brooke Martin, Jennifer Cox, Paul Williams. You are all my collaborators, but the mistakes are mine alone.

1

How Fantasy Means

The Shape of Truth

It cannot help having some meaning; if it have proportion and harmony it has vitality, and vitality is truth. The beauty may be plainer in it than the truth, but without the truth the beauty could not be, and the fairytale would give no delight.

George MacDonald, "The Fantastic Imagination", 1893

Fantasy is the lie that speaks truth. The lying part is easy to point to: dragons, spells, places that never were. The question of how fantasy tells truth is a little trickier, and more interesting. I will suggest three ways. First, it can be mythically true: true to the traditional beliefs and narratives through which people have long understood the world and ourselves. Mythic stories not only delineate the universe but also authorize social structures like clans, classes, and gender roles as well as rites and religious obligations. They are tremendously important whether we believe in them or not, but they often come packaged in ways that signify the past rather than the present or the future. They reside in books, covered in footnotes and dust, rather than emerging from living performance: dance, ritual theater, painting in sand or mud, stories recounted by elders. In *Stories about Stories* (2014), I argued that fantasy is one of the main techniques for reimagining our relationships with traditional myth—for instance, trying to move a mythic idea out of what Raymond Williams calls residual culture and into dominant or emergent culture (Williams 1977, 122).

A second way fantasy can be true is metaphorically. A dragon might not be a dragon but a human tyrant, or a desire to talk with animals, or an uncontrollable force of nature like a tidal wave or a volcano. Or all of those things at once, since a single text can support more than one analogical reading. This is the kind of reading that can look like allegory, but Tolkien warns us against equating the two. Allegories set up a one-to-one correspondence between, say, a historical event and a fantastic quest, and they are essentially closed systems. But metaphors, according to George Lakoff and

Mark Johnson in *Metaphors We Live By* (1980), are ways of using one entire realm of experience to puzzle out another, as when we compare love to a battleground. They are open-ended: limited only by our familiarity with what Lakoff and Johnson call the source domain and our ability to imagine the target domain. Most importantly, metaphors carry us across the gap between the known and the unknown. Metaphor is a mode of thought, a way to comprehend new experiences in terms of older ones without claiming identity between them—even though the classic verbal formula for a metaphor looks like a statement of identity: my love is a rose, your boss is a pig, the day is on fire. All those metaphors depend not only on our recognition of the aptness of the comparison but also on the incompleteness of the equation: on the "not really" implied in the "is." If I actually fell in love with a flower or you truly worked for a barnyard animal, there would be no shock of discovery.

Many of the core functions in fantasy—which is to say, the magical operations—can be read as literalized metaphors. George MacDonald, whose comments on fantasy and truth are quoted at the top of this chapter, understood this very well. His most transparent example is the tale "The Light Princess" (1864), in which the title character lacks gravity, both literally and figuratively. The metaphor is deftly sustained from the early scene in which the infant princess is inadequately secured to her crib and nearly floats out the window to the resolution in which love and sorrow finally anchor her to the earth. Lightness and weight, levity and gravity, restriction and freedom are running themes throughout, as MacDonald reminds us that the linkage is already there in our language but that we forget to imagine it concretely. He gives us back the living metaphor and at the same time reminds us that the claim "Love is Gravity" is as untrue as it is true, even according to the ground rules of his fantastic tale. To literalize a metaphor is not to collapse it into a tautology.

Many metaphors, and especially the ones we find in tales like MacDonald's, come from folk tradition, as myths do. Traditional riddles are based on unexpected metaphoric linkages: an egg is a box with a golden secret inside, silence is the thing that can be broken just by saying its name. Because such riddling is rare in contemporary culture, we are less adept at thinking metaphorically than our ancestors were. Folklorist Barre Toelken makes a strong case for the sophisticated metaphoric cognition recorded within traditional ballads such as "One Morning in May." Traditional singers and their audiences didn't need scholars to tell them that a fiddle and bow might stand for body parts, or that one could talk about sex in terms of making hay or plucking cherries. As Toelken says of a ballad in which a fiddle is smuggled out of Italy hidden in the fiddler's pants,

> The flap of the pants does indeed conceal something, but it is perfectly clear to everyone just what is being concealed. The concealment itself is not a secret, nor is it a euphemism. It is a culturally meaningful way of playing with what everyone knows is there.   (19)

What flatfooted, Freudian explanations of traditional songs and stories lose is the playfulness that comes from saying and not saying at the same time, and from relishing the paradox of the *is* that *isn't*.

This playful ambiguity carries over from traditional narratives to literary adaptations and imitations of them—that is, to modern, myth-based fantasy. Riddles and fairy tales are not myths, but they share with myth a complex perspective on meaning: in all of these oral forms, any object can take on unexpected significance, usually coded as magic, as the story surrounding it begins to generate meanings beyond the literal. Some images are almost impossible to separate from their mythic avatars: doves, flames, drops of blood. Others are unlikely bearers of metaphoric weight and yet in the right narrative frame, they begin to whisper oracularly and to offer glimpses of the numinous: a handful of pomegranate seeds in the story of Persephone, a spider's web in Navajo creation stories.

In that sense, all myths are also riddles, to which the answers are (depending on the seeker's questions) God, spirit, the universe, fate, ourselves. Riddles, in turn, are games, but they are games that can suddenly grow terrifyingly portentous. A number of fantasies incorporate traditional riddles and riddling ballads. Examples include *The Hobbit* (1937), with the riddling contest between Bilbo and Gollum; Ellen Kushner's *Thomas the Rhymer* (1990), in which the protagonist must solve ballads such as "The Famous Flower of Servingmen" and "The Unquiet Grave" as if they were riddles about his own experience; Diana Wynne Jones's *Fire and Hemlock* (1984), which challenges the reader with metaphoric connections between the heroine's life and the ballads of "Tam Lin" and "Thomas the Rhymer"; and Edward Fenton's children's fantasy *The Nine Questions* (1959), which takes its situation and structure from the first two ballads in Francis James Child's authoritative collection, "Riddles Wisely Expounded," and "The Elfin Knight." That last example (a lovely book, sadly forgotten) demonstrates that not only are the first two of my forms of fantastic truth, myth and metaphor, closely related, but the third, structure, is as well. Each of Fenton's chapters is modeled after a verse of the ballad; each verse poses a riddle; the final riddle unlocks the meaning of all.

The third kind of truth in fantasy is the one I want to explore in more depth here. Fantasy can be structurally true. It represents the shape of the world, and especially the shape of change. Such change can be reflected in the grammar of titles, with their frequent beginnings and endings: *The Ice Is Coming* (Patricia Wrightson, 1977), *The Dark Is Rising* (Susan Cooper, 1973), *Cloud's End* (Sean Stewart, 1996), *The End of the Game* (Sheri S. Tepper, 1986), *The Beginning Place* (Ursula K. Le Guin, 1980). Le Guin's title also shows how change over time can be represented spatially: with a place that is also a moment of transformation. Fantasy bookshelves are full (at least mine are) of titles naming liminal spaces: doors, gates, paths, roads, woods. If there is no word in the title designating a cosmic shift or precession, or the spatialized equivalent of one of those, the plot will almost inevitably hinge upon a prophetic utterance or catchphrase leading to a change of regime and scenes of destruction and recreation. This may seem like an obvious point: of course there is change; every story involves change. Yet the kinds of change represented in fantasy differ from the altered circumstances in realistic fiction, which more often involve the characters' external circumstances or inner lives rather than the sort of shake-up that alters the way the world works.

Again, such shifts can be portrayed in terms of transformed spaces rather than, or in addition to, changes over time. A good example is the wave of magic that rises in Elfland and sweeps over the previously mundane realm of Erl at the end of Lord Dunsany's *The King of Elfland's Daughter* (1924):

> And on the one side she saw the fields we know, full of accustomed things, and on the other, looking down from her height, she saw, behind the myriad-tinted border, the deep green elfin foliage and Elfland's magical flowers, and things that delirium sees not, nor inspiration, on Earth; and the fabulous creatures of Elfland prancing forward; and, stepping across our fields and bringing Elfland with her, the twilight flowing from both her hands, which she stretched out a little from her, was her own lady the Princess Lirazel coming back to her home. (237)

The power of this scene is in the simultaneous senses of recovery and loss it entails. Time has been traded away for eternity, and it is not entirely a good bargain. Elfland comes to Erl as Birnam Wood comes to Dunsinane, with all the consequence but none of the fakery. It is no accident that Dunsany describes the change in terms of different ways of experiencing time: "it came with all manner of memories, old music and lost voices, sweeping back again to our old fields what time had driven from Earth" (236). Anything that conveys decrepitude or loss gives way to agelessness and flowers blooming out of season, and the result is not so much comfort as eeriness. One island of mortality remains, a monastery around which the magical wave splits and passes, and it is described in a way that suggests all that Elfland lacks:

> For the sound of his bell beat back the rune and the twilight for a little distance all round. There he lived happy, contented, not quite alone, amongst his holy things, for a few that had been cut off by that magical tide lived on the holy island and served him there. And he lived beyond the age of ordinary men, but not to the years of magic.   (241)

Tolkien picked up on this contrast between mortal men, who long for deathlessness, and elves, who long for an escape from deathlessness. Yet in neither Tolkien nor Dunsany is it just a theme, but rather a structuring device for plot and setting and sequence, which are all of a piece. This is what M. M. Bakhtin means by *chronotope*: the time that is also space, and a corresponding range of possible character types (to occupy the space) and incidents (to take up the time). Bakhtin's chronotopes are features of genres, and the representation of the structure of change is something the fantasy chronotope does exceedingly well.

But what does it mean? How are we to take an inundation by magic as a truth about our own lives? We are none of us elves; our temptation is always going to be that of mortal beings rather than weary immortals.

Again, we can look to myth and see similar world-remakings: the Flood in Genesis; the succession of ages in Hindu myth from a golden Time of Truth to Kali Yuga, the Age of Strife; the advent of Ragnarök, the Norse Twilight of the Gods. Each of these transformations can be taken as a literal representation of the ancient past or a prophecy of end times, but it can also be seen as a way of locating ourselves in time and in the universe. The transformation is in the self as much as in the world, and fantasy provides a way to depict the structures even of inner changes like growth and desire and selfhood as well as more visible ones like the building of a castle or the fall of a kingdom.

Here it is worth pointing out a fundamental difference between form and structure. Form is evident on the surface, visible to the naked eye. For instance, two kinds of wings—that of a dragonfly and that of a bat—look equivalent in form and yet their inner anatomy and evolutionary history are nothing alike. Two houses can have the same profile and the same footprint on the ground, even be covered with the same paint or plaster, and yet be radically different in construction. Realism is very good at depicting form: social forms, forms of selfhood. Fantasy is better at probing hidden structure: fundamental building blocks and the way they articulate.

In another fairy tale by George MacDonald, *The Princess and the Goblin* (1872/1893), Princess Irene lives in a building that is in a perpetual state of transition: "a large house, half castle, half farmhouse, on the side of another mountain, about half way between its base and its peak" (1). Growing up, she is only aware of the main floors, until one day she gets lost and comes across a mysterious stairway leading to a tower where she meets a woman who is both old and beautiful, who introduces herself as Irene's great-great-grandmother. None of the staff are aware of this mysterious grandmother, who keeps a flock of pigeons as messengers, has a lamp that shines through the walls like a beacon, and spins a thread so fine as to be invisible—all forms of guidance for the Princess and the young miner Curdie who comes to be her friend and companion in adventure.

Beneath the house, by contrast, a gang of goblins has been tunneling through the foundations with the intention of kidnapping the Princess to be their prince's bride. The goblins are crude and impulsive, capable of violence but also comically inept. The place they break through into the house, significantly, is the wine cellar, where the butler is able to distract them by offering drink.

The Princess's house is thus arranged in tiers by class, upstairs-downstairs fashion, but also by virtue or wisdom. At the very top is the great-great-grandmother, wise and magical; at the bottom are the animalistic goblins, below even the servants in the kitchen; Princess Irene lives in between and is the only one who can move between the ranks, threatened by the goblins but protected by her ancestor. It is tempting—though anachronistic—to read the whole set-up as a Freudian allegory. Down in the depths is the id; up top is the superego; in between is Irene the ego, negotiating between primal appetites and societal constraints. But we don't need Freud to find symbolism in this edifice; MacDonald was trained as a minister but also educated in science; he attended lectures in medicine at the University of Edinburgh, where theories of the unconscious were being worked out before Freud. He was quite aware both of the power of symbols and of the tricks the brain can play upon itself, and many of his stories incorporate striking symbols of the psyche: the Golden Key that leads Mossy and Tangle on a lifelong quest in the story with that title (1867); the animal hooves and paws that Curdie is able to perceive under the hands of evildoers in the sequel to *Princess*; and especially the egglike space—essentially a sensory deprivation chamber—to which the title character of *Lilith* (1895) retreats to contemplate her own ego.

If we think of the self as a house, other forms of literature than fantasy are better at showing us its outward aspects. Realism confronts us with the daily travails, the emotions, the economic and social exchanges that we might think are the whole story. But fantasy can do something quite different. It looks at the soul from high above the roof, from deep in the foundations, from inside the walls themselves. By renouncing surface fidelity, a fantastic tale can reveal fundamental patterns of stress and support. It shows us the laying of foundation stones. It shows us where fatal cracks will appear, and what might crawl out of the ruins. Edgar Allan Poe's "The Fall of the House of Usher" (1839) is a perfect example of that last, and it is no accident that "House of Usher" is an ambiguous phrase, designating both the physical building and the family that erected it and will ultimately collapse with it.

In Poe's tale, the Usher family has come down to two individuals. Twins Roderick and Madeline are locked in a love-hate relationship that eventually results in their mutual murders. Roderick prematurely buries a catatonic Madeline, who rises from the tomb to strangle him and thus to bring down house and House. Essentially brother, sister, and dwelling share a single soul. This is one of the ways fantasy represents a complex selfhood: by dividing it among different entities, each of which stands for a single faculty or facet of the whole.

Another example of this sort of distributive psyche is the triad of Queen Orual, the goddess Ungit, and Orual's sister Psyche in C. S. Lewis's *Till We Have Faces* (1956). The text is full of indications that each is a part of the other, and all of a greater self. "I am Ungit," says Orual (276). "You also are Psyche," Orual is told by the voice of the god (308). And "We're all limbs and parts of one Whole," says the memory or vision of her tutor; "Hence, of each other. Men, and gods, flow in and out and mingle" (300–1).

Less explicitly, there is *The Lord of the Rings*, which Ursula K. Le Guin reads, in an essay titled "Science Fiction and Mrs. Brown," as an exploration of a divided self, with not only Gollum and Sméagol (who share a body) but also Frodo and Samwise as aspects of a single complex character. Le Guin points out that the technique comes out of traditional storytelling:

as traditional myths and folktales break the complex conscious daylight personality into its archetypal unconscious dreamtime components, Mrs. Brown becoming a princess, a toad, a worm, a witch, a child—so Tolkien in his wisdom broke Frodo into four: Frodo, Sam, Sméagol, and Gollum.... (103)

Here she is contrasting fantastic storytelling with the best of realism: Mrs. Brown is a character invented by Virginia Woolf to represent the hidden complexities and irreducible individuality of even the least prepossessing of humans. Tolkien's characters have the same complexity and individuality but split as if by a prism. Le Guin turns to Jung to name the parts of the self as *archetypes*, just as I reached for Freud to describe the house-self in *Princess*, but such splintered selves are too ancient and too common to fit any one psychological or psychoanalytic theory. The method should be credited to storytellers rather than analysts, and deserves a name of its own; I suggest calling it distributive selfhood.

Here are some other instances:

- the house of Gormenghast and its residents in Mervyn Peake's trilogy of that name (1946–59).
- alternative versions of individuals spread across the multiverse in Diana Wynne Jones's Chrestomanci books, beginning with *Charmed Life* (1977).
- the various "J" characters—all of the same genotype but raised in different societies—in Joanna Russ's utopia/dystopia *The Female Man* (1975).
- three recurring, possibly reincarnated characters who interact across a vast tapestry of history in Kim Stanley Robinson's *The Years of Rice and Salt* (2002).
- the multi-bodied, multiply gendered aliens invented by Eleanor Arnason in her story "Knapsack Poems" (2002).
- and, in a particularly vivid expression of the trope, the daemons of Philip Pullman's alternative universe in the His Dark Materials sequence.

We meet the daemons on the first pages of Pullman's *The Golden Compass* (1995; titled *Northern Lights* in Britain). They look like pets but function more like prosthetic extensions of selfhood: separable organs of the soul in animal form. The protagonist Lyra views her daemon Pentalaimon as a companion and fellow conspirator. Because Lyra is still forming as a person, her daemon is protean: sometimes moth, sometimes bird or cheetah. The alarming Mrs. Coulter uses hers, a golden monkey, to seduce and spy on others. Lord Asrael's daemon is a snow leopard; it reinforces his own inclination to intimidate others and attract their admiration. Pullman uses the same leonine imagery to depict both daemon and man: "All his movements were large and perfectly balanced, like those of a wild animal, and when he appeared in a room like this, he seemed a wild animal held in a cage too small for it" (13).

Pullman's model for the daemons is the mythic tradition of the familiar, with just a hint of shape-shifter. He was also inspired, he says, by the Renaissance fashion of having one's portrait painted with an animal prop, like Leonardo da Vinci's elegantly sinister *Lady with an Ermine* (Butler 2007). The daemons express inner truths about their human counterparts: for instance, servants all have dogs as daemons. A major part of the plot is an invention that severs daemon from master, leaving a maimed, witless husk. Human characters in the series can lie and misrepresent themselves, but their daemons always testify to an inner truth. This single narrative device allows Pullman to portray characters with remarkable depth, as if they were too large and various to be contained in a single body. It affects everything in the story, from setting to theme, and carries the reader through a number of less-engaging side plots. It also tells a truth about human nature: that selfhood extends beyond a person's skin and can even invade other living beings.

The converse of that truth is that a single individual can, as Walt Whitman puts it, "contain multitudes." Fantastic literature offers several rationales for positing multiple inner voices or personae. The Pixar movie *Inside Out* (2015) is both an instance of the trope and an examination of its use: a metafiction about popular psychology. It presents, without explanation, a version of selfhood in which each emotion or motivation is a different character—voiced by a different actor—inside the heads of the protagonist, her family, and everyone she meets (including a cat and dog). In science fiction, as opposed to fantasy proper, multiple selves are more likely to be accounted for through some sort of technology or (because science fiction allows itself certain pseudo-scientific premises) through telepathy or racial memory or possession.

One of the most rigorously scientific of setups is in Greg Egan's ironically titled "Reasons to Be Cheerful" (first published 1997). The protagonist of that story, Mark, has a brain tumor; the cure for his condition turns out to attack healthy tissue, necessitating an even more drastic intervention in the form of prosthetic brain tissue: "an elaborately tailored polymer foam...

that attracted axons and dendrites from surrounding neurons" (203) to replace the dying areas. This new artificial brain matter, however, is blank. To give him back memories and a personality, scientists program the tissue with neural patterns using "4,000 records from the database" from which he must select a new, individual self.

At the end of the story, Mark has a revelation. His selfhood may be a construct, a random selection from among the habits and desires of strangers, but so is everyone's. Looking at his father, he thinks,

> he's there inside my head, and my mother too, and ten million ancestors, human, proto human, remote beyond imagining. What difference did 4,000 more make? Everyone had to carve a life out the same legacy: half universal, half particular; half sharpened by relentless natural selection, half softened by the freedom of chance. I'd just had to face the details a little more starkly.   (227)

In this conclusion—one of the few genuine "reasons to be cheerful" in the story—Egan gives a scientific rationale for treating the psyche as a complex, contradictory, contingent thing. But fantasy offers other avenues to the same discovery.

Lois McMaster Bujold's Chalion series, and especially the set of novellas centered on the character of Penric, uses divine and demonic possession to account for the presence of more than one self within the head of a single character. In the world of the series, the five gods—Father, Mother, Son, Daughter, and trickster Bastard—can intervene in the affairs of humanity by taking over individuals temporarily. The possessed person is considered a saint and has extraordinary powers including the ability to see the true self or selves inside other persons. The gods are not necessarily benevolent from a human point of view, following plans beyond our knowing, and demons are not evil, though they are forces of chaos and disorder. In *Penric's Demon* (2015), a young nobleman inadvertently invites such a demon into himself when its host dies. Since Penric is unfamiliar with demons, the reader gets to learn their nature along with him:

> Demons were supposed to begin as formless, mindless elementals, fragments escaped or leaked into the world from the Bastard's hell, a place of chaotic dissolution.... All the demons possessed of speech or knowledge or personhood was taken from their successive masters, though whether *copied* or *stolen*, Pen was unclear.

Such knowledge suddenly becomes less abstract as Pen, or Penric, must learn to assert his own identity against the competing claims of a demon and as it turns out, its twelve prior hosts. All of those earlier carriers were female, including a mare and a lioness, as well as women of many classes and locations. The most recent are strongly present in Penric's mind; the oldest rather distantly there, faded over time.

Though he is in danger of being overwhelmed by this new interior crowd and especially by the demon itself, it is Penric's good nature that gives him the advantage over them. His first impulse is to engage in conversation rather than inner battle, and he charms the demon by giving it the first gift it has ever been offered, a name. In return he receives their respect and, eventually, access to their considerable and varied knowledge—he can speak and read multiple languages and use the skills of a physician, a priestess, and a courtesan. That last presents some difficulties for Pen, as the male occupant of twelve or thirteen female consciousnesses (since the demon—now Desdemona—itself has come to identify as feminine).

Penric's condition can be read metaphorically: as a way of representing acquired learning, or empathy, or indecision, as in such phrases as "She was of two minds on the issue." It can also stand for bisexuality in two senses of that word: having the nature of, and also being attracted to, both males and females. It is mythic, in that demonic possessions and tricksters as well as sudden and dramatic metamorphoses are common in oral traditional texts. The Norse trickster god Loki, for instance, changes sex on occasion and even gives birth, and the Greek seer Tiresias spends seven years as a female. In those cases, the transformation is physical, whereas Penric's is mental, although he does, in a later story, demonstrate considerable skill in performing as a woman.

Maria Nikolajeva (1988) has coined a term for what happens to mythic motifs when they pass out of oral tradition and into literary narratives. What once were *mythemes* (their designation in semiotic terminology) become what Nikolajeva calls *fantasemes*, irreducible but replicable chunks of fantastic world-building. According to Nikolajeva, "sometimes fantasemes coincide with what other scholars call motifs or functions. More often, however, a fantaseme is a wider notion..." (23). Examples range from individual enchanted objects or fantastic creatures such as witches' familiars to fundamental rules of magic, such as the principle of true names in Le Guin's Earthsea—which would constitute one of Nikolajeva's "wider notions." Most fantasemes originate as mythemes, which is to say that for any given magical principle or motif, one can find a version of it in oral tradition, using such tools as Stith Thompson's *Motif-Index of Folk-Literature* (revised 1955–58). Those fantasemes in turn invite metaphoric readings, as they interact with the characters and themes of fiction.

But a fantaseme such as Penric's acquisition of, as he says, "a council of twelve invisible older sisters" is more than either a mythic reference or a metaphoric link. It resets his nature as a character and alters the kind of story he is in. Like distributive selfhood, this sort of commingling of source identities represents something significant about Penric and about his world—which is to say, not only the imagined physical world but also his story-world, the entire set of possible interactions and implications that Bakhtin calls a chronotope. The change in Penric is structural, and the kind of structure it establishes is meaningful as a way of understanding what it is to be human. Like Mark in "Reasons to Be Cheerful," Penric must carve a life out of his legacy, as do we all. If Pullman's daemons represent the distributive capacity of the soul, Penric's demon represents its ability to merge and commingle. We are compound beings as well as extended ones.

Fantasy offers many forms of compounded selves, and many ways to acquire them. Some inner sharers are invited in, as Penric unknowingly welcomes Desdemona. Others simply barge in, like the Mockingbird in Sean Stewart's novel of the same name (1998): a spirit that invades the protagonist and rides her as spirits of the dead ride a medium. Others have always been there unnoticed, like sleeper spies, until roused by trauma or ritual or sexual awakening as in Alan Garner's *The Owl Service* (1967). Severian, protagonist of Gene Wolfe's *The Book of the New Sun* (1980–83), acquires a new second self and a new life trajectory through an act of ritual cannibalism enhanced by an alien drug and a miracle. In each case, the multiple selves must negotiate a new blended or kaleidoscopic identity. When they are able to do so successfully, the compounded being is stronger, more adaptable, and more self-aware than before.

Distributive and compounded psyches are not the only structures of selfhood that can be represented through fantasy, nor are selfhood and transformation the only categories that can be represented structurally through fantastic devices and narrative tropes. Anything that has a structure can have that structure set into magical form. Love has a structure, or rather many structures: Ovid's Metamorphoses represent a wide sampling. Death has a structure: graveyard fantasies such as George Saunders's *Lincoln in the Bardo* (2017) represent that structure spatially, while personifications such as Terry Pratchett's Grim Reaper (and the more specialized Death of Rats) in the Discworld books represent it as a humanlike enemy or guide. Gender has a structure, as does desire. All major life changes have structures. Injustice has a structure: a powerful example of the way fantasy can depict that is Frances Hardinge's story of genocide and resistance, *Gullstruck Island* (2009). Even meaning itself has a structure, and fantasy offers ways to represent semiosis, or the act of meaning, in such guises as magical bindings or Earthsea's True Speech.

Whether derived from myth or concocted from metaphor, fantasemes operate within larger systems. Fantasy is more than its component bits: its motifs take their meaning from the narrative patterns in which they are embedded. Fantasemes are the vocabulary of fantasy; stories are individual sentences; both depend on our knowledge of the syntactic and semantic codes of storytelling to give them order and meaning.

From just a few hints in a story, we start to hypothesize a world in which those clues form a coherent whole. The better we know the genre and its folk sources, the more quickly we can fill in the gaps and intuit a structure for the story-world. And once we perceive the "proportion and harmony" of that world, it can serve as a model or miniature simulation of the world of experience. We come to know it; we live in it as we read and remember the tale. And because of the way thought works, through logic and emotional association and perceived linkages, the fantasy world begins to offer insights into the world outside the fiction. In effect, it becomes a new source domain from which to extend metaphors.

To some extent, this is true of fiction in general. Realistic constructions such as William Faulkner's Mississippi become touchstones for readers' understanding of the world outside the fiction. Iconic characters like Dickens's Scrooge or Austen's too-proud Mr. Darcy stand in for whole classes of people. Social interactions we have read about start to show up all around us: the amusing misunderstandings of romantic comedy or the catastrophic decisions of tragic heroes.

Michael Saler notes, in *As If: Modern Enchantment and the Literary Prehistory of Virtual Reality* (2012), that some of these fictional worlds are so indelible as to be reusable by other writers: they become sandboxes in which anyone can play, virtual realities before virtuality became associated with the digital world. Significantly, all of his examples verge on, or cross the line into, fantasy. If we could travel in time, we might expect to see something like Dickens's London; but Sherlock Holmes's London is a more bizarre, fantastic space. H. P. Lovecraft's New England is a step further into the fantastic, with realistic geography but with impossible forces and alien beings lurking in its caves and attics. At the far end of the scale is

Tolkien's Middle-earth: wholly separated from history and inaccessible by any form of transport other than the imagination. Saler doesn't include L. Frank Baum's Oz among his instances of virtual spaces, though Oz is a perfect illustration of the process, as inviting to other creators as Lovecraft's mythos or Sherlockiana. All of these imagined worlds have inspired numerous sequels and adaptations and pastiches. Part of their appeal, I would suggest, is that each imagined world is organized around principles that are based in experience but that operate with a clarity and consistency not to be found in any real society. They are magical, though the magic may be covert, disguised as Holmes's deductive reasoning or Moriarty's malevolence. And magic throws everything into higher relief: makes the structure of meaning explicit.

The fantastic exerts a pull even on realistic story-worlds. The more inhabitable of these have been turned into overt fantasy by later writers. Faulkner's South is made magical in stories by Manly Wade Wellman, Terry Bisson, and Andy Duncan. Regency fantasy is an entire subgenre, turning Austen's England into a fairy kingdom. This genre-shift can be read as a sort of Doppler red shift: as the past recedes into the distance, it gets colored by imagination and wish-fulfillment. History begins to converge with story. Actual places—Austen's Bath or Baker Street in London—start to bilocate, showing up on maps of both primary and secondary worlds.

Fantasy is known for its use of maps, although Stefan Ekman points out in *Here Be Dragons* (2013) that the now obligatory map preceding chapter one was uncommon before Tolkien popularized the practice. One of the reasons for such maps is to give the reader room to exercise the imagination beyond the confines of the story. Named places to which the characters never go, warnings about dragons or dangerous forests, and even blank spaces on the map give the virtual world more depth and credibility. But the most important function of the map is to provide a sequence for exploration and for revisiting favorite spaces. To map something out is to plan an expedition. Maps arrange experiences in time and space, and thus allow us to organize meanings. An explicit use of this capacity is the Renaissance practice of creating a memory palace—a fantaseme that shows up in John Crowley's *Little, Big* (1981) and a number of other fantasy novels.

In Charles Sanders Peirce's semiotic theory, maps are icons: structurally similar to the things they stand for and thus useful sources of information. A city map tells us things about the city that we might not learn by walking its streets. A blueprint is a map of the building constructed from it. The blueprint for Princess Irene's house in *The Princess and the Goblin* might not have markings for "Here the goblins will tunnel in" or "Attic rooms for the magical Great-grandmother," but the spaces are arranged in a way that enables those discoveries. The blueprint is an icon of the house, and the house itself becomes an icon of other things: the kingdom, maturation, the soul.

Just as the Princess's house models the psyche, the house of Edgewood in *Little, Big* stands in for the structure of fantasy itself. Edgewood is a grand Victorian folly: an architectural game designed by the founder of the Drinkwater family. John Storm Drinkwater was both an architect and a spiritualist, and the house he has built serves as both a sample of his wares and a gateway to other realities. It is five-sided, and each of its façades is in a different high Victorian style, festooned with porticoes and dormers and bric-a-brac. The pentagonal shape leaves the interior full of odd angles and dead-end corridors: it is a building to get lost in. Like the Tardis on *Doctor Who*, it is bigger inside than outside. The grounds of the house abut a woodland that is home to supernatural as well as more ordinary wildlife. It is a liminal construction within a liminal space.

Crowley's story lets us know that Edgewood is both mythic and metaphoric. The myths range from the story of the sleeping king Frederic Barbarossa to Mother Goose, absorbing as well a range of more literary figures or fantasemes such as Lewis Carroll's Alice. The metaphors are myriad: Edgewood is the Drinkwater family itself, but also western civilization, domestic life, prophecy (including the Tarot deck wielded by Great-Aunt Cloud), memory, history, and art. Emily Dickinson's aphorism applies well to it and its neighboring wood: that "Nature is a Haunted House—but Art—a House that tries to be haunted" (Dickinson, 1971). *Little, Big* is unabashedly metafictional, and one of its messages is that all fantastic tales tend toward metafiction because they make us aware of their own made-upness, their artifice.

Above all, Edgewood is storytelling; it is the story we are reading, and thus a map of fantasy in all its possibilities. But storytelling is too large and various to be simply a metaphor: it is a realm, in the sense that Crowley uses that word in another novel, *Ka: Dar Oakley in the Ruin of Ymr* (2017). Edgewood fits the definition of realm *Ka* by being "Where we are when we are what we are" (76): in this case, the place we go when we find ourselves in stories. From the realm of story, one can draw an unlimited supply of metaphors: every X in the source domain can find a Y in any target domain. Hence we can go around claiming that X is Y in an attempt to understand love or violence or the numinous.

One of the essential functions of story is to generate ever more metaphors, and the metaphors of fantastic storytelling are especially useful because their artificiality is so transparent. Because fantasy is not life but lie, it can stand for the mysteries of life, for the hidden things and the underlying structures. In *An Experiment in Criticism* (1961), C. S. Lewis made the important distinction between "realism of content" and "realism of presentation" (57–9), maintaining that fantasy can do as well by the latter as any sort of fiction. I would go a step further and say that in renouncing realism of content, fantasy gains an ability to map the tectonic plates of reality. As Le Guin says in her 1974 essay "Why Are Americans Afraid of Dragons," "fantasy is true, of course. It isn't factual, but it's true." Though nothing prevents the fantasy writer from employing the representational devices of realism—all the facts, Ma'am, but not just the facts—it is the unreal that opens the way for deeper truths.

2

Realism and the Structures of Fantasy

The Family Story

What does realism look like from the vantage point of fantasy? It might appear surprisingly familiar, like an unknown relative. We tend to think of realist and fantastic fictions as a contrasting pair, but then there are many possible counterparts to realism. Fredric Jameson names a few:

> realism vs. romance, realism vs. epic, realism vs. melodrama, realism vs. idealism, realism vs. naturalism. (bourgeois or critical) realism vs. socialist realism, realism vs. the oriental tale, and, of course, most frequently rehearsed of all, realism vs. modernism. (2)

That last binary suggests one problem in formulating an answer to the question, "What isn't realism?" If "fantasy" is a vexed term, "realism" is positively schizophrenic. If the opposite is modernism, then realism is defined by its historical period. If, however, the opposite is romance or epic, then it is (assuming that we are talking about novels), a generic distinction. These are among what Jameson calls the antinomies of realism: the essential contradictions at its heart. Above, all, there is the unresolvable paradox that realism is seen as both description and judgment, or, as Jameson says, it is "an epistemological claim [that] masquerades as an aesthetic ideal" (5).

Yet, as I said at the beginning, fantasy and realism might be more closely related than we usually suppose. Samuel R. Delany's notion of subjunctivity (outlined in his essay "About 5,750 Words") is useful here. Think of a scale from literal truth to complete fabrication. No fiction, of any subgenre, sits at either end of the scale. Rather, all are conditionally faithful to experience; all stories lie to some extent and all testify to some truths. From George Eliot to George MacDonald is not a long journey but a short excursion down the road toward greater subjunctivity, or imaginative hypothesizing. The works of both start out with an "if" that marks them out as fictions; MacDonald's fairy tales (he also wrote domestic novels, which have more in common with his fantasy than one might expect) push the "if" a little further toward "what if?" or even "imagine that." Roland Barthes's useful phrase "l'effet de réel" reveals the secret at the heart of realism: we are never seeing reality but only the effect of the real, the effectively real, that which is real enough for the purpose. The production of such an effect is a matter of studied technique, like the style of painting called "trompe l'œil," or fool-the-eye.

So I will be exploring realism not only from the viewpoint of a reader of fantasy but also in the context of children's literature. As noted in chapter 8, children's literature is a protected space, wherein child characters enact a kind of innocence that belongs not to real children but to the memories and wishes of adults. Many things have traditionally been left out of that space to keep it functioning as a refuge: not only sex and violence but also economics and politics and cultural and racial outsiders. After the middle of the twentieth century, those things began to appear in realistic literature for older children, but they were always there in the forerunner to fantasy, the oral tale. To become more real, children's literature first had to become more like fairy tales while seeming to reject the fantastic components of such tales.

Elizabeth Enright was a critically acclaimed writer of children's books in a genre known as the family story: four books about the Melendy family, two about an abandoned Victorian resort town called Gone-Away Lake, and a couple of stand-alone novels, one of which, *Thimble Summer*, won the 1939 Newbery Medal. Those were not her entire output, however; she also wrote sharply observed short fiction for adults (appearing in *The New Yorker* and six O. Henry Prize anthologies), personal and critical essays, and a pair of short fantasies, *Zeee* (1965) and *Tatsinda* (1963). Her fantasies are competent and charming, somewhat unusual in having been published before the post-Tolkien fantasy boom, but by no means as beloved as her realist fiction. The characters aren't as memorable; the plots are a little more derivative; and the world-building is infused with whimsy, from which her other stories stay well clear. I would suggest that the real problem with her fairy tales is that she had already written fantasy of a richer, truer sort. Enright's best fiction is fantasy in realist guise, and her books and her comments on them reveal how much closer ordinary fiction is to fantasy than is usually acknowledged. Read in conjunction with the work of her contemporary Edward Eager, Enright's family stories reveal an affinity to fantasy that says much about how the real and the magical interact in fiction.

The family story is—or used to be—one of the major strands of children's literature along with varieties such as animal tale, school story, mystery, fantasy adventure, and Künstlerroman (an account of the development of a someday-artist). These subgenres freely mix and mutate, so that a foundational text like Louisa May Alcott's *Little Women* can depict both the March family as a whole and Jo as emerging writer. *Peter Rabbit* might be read as a family story as well as a beast fable. Edward Eager's comic fantasy *Half Magic* (1954) is equally the story of four siblings and their mother, thus paying homage to his acknowledged model Edith Nesbit's stories of the Bastable family as well as her magical misadventures. A family story is an episodic, mostly humorous account of life in a large-ish or extended family. Each child in the family is given the spotlight at some point, but the real protagonist is the family as a dynamic whole: overall plot arcs usually concern the family facing some crisis as one and reorganizing itself while reaffirming its central values. Major figures in the development of the form include Alcott, Nesbit, Arthur Ransome, Carol Ryrie Brink (who combined it with historical fiction in *Caddie Woodlawn*, 1935), Eleanor Estes, and writers of formulaic series such as the Boxcar Family, the Five Little Peppers, and the Famous Five—respectively, Gertrude Chandler Warner, Margaret Sidney, and Enid Blyton.

The mention of formula highlights one of the key differences between the reception of realist and that of fantastic fictions. Formula is an essential part of fantasy, which has its roots in traditional forms such as the fairy tale. Oral transmission pushes stories toward formula, as documented by Milman Parry and Albert Lord in their studies of classical and modern epic singers. The presence of formula in oral narrative is not a bug but a feature. Realist writers, by contrast, are expected to avoid formula—which, in practice, means disguising it. Their stories are supposed to feel organic and natural, based in observation and growing out of characters' foibles and desires, rather than dictated by some generic pattern. That is why some creative writing programs still insist that their students write only "literary" fiction; genre is not allowed.

There are myriad definitions of *genre*, ranging from marketing category to Wittgenstein's "language game," but whatever one's favorite definition, the idea that any text could fail to participate in some genre or other makes no sense. Genres represent tacit agreements between writer and reader about what a story is and how it should be read. As John Rieder says of science fiction, it "is not a set of texts, but rather a way of using texts and of drawing relationships among them" (197). Within any given generic contract are unwritten clauses about what is important for a story and what can be left out, what constitutes an ending, and how to tell good writing from bad. Genres are also enabling mechanisms: they reassure writers that certain kinds of experience are worth reading about, and they encourage particular ways of organizing those experiences. In that sense, Southern fiction is as much a genre as detective fiction, though its generic constraints have more to do with gothic sensibility, collective guilt, and exuberant style than with dividing the characters into detectives, suspects, and victims. As mentioned in the previous chapter, Southern fiction was authorized by the work of William Faulkner and later Robert Penn Warren and Eudora Welty, just as the classic mystery was authorized by Edgar Allan Poe and Agatha Christie. They made the South available for literature; they showed how to turn its history and tensions into story. Bret Harte and Owen Wister did the same thing for the West. Every successful writer similarly authorizes their own form while remaking the genres they have inherited. A text can be faithful to experience and still conform to generic expectations. Even autobiography is a genre, as is, Hayden White tells us, narrative history itself (83).

The pretense that realist fiction is purely representational and convention-free leads to peculiar critical judgments, and the family story form is a particularly revealing example. Surveys such as Carol Lynch-Brown and Carl M. Tomlinson's *Essentials of Children's Literature* (1993) equate the family story with realism, and then fault it for being insufficiently real. Books such as Enright's and Estes's, they say, pale in contrast with Louise Fitzhugh's 1964 *Harriet the Spy*, which opened up the possibility of "a more graphic and explicitly truthful portrayal of life" (135). The problem with this claim is not its praise of *Harriet* but its use of the word "truthful" to describe something that is merely darker and more satirical, as well as its assumption that realism must be "graphic." Similarly, Anne W. Ellis, in *The Family Story in the 1960's*, finds stories of troubled fictional families somehow more real than those of happy ones, and laments the fact that "sound material based on real life was sometimes spoiled in conjunction with impossible adventures" (76).

Phillip Barrish, in *American Literary Realism, Critical Theory, and Intellectual Prestige, 1880–1995*, refers to such judgments as "'realer-than-thou' one-upmanship" (4). Corinne Hirsch sums up the situation within children's literature similarly:

> Courses and textbooks characterize the children's and young adult novel as "fantasy" or "realism," regarding realism as a grab bag of all nonfantasy. Books are praised for their realism, condemned as unrealistic. Realism becomes a criterion for good literature, although it is rarely defined when used in this way." (9)

As Hirsch suggests, realism can hardly stand as a criterion for judgment when readers don't agree on what counts as real, either in fiction or in life.

One way to avoid such critical misfirings is to accept that realism and fantasy can coexist in the same text, and that such blended texts are neither inherently superior nor inferior to stories made up primarily of one mode or the other. Both C. S. Lewis and J. R. R. Tolkien took up the question of realism's place in fantasy, with Lewis, in his 1961 *An Experiment in Criticism* formulating the idea of a "realism of presentation" not dependent on "realism of content" (57–9). Tolkien went even further in his lecture "On Fairy-stories," claiming "That the images are of things not in the primary world ... is a virtue, not a vice. Fantasy (in this sense) is, I think, not a lower but a high form of Art ... " (47).

We are dealing with incommensurables here. More realistic does not necessarily mean less fantastic, nor the converse. Furthermore, realism can be executed well or badly, as can fantasy, and a single text may do both at once magnificently or incompetently. To get back to examples, I'd like to look at a family story in which a bit of fantasy is embedded within a predominantly realistic frame and one in which a realistic text is transformed into a magical episode. The first is the next-to-last of Enright's Melendy family books, *Then There Were Five* (1944). The second is Eager's *The Time Garden* (1958).

In an article about Enright as exemplar of the family story, I proposed five key components of her novels that are typically found throughout the subgenre, though any given work may not demonstrate them all. They are the most common "family resemblances," to use Wittgenstein's term for the markers that allow us to see groups of instances as a single category, though no one defining feature may be shared by all members of the category. Here is my proposed set of features:

1) a family story is a form of domestic comedy.
2) a family story is a bundle of parallel Bildungsromans.
3) the protagonist of a family story is the family as a whole.
4) each family story is an ethnography of a unique tribal culture.
5) the family story combines a fantasy structure with a realistic surface (125).

Two of those features are relevant to my argument here. I will come back to number five, but for now, the significant element is number two: the presence of multiple Bildungsromans. For three of the Melendy children, these are Künstlerromans, artist's development novels, since their education is primarily training in observation, empathy, and self-expression, preparing at least three of them to excel in the arts. The eldest, Mona, is an aspiring (and, by the third book, working) actress. Rush, the older of the boys, is a piano prodigy. Randy, the younger girl, dabbles in various arts, such as dance and painting. Enright says, "In Randy I recognize two of my long-ago best friends, as well as two of my long-ago best wishes: to be a dancer and to be an artist" (Introduction viii), an acknowledgment that also implicitly positions Randy as a stand-in for the author herself as a writer-in-the-making.

In the scene in question, after a picnic in the woods, Randy is entertaining the youngest sibling, Oliver, who deserves some pampering after he falls into a well. Oliver's trajectory is pretty clearly aimed toward science rather than the arts. He is modeled after Enright's sons, and especially Nicholas Wright Gillham, who indeed became a distinguished biologist—the chapter "Oliver's Other World" in *Then There Were Five*, depicting young Oliver's obsession with insect life, is revisited as a nonfiction sketch about her now "grown-up geneticist" son in "The Caterpillar Summer" (74). Though no budding creator himself, Oliver is an excellent audience for Randy's inventions. We are not given the full story but instead come into it in mid-improvisation:

> She was a little awed by the story herself, it came and came, like thread off a spool, and it was a wonderful story, all about an unknown volcano, near the North Pole, which was so warm that its sides were covered with flowering forests and warm streams, though it rose in the midst of a glacial waste of snow and ice.   (Enright 1944 (Then), 205)

With Oliver's encouragement, Randy gives her characters names and occupations: "Queen Tataspan, King Tagador, and Tatsinda, the heroine.... Also Tatsinda was a wonderful ice skater.... She used to go skating on the Arctic Ocean, on skates made of pure gold."

However, at this point Oliver falls asleep and the story ends abruptly—only to be continued almost two decades later as a stand-alone book. The characters still include Tataspan, Tagador, and Tatsinda, but they are joined by others: Prince Tackatan, a seeress and magic-worker named Tanda-Nan, and an invading giant named Johrgong. (That last name offers a bit of a relief from all the Ta- names of people and Ti- names of animals that Enright uses to set her fantasy world apart from reality.) We don't see the title character ice-skating, but everything else in *Tatsinda* develops from

Randy's story, including the veins of gold that attract the giant's attention and complicate the plot.

There may be an explanation among Enright's papers or correspondence for this unusual bit of intertextuality. I don't know why she decided to develop this one incident into a full-blown narrative. It could be that she was drawing on her own juvenilia, using and then reusing something she invented in childhood. Or she might have become intrigued by the unfinished tale and decided to flesh it out. As indicated above, I don't think *Tatsinda* works as well as Enright's family stories. The very factors that make it believable as the invention of an eleven-year-old—repetitive naming patterns, emphasis on decorative elements such as the gold, simple characterizations including a too-perfect heroine—make it less satisfactory as the work of an experienced adult novelist. Enright does throw in thematic elements that weren't in Randy's tale, such as Tatsinda's being ostracized because she differs from everyone else in having brown eyes and golden hair instead of blue eyes and ice-white hair, and she works out the invasion plot neatly, using the folk motif (also found in *The Hobbit*) of trolls being vulnerable to sunlight. *Tatsinda* demonstrates Enright's craftsmanship at the level of sentences and descriptive passages. It fits into a tradition of playful literary fairy tales, such as George MacDonald's *The Light Princess* (1864) and James Thurber's *The White Deer* (1945). Yet I think the main interest in the book is the light it casts on Enright's other work.

The scene in *Then There Were Five* shifts, once Oliver has fallen asleep, to the artistic ambitions of his siblings. Randy, who has, up to this point, envisioned other careers, thinks to herself, "Maybe I better be a writer too." This thought confirms Randy as Enright's textual stand-in. She is the Jo March of the Melendy books: the budding writer destined to write the story we are reading.

The comparison to Louisa May Alcott is not accidental: *Little Women* is an authorizing text for Enright's family stories. In her 1967 essay on "Realism in Children's Literature," Enright cites Alcott as the starting point of a new, more naturalistic body of fiction for children: "Then in our grandmothers' day there came Louisa May Alcott, that sensible revolutionary who opened the windows in all the overshuttered, overgimcracked, overplushed houses of children's literature. The boisterous air of life came in" (67). Like Alcott's March family, the Melendys number four, each clearly delineated and each with interests that shape the family's destiny. Like the March sisters, the Melendys squabble and snipe at one another, but the love that links them is constant. Both families delight in performance, rehearsing and performing theatricals in an attic space that is their own territory. Particular incidents in the Melendy books mirror those in *Little Women*: little vanities and come-uppances, comic misunderstandings, and the sacrifices the children make for a larger good (the backdrop of the Melendy books is World War II, as that for *Little Women* is the Civil War). Oliver's fall into the well echoes Amy March's fall through the ice, and Randy, though not directly responsible as Jo is, feels the same guilt:

> She was never much good in a crisis, and this time all the mean things she had ever done to Oliver came back to her. The times she had said, 'No, you can't come with us, you're too little. The times she had put things over on him, played tricks, laughed behind his back, because he was too young to know the difference.   (203)

The temptation is to read *Little Women* as a simple record of Louisa Alcott's own upbringing, and there are plenty of autobiographical elements in the book to support such a reading. Yet the novel is not a memoir and the telling is not simple.

Nor is Randy Melendy's story a transcription of Elizabeth Enright's childhood. For one thing, Enright was an only child, daughter of two preoccupied artists who eventually divorced. To fill in her fictional family, she drafted school acquaintances and cousins to form her imagined quartet of siblings. As she said in an introduction to the omnibus volume of the first three Melendy books, "It must be admitted that such a family, made of flesh and blood, whom one could touch, talk to, argue with, and invite to parties, does not actually exist. Yet in other ways...each of these people is at least partly real" (vii). Since her schoolmates were children of other artists, and her extended family included her uncle Frank Lloyd Wright, she had plenty of strong-willed and creative types to draw on. Rush, for instance, was modeled on Ira Glackens, son of the painter William Glackens. Ira, "the brother of my choice," shows up, instantly recognizable from his Melendy doppelganger, in a *New Yorker* sketch called "The Shush Rush" (21). She describes Mona as a composite of school friends and an unnamed favorite cousin who is perhaps the actress Anne Baxter (1944, viii). Oliver, as mentioned above, was based on one of her sons, and shared his name with another. In other words, the Melendy household was a fantasy in the non-genre sense: the kind of family Enright might like to have grown up in. In generic terms, though, she stuck strictly to the terms of realist fiction—or at least to the letter of the contract. A closer look at the structure of the adventures in the Melendy books and the later Gone-Away stories suggests a more complex negotiation at work between fantasy and realism. To get to that, I will turn to another writer who shared much of Enright's literary lineage.

Enright's contemporary Edward Eager made no secret of which writers authorized his children's stories. Every one of his books includes a discussion of E. Nesbit's fantasies, and L. Frank Baum is mentioned almost as frequently. Eager considered it a duty to point his readers toward the master; hence we have the children in the beginning of *Half Magic* reading Nesbit's *The Enchanted Castle* (1907) aloud as they walk home from the library—or rather, Jane, the eldest, does the reading, "because she could read fastest and loudest" (7). Another set of children in *Knight's Castle* (1956) discover Nesbit's *The Magic City* (1910) and declare it "one of the crowned masterpieces of literature which have advanced civilization" (57). Before venturing into writing children's books (he was already a successful playwright and poet), Eager wrote an essay for *The Horn Book Magazine* detailing his adventures in reading to and with his son Fritz. Beatrix Potter, Thurber, Tolkien, and Baum are all mentioned appreciatively, but Nesbit gets the highest praise of all, despite the fact that in America in the 1950s her books were hard to come by: he refers to "the magnificent works of E. Nesbit which I am now vainly chasing through New York's thrift shops and secondhand bookstores." (1948, 163)

Nesbit wrote brilliantly dashing fantasies, and encountering her work certainly unleashed Eager's fantastic imagination, but that is not all that he learned from her. In a later *Horn Book* essay, he expressed appreciation for Nesbit's realistic family stories:

> First in any listing of Nesbit's works always must come the three books dealing with the Bastable children, delectably titled *The Treasure Seekers*, *The Wouldbegoods*, and *The New Treasure Seekers*.... Who could forget the Bastables, particularly the noble Oswald? One sees them as perpetual pilgrims, marching forever down the road with peas in their shoes and a brave plan in mind to save the family fortunes, stopping by the way to dam the stream (and later cause a nearly-disastrous flood), forgetting in their zeal the cricket ball left lodged in a roof-gutter (which still later is to cause a flood of another kind).   (Eager 1958 (Daily), 3–4)

Eager's summary captures the fun had—and havoc wreaked—by Nesbit's children in their attempts to become rich and good. The Bastables are Nesbit's best characters, while her magic stories have the best plots: Eager combined the two.

Eager's plots, like Nesbit's, are episodic but within a larger arc involving, as he says of the Bastables, rescue of the family fortunes. Encountering some magical implement or entity, the children are granted wishes that go wrong, never quite to the point of disaster and always with some bit of wisdom gained and often an ally made. Some of the adventures take place close to home; others take them to places that are exotic and magical but also familiar from their reading: Camelot, the Arabian Nights, *Ivanhoe*'s Castle Torquilstone, Oz in the days before its discovery by Dorothy. This kind of travel into bookish realms gives the stories a metafictional dimension that reaches its peak in *Seven-Day Magic*, in which the magic item is itself a book that not only grants wishes but also records the adventures in the exact words of the text we are reading. At the end of *Seven-Day Magic*, one of the characters, Barnaby, having quarreled with the others, takes a trip into the book he has been writing, *Barnaby the Wanderer*, and, in a turn that anticipates the (also postmodern) 1999 film *Being John Malkovich*, ends up gazing Narcissus-like at his reflection in a pool and unable even to remember the name of his book:

> "I am Barnaby the Wanderer!" he tried to say again. But he had forgotten the right words. "I am Barnaby the Barnaby" was what came out. And after that, "Barnaby, Barnaby, Barnaby" was all he could find to say. He thought it was someone's name, but he had forgotten whose. (179)

This scene provides Barnaby with a lesson in cooperation, but it offers readers a lesson in genre as well. Without realism, fantasy can degenerate into solipsism; it requires continual infusions of resistance, the grit of the material world that keeps the machinery from running too smoothly.

The ability to enter into fantasy worlds by other writers is one of motifs Eager found in Nesbit (for instance, in *The Story of the Amulet* (1906), the future the children visit is the utopia envisioned by her friend H. G. Wells), but he took the idea further than she had done. Eager's children intervene, giving characters key information that allows those characters to change outcomes. And they revisit Eager's own fantasies: the children in *Seven-Day Magic* (1958) pop into a scene at the end of *Half Magic* just after the main characters of that book have left. But more to my point, these bits of intertextuality also include visits to places that are fictionalized but real. In *Seven-Day Magic*, that includes a trip to Laura Ingalls Wilder's prairie schoolhouse (mingled with the memories of the children's grandmother, who has unknowingly gotten her hands on their magic volume) and to a composite version Dickens's London.

That last adventure suggests that Michael Saler is exactly right to label such literary territories "virtual worlds." Referring to Sherlock Holmes's London (which overlays Dickens's) as well as H. P. Lovecraft's haunted New England and J. R. R. Tolkien's Middle-earth, Saler demonstrates how those fictional spaces became communal property, playgrounds for the imagination, open to all. "On the one hand," says Saler, "these worlds are autonomous from the real world, avowedly fictional spaces that provide an escape from a disenchanted modernity into self-subsistent realms of wonder. On the other hand, these worlds are inextricable from ordinary life and interpersonal engagements." And, most pertinent to my argument, "They challenge their inhabitants to see the real world as being, to some degree, an imaginary construct amenable to revision." (7)

Eager's children make Dickens's London and Wilder's Plum Creek into what game designers call sandboxes: shared, open-ended environments in which players are minimally constrained by whatever narrative the game-play asks them to follow. Writers use the same term to refer to the placement of their stories in someone else's imagined world, such as the Doctor Who-verse or the Star Trek franchise (the use of which, of course, is fiercely restricted by its corporate owner). Eager's fantasies show us is that imaginative children have always done this with their reading. So do Nesbit's stories, both realistic and fantastic: her characters not only model their behavior but also narrate their own adventures in heroic styles copied from their reading. Even the March sisters in *Little Women* act out John Bunyan's *Pilgrim's Progress*, and so they (or their creator) could hardly object to Eager's transformation of their fictional life into yet another fantasy world to be visited.

In *The Time Garden* (1958), a garden of magical herbs grants the ability to travel to the past, but not only the real past. Depending on the variety they pick—common thyme, wild thyme, Old English thyme—Ann, Roger, and their cousins Eliza and Jack might find themselves immersed in the American revolution, helping slaves escape via underground railroad, or meeting their own parents as children on their own magical adventures— Ann and Roger being the children of *Half Magic's* Martha and Eliza and Jack the offspring of Katherine. A visit to Boston inspires them to go back to the time of Meg, Jo, Beth, and Amy, even though, as skeptic Jack points out, "you couldn't go back in time to *them*. They weren't real" (73). To this, Eliza responds, "it's real-er than anything in your old history books!" And, sure enough, employing a sprig of golden thyme, they find themselves in a past Concord that is half history and half fiction, where (i)t was winter. And it was snowing. (For who can think of the March family without thinking of snowballs and mittens and skating on the pond and Christmas coming any minute?)

Meeting Meg and Jo and Laurie (Beth has a cold and Amy is visiting Aunt March, so they have to confront neither the specter of death nor their least favorite character), the modern-day children join them on the frozen pond.

The entire adventure hovers between history and fiction. Jo and Laurie feel as real as anyone from the past, and Ann inspires Jo to write about her own family. "*That* wouldn't make a story," Jo objects.

"It does, though," said Roger, not exactly sure at this moment whether he were addressing his remarks to Miss Josephine March or to Louisa May Alcott herself, but it didn't matter because they were the same person really. (76)

They are the same person only when both have entered into story-worlds. Eager is suggesting that the real becomes fantastic once it is transformed into story. Only generic constraints on some stories—the ones we class as realistic—keep magic from erupting into those worlds. For Eager's time-traveling children, the historical past is no different from the fictional, especially because neither is accessible except through the twin portals of magic and story.

Eager's characters are well aware of the narrative logic that allows them to travel across time or space or levels of fictionality. So long as they follow the rules, they can venture forth and return safely, collecting friends like Jo and Laurie and bits of grudgingly accepted wisdom. There is a clear structure to each adventure, acquired from Nesbit, who in turn borrowed it from fairy tales of the literary sort and from F. Anstey's comic fantasies for adults. The pattern is consistent: children acquire a magical agent of some sort, muddle about with near-disasters until they learn how the magic works, go on separate and then joint adventures, bring the magic a little too close to home, where it begins to resemble a less-innocent force of chaos, and finally make a bargain that frees the figurative genie and leaves them a little happier than they started.

This is also the pattern of Enright's family stories, only it is disguised with a veneer of ordinariness: magic rationalized. I'll try to demonstrate that through a point-by-point comparison of a couple of Eager's chapters, this time from his first fantasy, *Half Magic*, and two from the first Melendy book.

The Saturdays

The Saturdays most nearly resembles Nesbit's school of fantasy in that there is a sort of enabling charm. As we meet the Melendy children, they are hanging about in the top-floor playroom they call "the Office," bored because it's raining but enjoying the pleasures of being a child and having nothing in particular to do. Randy has an idea that sets everything off:

> "Each of us (except Oliver, of course) gets fifty cents allowance every Saturday. Now. You want to go to Carnegie Hall and hear some music. Mona wants to go to a play. I want to see those French pictures Father was talking about. Every single one of those things costs more than fifty cents. Now what I was thinking was this. We're all old enough to be allowed to go out by ourselves—except Oliver—if we promise to be careful and not get run over or talk to people or anything. So why don't we put all our allowances together once a week and let one of us spend them?"   (14)

Half Magic

The four children have returned from their weekly trip to the library, where the last E. Nesbit book was finally available. After Jane reads it to the others,

> There was a contented silence when she closed the book, and then, after a little, it began to get discontented.
>
> Martha broke it, saying what they were all thinking.
>
> "Why don't things like that ever happen to *us*?"
>
> "Magic never happens, not really," said Mark, who was old enough to be sure about this.
>
> "How do you know?" asked Katharine, who was nearly as old as Mark, but not nearly so sure about anything.   (8)

They go out to explore the neighborhood and Jane spies what she thinks is a nickel on the sidewalk. A little later, they are thoroughly bored:

> They sat there and couldn't think of anything exciting to do, and nothing went on happening, and it was then that Jane was so disgusted that she said right out loud she wished there'd be a fire.

The other three looked shocked at hearing such wickedness, and then they looked more shocked at what they heard next.

What they heard next was a fire-siren!   (11–12)

In best fairy-tale tradition, Jane gets her wish and it creates more problems than it solves.

The Saturdays: Randy's Adventure

Having come up with the idea of pooling their money, Randy gets the first Saturday expedition. On her own in New York with a dollar-sixty in her purse (showing how both prices and urban culture have altered since the 1940s), she walks up Fifth Avenue to the gallery where the French paintings are on display, but the adventure starts as soon as she's out the door: "being by yourself, all by yourself, in a big city for the first time is like the first time you find you can ride a bicycle or do the dog paddle. The sense of independence is intoxicating" (25). She savors the art, especially a painting of a melancholy little girl in a garden. She is immersing herself in the scene when an elderly and (Randy thinks) boring family acquaintance, Mrs. Oliphant, comes up behind her. Mrs. Oliphant comments that the portrait "isn't as beautiful as I remembered it. . . . But then I haven't seen it for sixty years. Not since I was eleven years old" (29).

Mrs. Oliphant, it turns out, was the girl in the picture, and over tea and ice cream, tells Randy the story of how the painting happened. It's a remarkable story about an overprotected and lonely child who runs away to see her first carnival, gets kidnapped by Gypsies, and is rescued by the artist, who asks to paint her portrait and intervenes to send her to a boarding school in England. The fur-clad, camphor-scented old woman not only turns out to have an adventurous streak but also becomes, through the rest of the series, a sort of fairy godmother to the Melendys,

Half Magic: What Happened to Martha

Each of the children gets a turn to wish on the talisman, with results as vexed but un-boring as Jane's fire, which turns out to be a sort of half-fire, a child's playhouse burning, providing the clue to the contrary nature of the magic.

A number of the wishes are made inadvertently, as is the case when the children go to the movies. Martha, the youngest, gets bored and wishes she weren't there at all. Granting half her wish, the charm makes Martha into a translucent, ghostlike figure who panics and runs from the theater. Her ghostly appearance spooks everyone and sets off a general hysteria reminiscent of James Thurber's "The Day the Dam Broke" (1933) or the aftermath of the Orson Welles 1938 *War of the Worlds* broadcast (with both references pretty clearly signaled in the text).

Running from the crowd, Martha ducks into a bookshop and meets the proprietor, who is unfazed by the apparition:

> "I presume this is a ghostly visitation? I am honored. Did you come out of one of the books? You might be Little Nell, I suppose, or Amy March, though the clothes don't look right."   (126–7)

The dapper little man turns out to have met their mother in a previous wish-misadventure, and, as before, responds to magic not with shock or disbelief but with ready acceptance born of the right sort of reading—in this case, not just Alcott and Dickens but also *Alice in Wonderland*:

> "Oh, there's never only *one* explanation," said the rather small gentleman. "It depends on which one you want to believe! *I* believe in believing six impossible things before breakfast, myself. Not that I usually get the chance. The trouble with life is that not enough impossible things happen for us to believe in, do you agree?"   (27)

The gentleman, Mr. Smith, turns out to be a reliable ally in negotiating both ordinary and magical complications and eventually becomes a non-evil stepfather to the children.

The Structure of Wishing

In both books, something extraordinary emerges from a determinedly ordinary setting. The impetus can come from a magical coin or a set of coins (the pooled allowance)—the important thing is not the form of the agent but its enabling properties. The siblings work out a way of exploiting their new powers, first singly and then, after a various mishaps, as a group. The agent allows them to go places and do things they would not have been able to go to or do otherwise. In *Half Magic*, the wilder adventures are part of the main plot, while in *The Saturdays*, they take place in embedded narratives, as when Mark goes to see *Siegfried* at the Metropolitan Opera or Randy hears Mrs. Oliphant's captured-by-Gypsies story. Though they take risks and encounter potential threats, the children come through unscathed, entertained, and enlightened. They bring back from the more-fantastic embedded narratives a heightened sense of mystery in the world, as when Rush, walking home through a snowstorm after the opera, starts to see snow-removal equipment as dragons:

> The machine would move its long neck, turn its head, and blow the snow it had consumed into the truck, then both would move slowly along again. It's just like an animal, thought Rush, looking at the machine. Like Fafnir, he thought, and began to laugh.   (58)

During one of the adventures, the children encounter a sympathetic adult whose friendship will alter their lives for the better even after the adventure is over. Throughout, they act and speak in a thoroughly believable way and their surroundings are vividly depicted and familiar, if a bit quaint to modern audiences.

Daily Magic

This particular blend of realism and fantasy might be called magical realism, except that that term has got itself associated with a very different sort of narrative, one in which a realistic setting is disrupted by impossibilities governed by no underlying magical system, no logic of the sort that Nesbit and Eager were so good at. Sarah Pincus has dubbed the Nesbit/Eager category "ordinary magic" and describes it thus:

> these novels straddle the genres of realistic fiction and of fantasy, and they are neither watered-down fantasy nor unbelievable depictions of reality. The magic and adventure present are just as extraordinary and powerful as in any fantasy, and the realist elements are just as believable as in any work of realistic fiction.   (3)

The problem with the phrase "ordinary magic" is that it is used in psychology to refer to a kind of resilience demonstrated by some at-risk children

(Mastern 2001). Nesbit's and Eager's children are frequently at risk and certainly demonstrate resilience; however, applying this definition to their tales would be a radical misreading that sucks out all the charm and lets the magical air out of the narrative. It would put them over into a category of books that Eager's children particularly loathe:

> "It calls itself *The Magic Door*, but there's not a speck of magic in it anywhere! It's just about this boy that learns to get along with these other people by being friendly and stuff. And the magic door's just the door of good fellowship or something. Man, do I despise a book like that!"
>
> (1954 (Seven-Day), 12)

In contrast with these bait-and-switch versions of realism, Eager's practice is to establish the recognizably real as a substratum for the undeniably magical. Eager's own term for this technique is "Daily Magic":

> if there is one thing that makes E. Nesbit's magic books more enchanting than any others, it is not that they are funny, or exciting, or beautifully written, or full of wonderfully alive and endearing children, all of which they are. It is the dailiness of the magic....
>
> The world of E. Nesbit ... is the ordinary or garden world we all know, with just the right pinch of magic added. So that after you finish reading one of her stories you feel it could all happen to you, any day now, round any corner.   (Eager 1958 (Daily)")

In order for such magic to take off, of course, it cannot be merely quotidian but must be thoroughly grounded in fresh observation and genuine feeling. Its dailiness is that of daily bread rather than daily routine.

Many of Eager's successors learned the same lesson from him or from Nesbit—Marcus Crouch's 1972 history of English children's literature is not called *The Nesbit Tradition* for nothing. Unlike adult fantasy fiction, which tends to get itself caught up in Tolkien imitations and fake medievalism, Nesbit-influenced children's fantasy has always employed magic to explore the here-and-now as well as the never-was. Writers such as Eleanor Cameron, Jane Langton, Diana Wynne Jones, and Frances Hardinge demonstrate the power and variety of "real world" or "low" fantasy. They have done so by invoking what Alexander dubbed the "flat-heeled muse"—a sensible, no-nonsense taskmistress in "good, sensible shoes," who demands research and logic in place of unbridled fancy. The result, as Eager's children know, is a sense that anybody, at any time, might find a talisman that looks like a nickel, or point out the road to Butterfield that turns out instead to be the road to Oz. Even if that never happens, the possibility is intoxicating.

Edited Reality

But what about Enright's books? They might seem to fall into the "true magic of friendship" sort of fraud, and yet they do not. Theirs is also a sort of daily magic, but to avoid recriminations from Eager's child readers, I will avoid the M-word and instead borrow a term from Enright. Her brand of realism uses careful selection and juxtaposition of details to take us out of the ordinary: she calls it edited reality. In an essay about realism in children's literature, she lists not only Alcott but also Hans Christian Andersen and Beatrix Potter as great realists—and thus implicitly as additional authorizers for her kind of fiction—and she insists that realism depends not only on "observation and experience," its "blood and bone," but also on "wish and memory [which] are the mind and heart that make book children real" (Enright 1967, 170).

Enright viewed wish as a guiding principle for the editing that is necessary to fiction. Because characters "cannot be allowed all the ragtag slack of daily life, all the humdrum coming and goings and yawnings and coughings and desultory chatter" (1967, 168), their adventures can be edited as well to make them

> neater, more just, and more exciting. Things turn out well in the end... unlike life, the end of the story comes at the high point. We do not have to go on with these people through high school, college, marriage, mortgage payments, child rearing, money worries, dental problems, old age, death, or any of the rest of it. It is our privilege to leave them in their happiness forever... (1967, 168)

Such editing has the power to create magic, just as cinematic editing, as Sergei Eisenstein discovered, can create connections simply by cutting from one image to another. The narrative connection isn't there and yet it is; just so, the magic in Enright isn't there but it lurks on every page.

Enright was aware of the degree of invention and intervention she was allowing her narrators. She believed that writing for children requires both "wish and memory," which is to say, fantasy and realism counter-balancing one another:

What can we promise them? Security? No, we cannot promise them that; now less than ever. The factory-magic we've contrived threatens them as it does us.

Happiness? How happy is this world? How can we promise them a thing like that?

But we can wish those things for them, and hope them and depict them, so that the child, who enters a book in a way no adult can, finds himself in a world which, though it may contain trial and conflict, also reveals security and reason and humor and a good measure of happiness.

(Enright 1960, 34)

What Enright means by "factory-magic" is technology unchained, the machineries of war and waste. She suggests that the time for fairy tales may be past, that "we have lost our taste for magic because we have ... made it come true. We've toiled and toiled to wrest the cloudy symbols out of the imagination and convert them into objects you can buy in a store. Or use in a war" (1960, 28). Hence her preference for disguising magic as luck, as benefaction, as editing. Yet magic it remains.

My fifth descriptor of Enright's version of the family story, that it typically "combines a fantasy structure with a realistic surface," is an attempt to describe this editing technique. Selection and juxtaposition let the Melendys and her other characters find dragons on New York streets and diamonds in caddis-fly shells. Editing selects the improbably delightful over the dreary norm. Creative juxtaposing makes any child into a fairy-tale hero, which does not mean making the world entirely safe or predictable. As Enright says of magic, "It is not a cozy commodity" (1960, 28).

Enright's story-worlds abut Eager's, though one batch of books might be labeled realism and the other fantasy. Both are, as Saler says of other fictional spaces, imaginary constructs amenable to revision. What they have in common is not so much the realism of presentation that C. S. Lewis talked about, though one can certainly point to bits of concrete reality amidst the flights of fancy. Rather it is the sense of discovery, of Keats's "wild surmise," that accompanies every turn of the page. In Eager's fantasies, the magic is on the surface; in Enright's, just below. One is presented seams out, the other seams in (Kelso). But the garment is the same enchanted cloak.

3
Neighbors, Myths, and Fantasy

Mythopoeic fantasy not only allows us to rethink our relationship with traditional myth but can also function as an argument and a model for a particular kind of community. Some of the most difficult social issues of the past few decades result from bringing together groups whose views are so different as to constitute alternative realities. Immigrants (including long-ago immigrants who resist assimilation) carry with them sets of religious beliefs, social structures, and habits of thought so deeply ingrained as to challenge the consensus underlying democratic systems. When fantasy builds on mythic traditions, it invokes some of those potentially disruptive folkways and world views. Yet the inherently reconciling dynamic of the fairy story—Tolkien's term for the modern genre of faërie or enchantment—offers scenarios for living in relative peace, side by side in different cognitive universes. Good fancies make good neighbors, as Robert Frost probably would not say.

The concepts of situated knowledge, developed by Donna Haraway, and cognitive minorities, proposed by Peter Berger, are especially useful in sorting out and thinking through the nature and functions of contemporary fantasy. I explored these ideas at length in *Stories about Stories*, but I am formulating them a little differently here as well as applying them to a range of newer examples by award-winning writers, including Helene Wecker's *The Golem and the Jinni* (2013), Aliette de Bodard's Dominion of the Fallen trilogy (2015–2019), and Laurie J. Marks's Elemental Logic quartet (2002–2019).

Definitions first. My working definition of myth, which I have woven bowerbird fashion out of threads plucked from folklorists and myth scholars such as Stith Thompson, Mircea Eliade, Barre Toelken, and Alan Dundes, goes like this:

> Myths are oral, traditional, sacred narratives, told as truth, about gods or godlike beings, set in the distant past or far future or outside of ordinary time altogether, which organize the natural universe and define humanity's place and obligations within it.

What I like about this definition is that it avoids a lot of unsupported speculation about ancient societies and mysticism about collective (i.e., Jungian) or repressed (Freudian) unconsciousness. It doesn't make everything into a myth but restricts the term to storytelling. And within the wide range of oral narratives, it distinguishes the genre of myth from related ones such as folk tale and legend. (Folk tales are stories offered as fiction rather than truth, and legends take place in historical time and are often secular rather than sacred.) However, like any statement about culture, this definition reflects scholars' (mine and those I draw on) own expectations. Once we venture beyond Europe and the ancient world, it gets harder to distinguish between mythic time and the here and now. Gods turn out to be tricksters like Anansi or Coyote, and comical folk tales can suddenly take on mythic dimensions. A lot of what we think of as myth turns out to be literature based on traditional myth. From Gilgamesh on, writers have meddled with oral texts and imposed their own order and interpretations. If any myth is there to be read, some writer or editor has been at work. Much of the collective wisdom of the ancients is really the interpretations of Sin-liqe-unninni (compiler of the fullest Gilgamesh text), the various writers of Genesis, Aeschylus, Ovid, Valmiki, and Snorri Sturluson. In many ways, modern fantasists are just continuing the pattern.

But that swerve into written literature suggests that it's time to move on to my second definition: of fantasy. Fantasy is the literature of the impossible, except when it isn't. Fantasy tells about dragons and wizards, but much of the best fantasy has neither. Since genres are always morphing and changing their boundaries, there is probably no safe, unchallengeable definition. My recourse is to define fantasy a little differently every few years. Here is my current attempt:

> Fantasy is a form of fiction that evolved in response to realism, using such novelistic techniques as represented thought, detailed social settings, and manipulation of time and point of view to revisit pre-rationalist world views and traditional motifs and storylines.

In other words, fantasy *is* myth—but it is also fairy tale and supernatural legend and romance and epic. And it's a return to all those things after they have already been declared archaic, after the rise of rationalism and the novel. Great fantasies are great novels but they are something more. Fantasy is not an escape from reality but a response to it, one that looks to other, more traditional ways of seeing and symbolizing. Writers of fantasy, science fiction, and utopia are, as Ursula K. Le Guin says, "realists of a larger reality" (Le Guin 2016, 113). These are the fictional forms that don't assume, for instance, that social institutions are real things. Or that the ordinary is the same as the true.

Fantasy needn't attempt profundity. It can be silly or satirical, trivial or topical, when it isn't serving as a vehicle for psycho-allegory or a disguise for history. But one of the oldest and most important strands of fantasy is what C. S. Lewis and J. R. R. Tolkien called mythopoesis. Though that term invokes one form of oral narrative while "fairy stories" invokes another, Tolkien's grounding in philology reveals that he sees the two as close kin. Mythopoeic fantasy makes new myths; only what it tends to make them from is old myths and tales. It isn't an accident that many pioneering myth scholars were also involved in the creation of modern fantasy: the Grimms; Andrew Lang; folklorist Katherine Briggs; Tolkien himself; the classicist Jane Ellen Harrison, along with her companion, fantasy writer Hope Mirrlees.

However, invoking myths, even in comic fantasies such as Thorne Smith's jazz-age romp *Night Life of the Gods* or Terry Pratchett's Discworld stories, means invoking older, non-materialist ways of seeing the world. And that's where Wecker's novel comes in. The title *The Golem and the Jinni* is a marvelous piece of disruption all by itself: there is a big crack between the two nouns. The set-up of the novel is like a movie in which two people who aren't even on the same continent get edited together as if they were in a conversation. A golem comes from one cognitive universe; a jinni evokes quite another. The novel is set in New York in 1899, but it's not exactly *our* New York. Along with wealthy financiers and Irish cops and fresh-off-the-boat immigrants from all over the world, this Manhattan has a handful of magical creatures. That makes the book part of an extensive shelf of New York fantasies, along with such works as John Crowley's *Little, Big* (1981), Tony Kushner's *Angels in America* (1991), and Chris Moriarty's *The Inquisitor's Apprentice* (2011). Literary New York is a fabled meeting place and transformative space, and one can see why writers find the stuff of fantasy in its history and geography. Moriarty, for instance, plays with historical names in her novel, so that the Astor family becomes the Astral family, the infamous Triangle Shirtwaist Factory becomes the Pentacle Shirtwaist Factory, and the great villain is J. P. Morgaunt.

But Wecker stands out among these authors in taking on the immigrant experience directly, addressing not only economic struggles and linguistic confusion but also clashes of world view. Her characters include Jews from Eastern Europe, who bring traditions about the artificial being called the

Golem, and Arabs from the Middle East, who bear stories and beliefs about *jinn*—better known to English-speakers as genies. (A minor note here: because the Arabic plural looks like a singular in English—the singular is *jinni*—one often sees references to *jinns*, but I am following Wecker's usage here.) These supernatural beings inhabit entirely separate universes. Golems are part of a cosmos that draws on Hebrew scriptures and Jewish folklore and the philosophy of the Kabbalah. Jinn are related to Islamic and, by cultural spillover, Maronite or Orthodox Christian belief. As Wecker says she came to realize, jinn are "an everyday truth for many in the modern Middle East and the Muslim world" (Q & A). With both magical beings, she faced the challenge of trying to respect communal beliefs and familial anecdotes along with their larger sacred contexts.

Readers must judge her success for themselves, but it clear that Wecker worked hard to respect those whose traditions she has built on, including her own family. She acknowledges that the novel is a sort of metaphorical autobiography, in that her family is Jewish while her husband's is Arab:

> so in that sense we come from two different (and, in many eyes, opposing) cultures. But I've always been struck by the similarities between our families, the way that certain themes echo between them. We're both the children of immigrants, with all that entails. As a result my husband and I both grew up in suburban, picket-fence America—but with the intimate and sometimes uncomfortable burden of another place's history, and the complications of living as a cultural minority, which affects our relationships with those we love and those we meet.   (Q and A)

She started writing stories about the meeting of these two cultures, but nothing really clicked until she combined that theme with a lifelong love of the fantastic. Hence the creature of clay and the demon of fire, interacting with and revealing the human characters around them.

Significant fantasy, the kind that lasts, must be doubly grounded: in the textures of real everyday experience, on the one hand, and in the immaterial world of stories and beliefs, on the other. Far from making everything up, most fantasy writers do a tremendous amount of research, especially writers of historical fantasy, who are trying to recreate the past that people thought they lived in, rather than the one we reconstruct from legal documents and physical remains. The difference is that the experienced past, unlike the documented one, unambiguously included things like ghosts, demons, miracles, and fate. Or golems. Or jinn.

In the definition of fantasy I have given, I deliberately avoided some terms that often come up in discussions of the genre: the impossible, the marvelous, the unreal. The trouble with these terms is that they suggest we all know what is possible, un-miraculous, or real. We do know those things, but what we know does not necessarily match up. Kathryn Hume has proposed a good fix for the definition problem: she suggests that there is enough overlap in our sense of the possible that we can identify a "consensus reality," or what Lily Tomlin once called "a collective hunch." We generally agree that unsupported objects fall to the ground; that everyone needs to eat; that things don't suddenly turn into other things without physical cause. Fantasy is anything that denies one of these commonly held assumptions—or rather, that imagines a pocket universe in which the assumption isn't valid.

But consensus sometimes breaks down. My reality doesn't include guardian angels, but some of my neighbors' does. Your earth might be six thousand years old, while mine is a few billion. If I write a story about demons, it's a fantasy; if someone else does, it might be sober realism. Differences in world view mean different genre boundaries, and hence different ways of reading. There are books I think of as pure fantasy that to many readers are prophetic truth: for instance, the apocalyptic thrillers in the Left Behind series. Here is where Peter Berger's idea of cognitive minorities is handy. Looking at America in the late 1960s, Berger saw traditional forms of belief being replaced by secularism (1970, 6). The devout were no longer in charge; their beliefs made them exceptional. Berger did not anticipate the pendulum swing in the 1980s and 1990s that made religious rhetoric (if not necessarily sincere faith) a requirement for holding public office and created a fad for popular entertainments like the TV series *Touched by an Angel*. Minorities and majorities can easily change places. Yet his insight remains valid: there are groups that can be defined not by race or economic status or heritage but by assemblages of distinctive beliefs. The cultural minorities Wecker talks about are also cognitive ones.

In the Manhattan of *The Golem and the Jinni*, many cognitive minorities live in close proximity to one another. Orthodox Jews are one. Maronite Catholics are another. In and among them we find Eastern Orthodox Syrians, Muslims, secular Jewish social reformers, and even a few white Anglo-Saxon Protestants. What doesn't seem to exist is a cognitive majority. The result, within the novel, is that hardly anything one's neighbors say or do seems completely outlandish. Whatever someone believes in is, by definition, believable. Maybe a golem is impossible in *this* neighborhood, but a few blocks away, who can say. Here we have only a man who was a doctor in the old country but whose possession by an evil spirit leaves him unable to function. Oh, and a jinni who works as an assistant tinsmith.

Wecker is very good at shifting among these perspectives, which are both characters' points of view and competing models of the universe. She fits the fantastic into the cracks between realities. Like a parliament made up entirely of minority parties, her world always has room for one more splinter, single-issue representative, who might even be called on to form a governing alliance. From a reader's perspective, we can each find somebody in the book to ally with, but we should not feel entirely confident that our chosen character is right about what is or isn't possible.

That last uncertainty says that this is more than just a book full of cognitive minorities. It's also a book about the way prior experience and current situations shape one's response to the unexpected and the unexplained. Wecker's characters continually find themselves having to adjust their thinking, and they often debate beliefs and assumptions. A character might move from one cognitive minority to another—although they can't evade their own ethnic or religious identities, and what they believe is always intertwined with who they are or think themselves to be. The same is true of readers. When I said just now that the novel depicts a meeting of Jews and Arabs, consider your own reaction. Did it sound like appropriate material for fantasy, or like a situation likely to find a happy ending?

Wecker makes the fantasy work and even finds a reasonably happy ending, because of the way she frames these interactions. Fantasy deals with explosive materials by claiming not to be real, not to matter. It's just an entertainment, just a game, just a fairy tale. Stephen Greenblatt says that the Elizabethan theater got away with representations of regicide or sexual ambiguity or blasphemy in more or less the same way: it was "powerful and effective precisely to the extent that the audience believe[d] it to be nonuseful and hence nonpractical." (1988, 18)

Within this apparently trivial context, differing beliefs about God and fate can be kept from reacting explosively, especially if they are further buffered by being assigned to different characters. Where one character sees God's will, another sees a force of nature or a convenient rationalization. A lot of fantasy does this, including the whole subgenre of science fantasy. In older science fantasies, the less sophisticated characters typically believe in magic, while the author's representatives and the narrator trust in science. More recently, though, fantasy writers have been leaving things open, as Wecker does. This is a postmodern move: to allow different discourses to remain in equilibrium, and to recognize that perspective matters. To describe it as a narrative technique, I have repurposed Haraway's "situated knowledges." I understand her term to mean not that anything goes and all views are equally valid, but rather that whatever we know is always known from a particular standpoint. We all experience gravity: its effects can be measured and predicted. But we all experience it in our own bodies, with our different heights and weights and genders and burdens. Gravity means something different to each of us: our knowledge of it is situated in our individual being.

If there are situated knowledges, then there can be situated fantasy, which is what Wecker and a number of other contemporary fantasists are writing. If even gravity can be experienced differently, then anything created by humans is irreducibly situated and contingent. Knowledge, even our knowledge of ourselves, is limited and filtered through the narratives we have absorbed. There's always another way to tell it. To quote John Crowley's *Ægypt* (aka *The Solitudes*, 1987), "There is more than one History of the World" (73).

The Golem and the Jinni presents many instances where this contingency is acknowledged and commented on by the characters themselves. The novel opens with the animation of the golem on board a ship bound for America and then flashes back to a Polish shtetl where everyone already knows what a golem is and knows the story of how Rabbi Loew created one to protect the Jews of Prague. But in New York, only Jews from the same cultural group know the stories, and even they are likely to have left many of their beliefs behind in the Old World. In the New World, the golem becomes a blank, an undefined quantity. Golems are usually represented as neuter or masculine, but the man who commissioned this one wanted a wife. Thus she looks like an ordinary woman, though she is also enormously powerful, able to read others' desires (part of the magic: necessary to accomplish her tasks), subject to everyone else's interpretations, intelligent, curious, and uncertain who she is or what she herself wants. Putting all of that together with the turn-of-the-century setting, I suggest that she is a metaphor for the so-called New Woman, a term coined in an 1894 essay by Sarah Grand. Like the suffrage-seeking New Woman, the Golem might become anything at all, might challenge any power or topple any monument.

Wecker addresses the sex of golems in a note on her website:

> Golems in legend are almost always male. However, in one tale, an 11th-century poet and rabbi named Solomon ibn Gabirol creates a female golem out of wood, to be his servant. When the authorities question him about his new serving girl, he explains that she is merely a golem. He then removes the life from her, and she collapses once again into a pile of wood.   (Q and A)

To Wecker's example we could also add the female robot, the false Maria, of Fritz Lang's 1927 film *Metropolis*, which is itself a work of science fantasy or situated fantasy. The gadget-filled laboratory where Maria is made says, "Science," but the look of her inventor and his ancient cottage suggest medieval magic. The inventor's name is Rotwang: in Wecker's novel, the customer who orders a golem wife is named Rotfeld. I suspect indirect influence if not deliberate allusion.

When Wecker's golem strides onto the streets of Manhattan, only one person recognizes what she is. Rabbi Meyer is a New-World counterpart to the Kabbalistic magician who created the golem, except that his studies of the occult are benevolent and directed toward inaction rather than action. Everyone else sees a tall, oddly dressed women: only he and a passing sparrow see the figure of clay. But Rabbi Meyer decides to treat the golem as the woman she appears to be, as an innocent soul rather than a dangerous monster. He gives her a name: Chava, or Life.

The jinni's gender—and thus its humanity, which we bestow along with gender in our choice of pronouns—is likewise a matter of observers' expectations. It appears to be a man, but Boutros Arbeely, the tinsmith who accidentally frees it, knows otherwise, because he "remember[s] his grandmother's stories of flasks and oil lamps, all with creatures trapped inside" (21). And even he wonders if he has gone mad. Interestingly, it is the jinni who says in wonder, "It's real. This is all real" (21). Later the jinni explains.

> "Imagine," he said to Arbeely, that you are asleep, dreaming your human dreams. And then, when you wake, you find yourself in an unknown place.... And then, a strange creature finds you and says, 'An Arbeely! But I thought Arbeelys were only tales told to children! Quick, you must hide, and pretend to be one of us, for the people here would be frightened of you if they knew.'"   (44–45)

We accept the strangeness of the jinni because we see how strange we humans look to him.

The jinni's viewpoint is based on centuries of experience, which he uses to try to understand all the alarming changes that took place during the thousand years he was imprisoned and unconscious. The golem looks at things from the opposite position. Everything is new to her, since she herself is only a few days old. From the perspectives of most onlookers, any strangeness within golem or jinni is hidden within the teeming mass of newness that is Manhattan. Both jinni and golem are constantly reading other people's reactions, offering glimpses of yet other perspectives. Some readers have suggested the novel would be better without the magic, that what Wecker was really interested in was the historical experience. I could not disagree more. We learn a lot about historical New York by looking through the eyes of these two nonhuman beings, each encapsulating—literally embodying—an alien belief system.

To a folklorist, stories about jinn and golems are legends: they take place in real locations, within human memory, and they are told as truth. But legends, like fairy tales, are next-door neighbors of myth. Jinn may show up in one's own tent, but they also interact with King Solomon and with Muhammad. Golems are animated by writing God's name in the clay: to make one is to recapitulate the creation of Adam in Genesis. Both present theological problems regarding souls and immortality. Oddly enough, this Golem—the being of inert clay—is devout, accepting restrictions on orthodox women's behavior and relying on Rabbi Meyer for spiritual advice, while the jinni—a spirit made of fire—is a skeptic. To him, "God is a human invention" (240), but when he asks the Golem if she believes in God, she replies that Rabbi Meyer believed, "And he was the wisest person I've ever met. So yes, maybe I do." (241)

Similarly, different characters have different views of angels, which traditionally occupy the same cognitive space as jinn or demons. The only angel that actually appears in the story is the Angel of the Waters statue, in the Bethesda Fountain in Central Park (which also features prominently in *Angels in America*). Looking at the statue, the Golem comments, "I read about angels, once. In one of the Rabbi's books.... You don't believe in them, I suppose."

"No, I don't," answers the Jinni. "[H]e didn't want to talk about angels, or gods, or whatever else the humans had invented that week" (276–77). Yet the Jinni himself is associated with angels by, of all people, Yehuda Schaalman, the magician who created the Golem: "Was it this mysterious Ahmad? Or the Angel of Death, playing with him?" (400).

The only ultimate truth in all these different beliefs is that, as Schaalman concludes, "truths were as innumerable as falsehoods—that for sheer teeming chaos, the world of man could only be matched by the world of the divine" (441).

Posing truth against falsehood, matching humanity with the divine—this is the ultimate expression of situated fantasy, but it isn't the final word from the book. In the Golem's final musings, she expresses hope for some middle ground, "a resting place between passion and practicality. She had no idea how they would find it: in all likelihood they'd have to carve it for themselves out of thin air" (484). But the only thing we can actually carve out of thin air is speech, or speech shaped into story, as in the first recorded use of "thin air" in a speech by Prospero in *The Tempest*:

> These our actors,
> As I foretold you, were all spirits and
> Are melted into air, into thin air.
>
> (Act IV, Scene 1)

What Shakespeare sets up in the scene is not only an extended metaphor for the theater and the power of the imagination but also a way to link the mortal world to the realm of the goddesses who bless the union between the young lovers. The insubstantial pageant, like the whole of *The Tempest*, is a story about stories and the way they situate and validate belief.

Myths and sacred legends are way up there, unreachable and eternal. We're down here, amid confusion and change. But stories bridge the gap. The middle ground the Golem is hoping for, between passion and practicality, is also a mediating narrative between human existence and the divine, or between realism and myth. John Stephens and Robyn McCallum describe retold myths as "re-versions" (4): they have been reframed and reassembled in ways that can challenge or even reverse their ideological significance. Part of that reframing is the addition of a metanarrative, a story about the story. Metanarratives arise within traditional cultures as well as literate ones.

Barre Toelken, who spent decades working with Navajo storytellers and trying to find his way into their world view, talks about the way those storytellers adapt myths. He gives the example of a healer who incorporated horses and sheep into a creation narrative that is part of a healing ceremony. The storyteller knows that those animals were not native to North America: they came over with the Spanish. But, the teller reasons, "how can it be a sacred story if it doesn't include all the important beings in our world?" (89). Toelken says we have not paid enough attention to traditional cultures' "capacity to adjust and reconstruct mythic constellations" (89). He compares this kind of self-conscious adaptation of myth to Talmudic commentary on Hebrew scriptures. It keeps myths alive and relevant and thus represents the kind of renegotiation that is always going on between cultures and their foundational stories.

Fantasies like Wecker's reframe and reinterpret myths, but at the same time update and revalidate them. Fantasists in essence add the horses and sheep to the creation story, because those are here now and need to be incorporated into sacred space. And, like sheep and horses, we have to be brought in as well. We do so by telling our own stories about the stories, creating our own glimpses of the cosmic and the profound. But this is only fantasy—as trivial as Shakespeare, or Milton, or Dante. Situated fantasy invites us to take our myths and legends lightly, to edge up against them in fantasy. If we can let go of the literal and the absolute, we can meet one another as Golem and Jinni meet, in the neighborhood and on the equal ground of the imagination.

As I suggested above, our usual sense of how such meetings will play out is less optimistic than Wecker's story: recent and ancient histories alike suggest devastation and genocide as more likely outcomes than romance. We see fortified Belfast neighborhoods during the Troubles, or bombed-out Beirut after the Lebanese civil war, and we suppose that those are the inevitable results of cultural juxtaposition. China Miéville's *The City and the City* (2009) offers a powerful image of irresolvable differences in world view within a confined space. The two cities of the title, though designated by the same noun, are as different as the two nonhumans in Wecker's title. One city is Eastern European, run-down, historically Christian; the other is more prosperous, more Middle Eastern, and unofficially but strictly adherent to the Temple of the Divine Light. Yet by rights they should be a single city: Ul Qoma is in the same location as Besźel. One neighborhood will have Besź architecture and signs in its Cyrillic-like alphabet; the next one over will feature Ul Qoman writing and construction. Miéville's brilliant conceit is that the two riven cities are by custom invisible to one another, that one can only cross between them at a few designated checkpoints, and that different ways of seeing can separate us even more effectively than physical distance. If *The City and the City* were a mythopoeic fantasy, one might expect the situation to be altered by the end, with some rapprochement between the believed worlds. However, because despite its vaguely fantastic set-up it is essentially a hard-boiled police procedural with a tinge of spy novel—two forms that depict only local, temporary victories within an inalterably corrupt world—there is no bringing together of neighbors, no shifting of belief systems, only the discovery of ever deeper plots and subtler misdirections.

Aliette de Bodard's Dominion stories take place in an alternative Paris that is as Balkanized and as bleak as Miéville's double city, and yet because her storytelling is based in legend and myth rather than the accounts of crime-fighters and spies, it not only allows for but requires some sort of breaking down of barriers by the end of the third volume. The premise of the stories is that angels have started falling from Heaven to the streets of Paris, to which they bring powerful magic and devastating disorder. Theirs is a different kind of corruption from the institutionalized cynicism of hard-boiled fiction and film noir. These are, after all, fallen angels, which is to say beings whose beauty masks a lack of empathy for humans and an implacable bitterness over their exile. Their leader is Lucifer Morningstar, who has made himself head of House Silverspires, a fiefdom in the heart of the city. Another prominent Fallen is called Asmodeus, but not all take demonic names. Several have names chosen by the first and foremost among them from among non-Christian myths—the narrator explains that "Morningstar had liked old-fashioned names, drawn straight from the pages of some of the obscure books he'd favored: Selene, Nightfall, Oris, Aragon . . . ." The Houses are fortified neighborhoods within which the Fallen rule with impersonal cruelty. Humans must make a choice between submitting to one of the Houses or remaining Houseless and thus defenseless. The angels' favorites are gifted with lesser powers; they can become alchemists or healers or magical warriors. Angel breath bestows temporary vitality and control over the elements; the ground-up bones of an angel become an even more powerful magical enhancement but also a highly addictive drug—literally angel dust.

As we come into the series, Paris is already scarred by a war between major Houses. Streets are barricaded, monuments lie in ruins (images of the burned-out shell of Notre Dame are eerily prescient in a work written four years before the 2019 fire), gangs scavenge for Fallen relics, the Seine is polluted by magical residue from the war. Yet de Bodard introduces elements to the narrative mix that will ultimately destabilize the rule of the Fallen and thus offer at least a hope of redemption to the city. Like Wecker, she draws on personal family history. Reflecting her French and Vietnamese ancestry, she features characters who confound binary thinking that would insist that everyone must be either insider or outsider, predator or victim, ordinary human or angel. In the first book, *The House of Shattered Wings*, after a brief vignette from the perspective of a newly fallen angel, the viewpoint shifts to that of Philippe, who is revealed to be not the young man he appears but an ageless sage expelled for disobedience from the Imperial Court of Heaven and then taken as a conscript in the war of the Houses from his Vietnamese home-in-exile. The presence of non-Europeans—not only Vietnamese or, as the text calls them, Annamese, but also Senegalese, Maghrebi, and other formerly colonial peoples—dilutes the power of the Fallen and offers the possibility of pockets of resistance to their power.

"There *were* others," Philippe muses, "from other countries, other magics that weren't Fallen." However, the Fallen are currently dominant as those who believe in them are dominant: magical systems in the series mirror the political realities of a colonialized world. Though Christianity itself is a shambles as Paris is in ruins, the cultural hegemony that raised its world view above other cognitive systems is still in play in the magical dimension. Philippe can resist the power of the Fallen but he cannot challenge them directly; he must work indirectly, performing spells by sensing and guiding the elemental power called *khi* in the book—more recognizable in the transliterated Chinese word *chi*.

Philippe's awareness of *khi* gives the first hint of another group, another cognitive and racial minority living unnoticed by the Fallen:

> There was—a flash of something familiar: the magical equivalent of the smell of jasmine rice, a touch of something on the nape of his neck that brought him, instantly, back to the banks of the Red River, staring at the swollen mass of the river at monsoon time—breathing in the wet smell of rain and churned mud. Had some other Annamite been there?

But the familiar sensation is not awareness of another human immigrant like himself, but rather a glimpse of yet another magical power hidden in the rivers of Paris: dragons.

Philippe's response to the watery *khi* currents he has sensed is cautiously optimistic: "Good. Not everything in the world was subject to the Fallen." He does not yet believe that there might be an entire dragon kingdom transplanted to the waterways of Paris. It seems impossible that the Fallen themselves would not be aware of such powerful rivals. Yet the dragons are there—though their underwater realm is tainted by magical fallout from the war—and their elemental magic allows them to stay clear of the Houses and eventually to emerge as a challenge to the Fallen and their world view.

The interactions among diverse immigrant communities, racial identities, and belief systems force change even on the Fallen, and that capacity for change is the main source of hope in the series. Philippe plays a role in humbling House Silverspires and pushing Morningstar toward self-sacrifice. Eventually Philippe joins his fellow Annamese, whose traditions and communal ties have allowed them to survive without the sponsorship of a House. A similar role is played in the second book, *The House of Binding Thorns*, by the young dragon prince Thuan. Thuan starts out as a spy (in his human form) in House Hawthorne and ends up as consort to its Fallen leader Asmodeus. Angels are represented by convention and theology as both unchanging and implacable, characteristics that in the Fallen manifest as arrogance and cruelty toward mortals. Yet as they live among humans and confront dragons, the Fallen begin to form familial and romantic relationships with both, and those relationships result in very un-angelic alteration and accommodation. They have become neighbors, and neighbors must make adjustments even to the universes they have constructed around themselves.

Laurie J. Marks's Elemental Logic quartet shares with de Bodard's Dominion stories a tough-minded view of human history and behavior but similarly finds its way toward a cautiously optimistic conclusion. Whereas both de Bodard and Wecker set their stories in alternative versions of our world, Marks's series is secondary-world fantasy, epic in scale and meticulous in its world-building, in the tradition of Tolkien and Le Guin. Like those writers, she lets the grand historical narrative stay mostly in the background while she focuses on personal choices and relationships: the small tipping points that change history. A few pages into the first volume, *Fire Logic*, we are confronted with a genocide. The Ashawala'i, an isolated pastoral people in a mountain region of the continent of Shaftal, are attacked by the aggressive Sainnites for no obvious reason. Zanja na'Tarwein, their emissary to the larger world, tries to warn her people and to help them fight off the attack, but to no avail:

> The war horse trampled her into the stones and dust. The *katrim* died all around her. The peaceful history of the Ashawala'i reached a bitter, bloody conclusion. Zanja lay with the others, her blood soaking the dry soil, and the dust slowly settled around her.   (Marks 2002, 47)

Zanja survives, the last of her people, and allies herself with the Shaftali against the Sainnites. The latter are recent arrivals on the continent who are determined to remake their new home in their own image while remaining apart from its people and their traditions, like Roman legions in Britain or Spanish conquistadors in the Americas.

In a recent reassessment of the series after the long-awaited publication of its final volume, Lee Mandelo sums up its accomplishments:

> Kindness and generosity, as well as a willingness to learn, evolve, adapt: these are all part of the practice of hope, in contrast to revenge, dehuman-ization, and stagnation. *Fire Logic* struggles through a morass of trauma, both personal and communal, but comes out whole with an optimism not gutted by pain but tempered in it. It's a powerful challenge to

oft-fashionable grimness for pessimism's sake, and two decades later, that's
still excessively relevant in literature as well as the world at large. (2019)

The traumas Mandelo mentions are deep; the cure is correspondingly slow
and complex. Even after four volumes, not everything is fixed and not
everyone gets a happy ending.

Epic fantasy is often characterized in terms of a battle between good and
evil, but the best fantasy has always muddied those categories. Marks has us
start out seeing Sainnites as classic villains and Shaftali as plucky heroes, but
she gradually makes the reader question those initial impressions, though
there is no question that the Sainnites do commit atrocities, not only
massacring Zanja's people for no apparent reason but also attempting to
extinguish Shaftal's culture along with its civil systems. *Fire Logic* begins
with the destruction of Shaftal's cultural center and library, part of a
deliberate attempt to stamp out Shaftali beliefs and practices. The
Sainnites also attempt to kill all practitioners of Shaftali magic or "logic,"
which is based in the four elements of earth, air, fire, and water as a family of
metaphors something like the four humors of medieval medicine.

In Shaftali culture, everyone has a natural inclination toward one of the
elements, but only a few individuals can take that inclination a step further
toward control over natural phenomena and other people. It is these earth or
air witches who are targeted by the Sainnites as potential sources of rebellion, and rightly so, since the witches who escape their culling do indeed
form the heart of the resistance. Of the main characters, Zanja and the
scholar Emil represent fire logic, which involves intuition and facility with
languages as well as passion. The alarming Norina is an air witch and a
Truthken, someone who can detect others' lies. Water witches are rare; their
powers include manipulation of time and weather. Earth witches are mostly
humble and practical homebodies, but one of their number is the invested
G'deon, who stands for the land of Shaftal. The idea of "standing for" is at
the heart of the logics. Marks has carefully worked out her system so that
what initially seems like a sort of "what's your sign" game like astrology
turns out to be instead an investigation of the way people embrace particular
metaphors and turn them into what the philosopher Wilhelm Dilthey called
Weltanschauungen, world views (or world perceptions or intuitions).
Dilthey saw Weltanschauung as both a basic temperament and a cognitive
stance: a way of processing experience. He believed national cultures as well
as individuals could be oriented toward one Weltanschauung or another;
religious systems reflect the dominant Weltanschauung of the folk.

Marks essentially combines Dilthey's philosophical and historical analysis with George Lakoff's linguistic one to posit that belief and behavior are governed by temperament and metaphoric habit. One's element is a source of strength but also makes one subject to that element's weaknesses. She explains on her website that the notion is grounded not only in her study of Shakespeare and the doctrine of humors but also in her experience of teaching writing and observing the different styles of learning and expression among her students:

> I also began to see how these propensities were not just writing propensities, but living propensities; or, as a Buddhist might put it, "How you do anything is how you do everything." And at some point, during one of many complete overhauls of *Fire Logic*, I began to write about the four kinds of magic as four kinds of thinking. I didn't begin using the word logic to describe this scheme until I was (or thought I was) nearly finished with the novel.   ("Elemental")

The Elemental Logic series plays cognitive dissonance against political conflict: the devastating Sainnite invasion reveals hidden fractures within Shaftali society and forces realignments and compromises among the temperaments. At the same time it imposes on the invading army a new magical reality; elemental powers begin to appear in their ranks, especially among the offspring of the inevitable liaisons between occupiers and occupied.

In the second volume, *Earth Logic*, Marks clearly signals the kind of transformations that will be and have been forced on both peoples (and incidentally but significantly on border tribes such as Zanja's). The half-Sainnite seer Medric sums it up in a history he is writing of his father's folk:

> The worst thing they have done to you, who are my mother's people, was not to destroy your government, take your food and children, deny your traditions, or outlaw your greatest powers. The words thing they have done is to replace your version of honor with theirs. They are making you, the Shaftali people, into Carolins [the Sainnite warrior cast].   (265)

Medric identifies the core of Sainnite culture as honor: it is their controlling metaphor, their element. Sainnite honor is a warrior code; it demands loyalty to the unit, to the army, to the race, and repudiates individuality and innovation. Medric pinpoints the worst aspect of the invasion as the transformation of Shaftali into Sainnites. The Shaftali war leader Mabin is indistinguishable from her Sainnite counterparts: she even writes a treatise on warfare.

The only effective countermeasure is not to become Sainnite but rather to let the Shaftali cultural tradition of hospitality complete its work of turning the stranger into a friend. Shaftal is a harsh environment and its version of hospitality is correspondingly extreme, as it tends to be in places like the Arctic. The description of Shaftali traditional practice resembles travelers' accounts of many tribal people, including Homer's Bronze Age Hellenes. In Greek and Roman myth, those who practice *xenia*, guest-friendship, are rewarded; for instance, when the aging couple Baucis and Philemon welcome strangers who are gods in disguise, offering their own meager portion to the guests, they are rewarded with an everflowing pitcher of wine and made custodians of a sacred shrine. Those who violate the sacred duty of *xenia*, such as Penelope's rowdy suitors, are punished.

In Medric's book (which is positioned in the text as the counter to Mabin's treatise on warfare), he writes about the differences between his father's warrior culture and the practices of his mother's people:

> The Land of Shaftal is unforgiving, a place of harsh winters and brief summers, where sometimes only luck might decide the difference between death and survival. In such a brutal place, it seems the people should also become brutal. That once was the case, long ago, in the time of the first G'deon, Mackapee. But as Mackapee sat in his isolated cave by a peat fire, watching over his sheep, he imagined Shaftal as a community based on mercy. Kindness and generosity, he wrote, can never be earned and will never be deserved. Hospitality is not an act of justice, but of mercy—a mercy beneficial to everyone, by making it possible to depend on and trust each other.   (Marks 2004, 354–55)

Shaftali tradition ascribes this transformative insight to a legendary founder, like Robert the Bruce learning persistence from a spider in his own cave of exile. Legends validate present-day practices by giving them a divine or heroic pedigree while also allowing storytellers to locate themselves and their listeners within the dimension of myth. In essence, Medric is telling his readers that they too are Mackapee before the peat fire; each time they hear of his epiphany it is reenacted. Thus the difficult folk-art of hospitality is maintained; thus it will be taught to the invaders, will they or nill they.

We see this process with characters such as Clement, the Sainnite general, as she sits with a Shaftali family who have taken her in for the night. She muses on her hosts' words of welcome: "And if it hadn't been a good year, Clement wondered vaguely, what would the farmer say instead? That there was always enough to go around, or that what is given comes back eventually?" (Marks 2004, 231). She is learning from example, and it is the shared— and sharing— attitude even more than the food and warmth that makes "the fear in her slowly [come] undone, like an old stiff knot" (231). She is one of the first Sainnites to acknowledge that she has become Shaftali; she leads by example. In Marks's fairy-tale structure, the best will ultimately win out over the worst, though it takes much work and even more sacrifice of personal honor to make it happen. Some Sainnites refuse to follow their leaders; the Shaftali who have become effectively Sainnite do not immediately revert to the practice of radical hospitality. Yet one by one the resisters begin to bend; it is partly their connection to the mythic realm that nudges them in the right direction.

In Marks's version of mythopoeic fantasy, there are no gods directing the action or enforcing codes of behavior. Sainnites seem to be atheists; Zanja's people do have theriomorphic trickster gods such as Raven, but their attitude toward those gods is wary respect rather than personal worship; and the Shaftali religion is based in the land and its elements rather than in a pantheon or an angelic hierarchy such as Tolkien's Ainur. These three rival cosmologies (and others hinted at among the border people of Shaftal) might well have been used to justify further violence between tribes. As the Sainnites go from being an occupying force to a dwindling and unpopular minority, the Shaftali could easily turn to revenge, murdering the infidels as their own witches were murdered. It takes a further discovery— which in Marks's world means another rediscovered book—to force the recognition on both groups that they have more in common than they believe, and that Shaftali and Sainnites are not only neighbors but also kin.

Each of these fantasy scenarios involves diverse groups forced by proximity and circumstance to become not merely tolerant of other beliefs and other ways of life but open to alternative stories. People are not asked to convert to this or that cosmology but only to listen to its narratives and to acknowledge their validity for someone else. They must recognize that their own knowledge is situated within a particular history and culture, and be willing to grant the same recognition to others. That is easiest when there is no cognitive majority, but only a cluster of minorities, as in Wecker's turn-of-the-century lower Manhattan. It is most difficult when either a majority or a powerful minority ascends over other sectors, outlawing religious practices or imposing creeds and tests of faith.

Because these are fantasies, the narrated world itself favors accommodation and renewal. The fairy-tale structure of fantasy requires resolution: it is part of the form, like the concluding couplet of a Shakespearian sonnet. Other storytelling formulas lead to other forms of closure—the unmasking of a killer in detective fiction, the conceptual breakthrough of science fiction, the long-delayed kiss of romance, the shoot-out of a Western—but none are so demanding of creative solutions as fantasy. A fairy story, with or without fairies, must end in what Tolkien called eucatastrophe, the sudden breathtaking turn toward harmony and wonder. Meeting that demand, it seems to me, is more challenging than writing the most rigorous of hard science fiction and worthier of respect than the most faithful reproduction of everyday reality.

Literary fantasy keeps the fairy tale's happy ending but complicates and distributes it, so that is not just a single princess who finds a new home, not just one ogre who is killed, but a whole world that is redeemed by trust, love, determination, kindness, and kinship. The writer who contracts with readers to provide such a tale must find a way both to acknowledge the world's terrors and traumas and to find a convincing path toward transcendence. Not all writers manage; not every poet finds the perfect rhyme to sum up a sonnet. But those who do succeed offer us scenarios for survival. And a scenario that transforms armed camps into neighborhoods is a magical spell much needed in our troubled time.

4
If Not Conflict, Then What?
Metaphors for Narrative Interest

To understand how fantasy means and what kind of cultural work it performs in the world, a good way to start is by identifying some of the ways we perform fantasy as readers. What it does is largely a matter of what we do with it.

A how-to website on novel-writing (one of many making the same claim) asserts that "Conflict is at the heart of all stories" ("6 story conflicts") It then goes on to list the six types of conflict, from "person versus person" (at least they didn't say "man against man") to "person versus supernatural."

This may be good advice for getting published, but it isn't true. The only essential requirement for narrative is change over time. Other types of texts, such as arguments and descriptions, don't entail such change. Seymour Chatman suggests that for a narrative to be perceived as not just a story but a meaningful story, the change must be motivated. There must be causal connections between events and a reason to recount them: what he calls a "point" (1993, 11). Chatman disputes E. M. Forster's claim that "The King died and then the Queen died" is merely a story, while "The King died and then the Queen died of grief" is a plot. Forster voices a modernist prejudice against storytelling—"Yes—oh, dear, yes—the novel tells a story," he says—but his definition is less convincing as a distinction between story and plot than as a capsule description of narrative art. Furthermore, according to Chatman, readers will infer connectedness and consequence even when the text seems to offer only sequence: "In E. M. Forster's example . . . we assume that the queen was in fact the wife of that king. If not, there would have to be some explanation of the queen's death, for example, 'Though she did not know him, she died of the grief she felt for the decay of royal houses'" (Chatman 1978, 30–1).

Joan Aiken similarly argues that "What E. M. F. refers to so disparagingly as a story is, in fact, not a story at all but a mere narrative. His definition of *plot* is what *I* would call a story":

> The difference between life and a story is that life is flat and goes on and on, whereas a story has a shape, which resists alteration. Take out one piece and it pulls the whole structure lopsided; it has a frame, a climax; you listen in confidence because you know that *something is going to happen*, it will all work out in the end.   (40–1)

Forster's second sentence is a complete story, a shapely story, a story with a point. It has characters, an implied setting (Where do we find kings and queens? In the counting house and the parlor, of course), and motivated change over time. Of course, we can question the motivation and, as Chatman says, we can scarcely help drawing inferences. Was the Queen grieving for the loss of her husband, or did she not look forward to becoming a dowager? Is the statement ironic, representing not the Queen's real feelings but those attributed to her by the court? That last is essentially the plot of Kate Chopin's "The Story of an Hour," minus the royalty.

Whether one claims plotting or storytelling to be the higher art form, a more pertinent question is, Where in Forster's example can we find the conflict that is supposed to be essential? There is change, there's emotion, there's consequence, but where are clash or combat, which are the core meanings of *conflict* and its Latin predecessor *conflictus*? Our writers' website would have us believe the conflict to be within the Queen herself, or between the Queen and whatever caused the King's death, something natural or supernatural. I don't buy it. All but a few of those uses of the word are metaphoric, and the metaphor has colonized a whole realm of experience.

Every successful story has an engine of impulsion, an emotional mainspring (to suggest an alternative metaphor). Something keeps us going, engages our attention and sympathy, stimulates anticipation and suspense. To call that something "conflict" is to choose among analogies. And it's a dubious choice for a number of reasons.

Ursula K. Le Guin's short essay "Conflict" addresses exactly my topic. This chapter is essentially a sermon on her text. Le Guin even uses the E. M. Forster example that Chatman quoted, asking with regard to the pair of royal deaths, "Who is pitted against what? Who wins?" She also mentions a couple of examples that one would think make the case for the "conflict" fans: *Romeo and Juliet* and *War and Peace*. In neither case does she deny the presence of conflict, but she questions, of the former, "is that all it involves? Isn't *Romeo and Juliet* about something else, and isn't it the something else that makes the otherwise trivial tale of a feud into a tragedy?" (191).

I take her question as an invitation: to look at a number of examples of fantastic stories and see how their narrative shape and impetus might be described other than through what Le Guin calls the "gladiatorial view of fiction." If not conflict, then what?

I'll begin with Lewis Carroll's *Through the Looking-Glass*, which, like *War and Peace*, is a story with battle as backdrop. Instead of the Napoleonic wars, we have a chess game: symbolic combat. A less quirky writer than Carroll might have focused on the conflict between red and black, made the rival queens into enemies, and dramatized the individual contests between knights. The result might have come out something like George R. R. Martin's *Song of Ice and Fire*: epic, gritty, violent. Instead, we have a number of narrative trajectories involving a White Queen who is occasionally a sheep, a pair of nursery-rhyme twins who spend a lot of time preparing for combat only to be distracted by the shadow of a crow, a garden of argumentative flowers, and a knight who would rather invent than fight. But the main narrative engine is Alice's journey from pawn to queen, which is marked out by the series of squares she must cross to the final row on the board. Like many fantasies, *Looking-Glass* first unfolds its plot in the form of a prophecy: the Red Queen tells Alice exactly what she is to go through, from a quick railway journey through the Third and Fourth Squares to the forest of the Seventh and then the Eighth where "we shall be Queens together and it's all feasting and fun."

The journey is the plot, and the complications that make it interesting have less to do with conflict than with misunderstandings, cross-purposes, and sudden transformations. Much of the interest is in seeing how Carroll transmutes common objects into characters and institutes frustration as a natural law: as the Rose advises Alice, to get to a goal, one has to "walk the other way." In place of conflict, Carroll uses misdirection (in several senses) to propel his narrative.

Another fantasy with a similar structure is Edward Eager's comic fantasy *Half Magic*. In that case, the journey is toward mastery of a magical artifact that grants exactly half of what one wishes for. Or we could say (as I did in a previous chapter) that it is a journey toward self-discovery for each sibling and reformulation of their family into a new and more satisfactory order. Each adventure involves negotiating with a resistant adult world and a refractory magical servant. There is no adversary, no battle of good and evil, no tragic fate. The one fight sequence pits Katherine, the poetic sibling, against Sir Lancelot, and the scene ends up being not about strife but about pride: both Lancelot's and Katherine's. The four children bicker throughout and often disagree about means and ends, but even those mild conflicts aren't the main interest. The emotional mainspring is our pleasure in watching the wishes unfold: what will go wrong this time, and what will the children learn from another narrowly averted disaster?

Diana Wynne Jones was another master of the frustrated wish. I could pick any of a number of her books, but a good test case is *Witch Week* (2009), in which a comic surface masks a situation of real horror, a world governed by persecution and paranoia. The story takes place in a deceptively ordinary boarding school. Someone in Class 6B leaves a note accusing a classmate of being a witch; someone else proves the point by working a spell, for this is a world in which actual witches are hunted by actual inquisitors and burned at the stake. The story focuses on the outcasts of Class 6B, all of whom are trying to get by through strategies of deflection and self-disguise—in other words, it is a realistic story of school life except for the presence of magic and the danger of immolation.

A determined reader could describe this as a story of conflict: there is plenty of simmering hostility with a few outbreaks of overt malevolence. The scapegoating of witches is a kind of conflict, reminiscent of plenty of real-life clashes such as antisemitic campaigns or the Red and Pink Scares of the 1950s. However, that level of reference remains mostly in the background, in the form of scenes remembered or overheard. It is more accurate to call it a story of connection and (forced) cooperation, The main characters must learn how to work together, letting the strengths of one compensate for the failings of another. The emotional engine of *Witch Week* has to do with not-quite-buried grief, resentment of the popular by the unpopular and vice versa, hypocrisy among both children and adults, discovery of powers the children don't know they possess, and a final turn toward justice. Those last two fuel many fantasies. Coming into one's powers is a classic fantasy trope, and the restoration of justice (sometimes emblematized as the return of a king) is familiar from *The Lord of the Rings*, Le Guin's *The Farthest Shore* (1972), and a thousand others.

A particularly powerful fantasy of scapegoating and deception, Frances Hardinge's *Gullstruck Island* (2009), shows how easily difference can lead to violence and abuse. The precarious truce among different races on Hardinge's imaginary island is broken by an act of treachery and soon ramps up to near-genocide. The protagonists consider retribution, the return of violence for violence, but ultimately take the harder path toward reconciliation. It would be easy, but misleading, to analyze the power of the novel in terms of conflict; the conflict is there but again the more significant movement is toward self-knowledge and acceptance of the Other. Along the way, Hardinge provides enough moments of beauty and humor to remind us that life is more than battles and betrayals.

In his study of *Justice in Young Adult Speculative Fiction*, Marek Oziewicz has identified the creation of new scripts for justice as a central theme in, and an essential function of, fantasy. By "scripts," he means stories that dramatize the relations between perpetrator and victim, tyrant and rebel, usurper and rightful heir, and all the other interactions that constitute injustice. To be useful, those scripts must be memorable enough to stick in our minds, transparent enough to be held up against the world for comparison, and innovative enough to offer alternatives to the old, destructive scripts such as vengeance. And that is part of my dissatisfaction with conflict as a measure of storytelling success. By itself, conflict offers nothing constructive. It must be paired with resolution, like war with peace. And the resolution is, or should be, the more significant half of the pairing.

It may seem like a pretty far reach to get from Looking-Glass logic to new models for justice, although I got there in only four examples, or three degrees of fantasy separation. More to the point, a focus on conflict as the sole source of interest in fiction means that writers need to keep upping the stakes, and the stakes in Harding's novel are certainly higher than those in Carroll's dream fantasy. Conflict in a story is like action on the screen. Audiences get jaded. They begin to want more violent fights, longer chases, bigger explosions—and Hollywood is happy to oblige. Yet too often, action sequences are times when nothing happens storywise: no one learns anything, nothing is revealed about characters, and nothing moves forward. There are exceptions, of course, and action can be kinetically beautiful in its own right (for instance the fight with Zhang Ziyi's lethal sleeves in *House of Flying Daggers*, 2004), but there are only so many minutes in a movie and every minute devoted to blowing things up means fewer minutes for flirtation or contemplation or regret.

Which leads me back to conflict in fantasy. Of course there is conflict in *Lord of the Rings*, in A Song of Ice and Fire, even in Le Guin's Earthsea. G. Willow Wilson's World Fantasy Award-winning novel *Alif the Unseen* (2012) explores several kinds of conflict: between humans and jinn, religious hard-liners and reformers, oil-rich Middle Easterners and south Asian servants, contemporary Western technology and traditional Arabic world views. Given that the setting is an unnamed Emirate on the Gulf, it is no trick to find conflict. The challenge Wilson takes on is the opposite: to move beyond conflict into something more constructive, perhaps even one of Oziewicz's new scripts for justice.

The first step toward meeting that challenge is to find a way to represent Alif's city as something more than a battleground. It is also a community, a place where people find ways to connect socially, romantically, electronically. Though Alif initially sees himself as a lone warrior—Internet hacker as knight errant—he can only survive and prevail with the help of a wide range of relationships. Where some might locate the narrative interest in the conflict itself, I suggest we look instead in the process of finding allies, in discovering unforeseen resources, and in re-evaluating oneself and one's surroundings. I am much more interested in discovery than in conflict, and in wonder rather than hostility, as emotional mainsprings, which is why I am a reader of science fiction and fantasy.

Earlier, I claimed that "conflict" is a metaphor, although it is mistaken for literal description of how stories work. George Lakoff and Mark Johnson have shown us that any choice of metaphor is vital: we think with metaphors and we live by them. "Argument is war" is one of the metaphors discussed by Lakoff and Johnson, and they suggest that we "(t)ry to imagine a culture where arguments are not viewed in terms of war, where no one wins or loses, where there is no sense of attacking or defending, gaining or losing" (5). How can we do that? "Imagine a culture," they suggest, "where an argument is viewed as a dance, the participants are seen as performers, and the goal is to perform in a balanced and aesthetically pleasing way." The implication is that a change of metaphor might lead to a change in behavior: we act out the stories or scripts we have distilled into metaphor and internalized.

I'm not sure if I can see all sources of narrative tension in fiction in terms of dance, but there are other related metaphors to try out. How about a musical metaphor: dissonance? We already use that metaphor for the kind of internal conflict called cognitive dissonance. Again, we forget we are using metaphor: the operations of the brain involved are neither fighting nor music-making. Of the two arts, music and dance, I find the analogy with music more compelling, maybe because I am a musician. Daniel Melnick has identified dissonance as a key metaphor in the aesthetics of modernist fiction, tracing the notion back to Nietzsche but also to the cross-influence on literature of musical innovators such as Debussy or Stravinsky. This metaphor offers myriad insights into the experience of fiction. For instance, dissonance implies an absent or violated, but still implicit underlying harmony—atonality does not produce dissonance per se. It is also temporary: one of Mozart's string quartets is known as "The Dissonant" because of the disturbing musical "errors" among the opening chords, but over time, those discords are resolved into new, more complex kinds of order. One generation's dissonance might be the next's consonance, and one culture will accept as harmonically allowable what another shuns: quarter tones or minor seconds or augmented fourths.

There is much dissonance in *Alif the Unseen*, frequently involving the inability of characters to see what they don't already believe in. Alif himself doesn't see the networks of community that sustain him, especially the work performed by his mother and other women. Imprisoned by the Emir's agent and thinking he has lost everything, he comes to the realization that "the ritualized world he had dismissed as feminine was in fact civilization." Another character, the American referred to only as the convert (partly a satirical self-portrait by Wilson) retreats into a drowsy fog when confronted by genuine magic, which contradicts her world view:

> Alif glanced at the convert: her eyes were glassy and she kept swaying back and forth as though falling asleep and catching herself each time she dozed off.
>
> "She's an American," said Vikram, apparently by way of explanation.
>
> "Ah." The woman gave the convert a look of pity. "Half in, half out. She may not remember much of what passes here."

Both the convert and Alif move past their respective cognitive denials to form new intellectual models and to find beauty in things they previously could not perceive. One of the strengths of dissonance as a metaphor is that there are many ways to respond to it, unlike conflict, which can only be mediated or fought to the end. A dissonant note can be changed or the notes surrounding it can shift to make it the root of a new chord. The listener can learn to hear more subtle harmonies: polytonality, for instance, in which clashing notes each make sense in overlapping harmonic structures. The ending of *Alif the Unseen* is polytonal.

A second metaphor we can try on is friction. This one has been used by many commentators, and it's especially apt for the impediments to love that are the stock-in-trade for popular romance. A popular writer of male-male romance points out on his website that friction not only impedes movement but also generates heat (with a strong suggestion of sexual activity). He explicitly contrasts friction with conflict: "obsessing about conflict," he says, "can lead to monotonous, silly choices," whereas

> friction in fiction operates exactly as it does in intimacy...as a shifting dynamic interaction of differing things, as rough, soft, fast, slow, cruel, gentle as necessary...but never inert.   (Suede 2010)

Friction implies proximity, movement, pressure, resistance, and change. You can't win a friction, as you can a conflict, but you can adjust the parts, introduce lubrication, or let the friction itself smooth down the rubbing surfaces. Friction is also traction, which allows the story to gain momentum.

Looking again at *Alif the Unseen*, sources of friction include non-meshing desires, misinterpretations (between languages and between discourse communities), and many forms of injustice. Alif desires the aristocratic Intisar, but she desires other things more than she desires him. His childhood friend Dina desires Alif's love but he does not notice her desire.

There are plenty of other social, emotional, and political forms of friction in the novel, but I am going to focus on semiotic frictions: differing meanings that rub together to produce complexity and narrative heat. The plot revolves around a book—a sequel to the *Thousand and One Nights* but written by jinn rather than humans—that is a translation of a translation,

> first into Persian from the voiceless language in which the creature spoke... Then from Persian into Arabic, the language of Reza's education, as mathematical and efficient as the creature's speech was diffuse.

The Arabic version has been lost, and the world knows the text only through a further translation into French generally believed to be a fabrication by the supposed translator, François Pétis de la Croix.

Some of the most interesting conversations in the book involve the way meanings shift and multiply, even in a stable text like the Quran. The jinn Vikram says, "All translations are made up.... Languages are different for a reason. You can't move ideas between them without losing something." Vikram also points to the word translated as "atom," which could not have meant *atom* when the Quran was written and yet

> [i]n the twentieth century, *atom* became the original meaning... because an atom was the tiniest object known to man.... tomorrow it might be a quark. In a hundred years, some vanishingly small object so foreign to the human mind that only Adam remembers its name. Each of those will be the original meaning of ذرة.

Thinking of these linguistic challenges as forms of friction rather than conflict, we can see that each makes the text less predictable and its meanings more open-ended. It is no accident that Alif is a computer programmer:

the story is about coding and metaphors and multivalent symbols. Those are dangerous. Early in the novel, Dina objects to the metaphors in Philip Pullman's *The Golden Compass*, which Alif has lent her, as "just a fancy way of calling something by a false name." Yet at the same time, metaphor— and its more sustained cousin, fantasy—may be the only way to represent the complex, deceptive, shifty nature of reality. A wise cleric in the novel says, "If man's capacity for the fantastic took up as much of his imagination as his capacity for cruelty, the worlds, seen and unseen, might be very different."

So far I have been using metaphors that were already lying around, so now I want to try my hand at manufacturing a new one. I will also describe the process by which I got there, since sometimes the path is more important than the destination.

I recently reread Patricia McKillip's 2010 fantasy *The Bards of Bone Plain* in preparation for teaching it, and in the process I finally figured out something important about McKillip's brand of fantasy. She is another writer who can and does employ conflict very adroitly, very unexpectedly, as in her Riddlemaster trilogy (1976–79), which involves a longstanding dispute between shapeshifters and land-bound humans. Yet there is always, in Le Guin's words, "something else" going on in McKillip, and it is a mysterious something else. Nothing is what it seems in her novels, and enemies and friends switch identities with dizzying speed. There is also dissonance in her stories: again, as when the Riddlemaster's Prince Morgon has to revise his world view each time he encounters a being who doesn't fit the categories he has inherited or devised. Most strikingly, his division of the world into good and evil camps increasingly breaks down as he finds elements of both qualities in himself and his seeming enemies. Since music is an important part of the plot, as in much of McKillip's work, there is literal dissonance as well. Friction comes in most particularly in McKillip's dialogue, which can be frustratingly indirect. Characters say what they don't mean and mean what they don't say. Intentions rub against circumstances; frustrations polish the characters like sandpaper.

But neither of those quite conveys McKillip's particular form of narrative engagement, any more than *conflict* does. The first metaphor I came up with for *The Bards of Bone Plain* was "blur." Going through the book the first time, we are likely to be confused or misled by our initial expectations and subsequent misinterpretations of scenes in the book, until the realities of the situation eventually come into focus; till then we see "through a glass, darkly." But a more careful reading of *The Bards* reveals that it is never really blurry. The language is vivid and precise and the narrative tells us exactly what is going on, although we, and the characters, fail to comprehend. Sticking with optics as what Lakoff and Johnson call a metaphoric source domain, I found another, apter metaphor: occultation. That term undoubtedly calls for a definition for us non-specialists. According to the Merriam Webster dictionary, occultation is, first, "the state of being hidden from view or lost to notice," and, second, "the interruption of the light from a celestial body or of the signals from a spacecraft by the intervention of a celestial body [;] *especially*: an eclipse of a star or planet by the moon." Primary, nonmetaphoric uses of the term are now mostly in astronomy, but metaphoric extensions of that use give it back some of its original meaning of any act of concealment.

The core meaning of occultation is that one thing is hidden by another. That is McKillip's technique to a T: the clues are present, not blurred, but obscured by something that comes between the observer and the thing observed. The process of hiding is reminiscent of Poe's "The Purloined Letter." The truth is there in plain sight, but it has been disguised as itself, or rather, as Jacques Lacan informs us, the original letter is replaced by another version of itself, turned inside out and re-addressed, an act which changes nothing and yet changes everything: author, addressee, signification, use (1972). A character named Kelda engages in just this sort of occultation in the book: he is a magical bard who disguises himself as a magical bard, but a less impressive and less dangerous version of himself.

More often, there is no deliberate intent behind the hiding, but rather the characters and reader are misled by habits of thought. The thing we expect to see "interrupts the signals" from the actual object. In *The Bards*, for instance, one important plot point involves a set of monoliths. We meet the standing stones in the third sentence of the book:

> Tide washed softly along the flank of one of the great, weathered standing stones scattered so randomly on both sides of the river that some said they moved about restively at night when the moon was old.

But we have already unknowingly met one of those stones in the very first sentence, which is, "Phelan found his father at the river's edge." McKillip's narrator has given us important information and then obscured it with phrases like "some said" and "one tale of the stones." Phelan's father Jonah is, sometimes, one of those standing stones.

Again, the truth is concealed in plain sight when the narrator says that another tale of the stones "was drifting drunkenly behind a pile of rubble from a wall that had collapsed wearily into the conjunction of water and earth," and then when the hidden voice speaks the words of a traditional riddle-song:

> I was there when they went to war,
> The stones of Bek, the stones of Taran,
> And the doughty stones of Stirl.
> I saw them rage and thunder. I lived to tell the tale.
> Who am I?

The hidden voice is that of Jonah, giving Phelan clues to the mystery that is himself. But Phelan thinks he already knows the answer: Jonah is simply drunk again, he is hidden behind the pile of rubble rather than being part of it, and the riddle is simply treating the stones as a metaphor for something else, some other conflict.

Yet if we don't accept all those common-sense assumptions—and in rereading the story, we don't—then they give us a completely different account of who Jonah is and what is happening. The scene goes on:

> Phelan might have been alone in the mist, and the world itself beginning all over again but for his father's voice.
> "Who's there?"
> "Much you'd care," he reminded the pile of stone, and got a soft chuckle out of them.

All of that tells us important things that neither we nor Phelan are ready to see. He is and is not alone in the mist. The world is indeed continually beginning all over again as part of what the story calls the Circle of Days. Jonah is both man and stone.

Many key elements of the story are similarly concealed in plain sight, including a legendary set of tests called the Three Trials of Bone Plain. The tests have well-known names: the Turning Tower, the Inexhaustible Cauldron, and the Oracular Stone. But the Turning Tower is concealed behind or within an actual ruined tower at the school for bards; the Cauldron goes unrecognized in the cooking vessels that nurture Phelan and other residents; the Stone is silent because no one can read the ancient runes inscribed around the city; and no one understands Bone Plain to be a version of the landscape all around them. Teaching a history lesson to the student bards, Phelan tells them something he himself does not realize at this point:

> "Your muses are everywhere around you … Sun, wind, earth, water, stone, tree. All speak the language of the bard. Of poetry."

Misunderstanding his own lesson, he explains, "As we know, stones do not speak, nor do cauldrons yield an unending supply of stew except in poetry." He doesn't realize that his world is poetry and that magic is hidden in the songs he has learned, in the stones of the plain, in his own heritage as son of an immortal bard, and in the daily round of activities that bring bread and soup to the table and good cheer to the community of students and masters.

One of McKillip's most magical tricks is to render the same images and objects simultaneously everyday and enchanted, and the key to her technique is occultation, which can also mean rendering something occult, the object of secret knowledge. She uses several extended metaphors to represent that knowledge and the ways it is disguised: the stones, the songs of the bards, legends about the bards Nairn (who is also Jonah) and Declan, and the runic writing that is both occult and everyday. We see those runes not only inscribed on monoliths but also decorating loaves of bread and marking the tops of jars of preserves: they are part of housewives' lore. Jonah/Nairn asks Declan, "Why are you teaching me to write 'water' with scratches … that nobody understands anymore?" The answer is that "The word only looks like 'water.' Beneath the surface, it becomes something else entirely." And there is a good definition of occultation, as McKillip uses it.

The process also applies to people. Jonah despairs of ever understanding what Declan is trying to teach him, when the lesson is already laid out in front of him: "[Jonah] was silent, trying to hear what Declan wasn't saying, what might lie within the words. He gave up. The bard was too subtle and he too ignorant to understand …" The problem is not that Declan is subtle or Jonah ignorant, but that Jonah thinks in terms of subtlety when Declan is being straightforward. Music is magic; Jonah is, or ought to be, a wizard; and only his mistaken sense of himself stops him from perceiving or employing his own power. As with power, so too with love, and with conflict. Jonah is a Jonah, in the proverbial sense—a man cursed for his unbelief—because he has mistaken his ally for an enemy. That ally is the bard Welkin, whom he once tried to kill in the belief that Welkin was a danger to him and to the land.

In the second bardic competition that serves as climax to the book, Welkin returns, calling himself Kelda, and Jonah once again sees him as a threat, but the battle of the bards turns instead into an ensemble piece for Kelda, Jonah, Phelan, and a friend of Phelan's named Zoe. As one character sums it up, "All this time I thought it was Kelda, playing with Zoe. I couldn't see anything very clearly until now. I've never heard your father play before." As for Kelda,

> "He turned back into Welkin and reminded my father how to play again. Then he turned himself back into that."
> He gestured to the boulder breaking out of the grounds.

All these characters ought to know better than to engage in combat against a character who is a stone, whose names, Welkin and Kelda, mean, respectively, sky or cloud and wellspring. This seeming enemy is an embodiment of the land itself and its movement through the Circle of Days. If Welkin/ Kelda were an enemy, we could analyze the scene as conflict between humans and nature. But, as I said at the start of the chapter, nature is not a combatant; we only think so if we engage in our own form of occultation, putting some sort of human enemy in front of the environment so that we can't see it.

A story is both an aesthetic object and a simulation game: a way to rehearse what hasn't happened yet and to interpret what has already occurred. Stories in general are as China Miéville says of the fantastic specifically, "good to think with" (46). The idea that literature has a use value of this sort is reinforced by recent studies of the way the brain processes fiction. Patrick Hogan, for instance, tells us that:

> One basic principle of cognitive science of literature and the arts is that the human brain operates using the same structures and processes regardless of whether it is addressing literature or life ... [T]he neurocognitive architecture is constant.   (3)

Simulation is modeling, a way of finding underlying patterns that help us predict, interpret, and evaluate one another's actions. The various metaphors for narrative interest are thus also models. A conflict model not only generates an emotional response by pitting characters against one another or against some outside forces but also invites us to understand characters in terms of such conflict. And favoring conflict as an aesthetic technique encourages us to see conflict as the basis for all interactions, fictional or otherwise. Models are also scripts.

So what do my other metaphors offer in the way of models? What do they invite us to *do* with the texts? Looking for dissonance involves searching for underlying harmonic structures that the dissonance transgresses. It can also involve integrating the dissonance into new, more complex forms of harmony. It encourages us to see characters relationally, not as opponents but as collaborators—like the harpists of *The Bards of Bone Plain*, once they give up the idea of winning and losing. It encourages us to think of stories symphonically: to think of individual choices as variations on musical motifs (or motives) and different temperaments as instrumental timbres: oboe characters will register very differently from harps or violas. Finally, though we say of both conflict and dissonance that they can be resolved, the natures of those two kinds of resolution are very different.

The friction metaphor emphasizes texture and movement. Stroking a kitten is a completely different experience from gliding over ice, though both involve friction. Thinking in terms of friction invokes senses other than sight and hearing, both of which operate at a distance and thus let us remain uninvolved. Other choices of model invite different kinds of imagery. Friction nudges writers toward touch and heat and pain—and also invokes the smell of burning rubber and the taste of grit and the feeling of giddiness or arousal: all with the effect of encouraging very close reader identification. In terms of interpreting intentions and meanings, a friction model is also relational in a way that conflict is not. Friction requires mutuality. To develop friction in a scene where a character is alone, the character must rub up against *something*: circumstance, or memory, or blocked desire. Friction also involves movement. The opposite of friction is not frictionless-ness but stasis. The cure for something that rubs you the wrong way is to figure out the right way to rub. In *Alif the Unseen*, there will never not be friction between classes or religious systems or conceptual orders. Neither people nor jinn will suddenly develop glassy-smooth temperaments. If they could, there would be no traction and nothing would move forward: there would be no stories.

Finally, occultation not only sets plots moving and throws obstacles in front of characters but also creates meaning by hiding it. Every revelation involves finding a way to incorporate the older misunderstanding into a new cognitive structure. Importantly, the structure of occultation is not binary, but trinary: every instance of occultation requires a concealing object, a concealed object, and an observer. Change the position of any one body, and you have something other than occultation. We would not have solar eclipses if the sun and moon were not where they are in relation to Earth. And early astronomers would not have been able to learn something about the sun, the moon, and the earth from their conjunction: occultation is an important source of new observational data about all three players.

This sort of nonbinary relation is reminiscent of Charles Sanders Peirce's system of semiotics. For Peirce, meaning occurs only when a sign and its object are accompanied by a third thing, which he calls an interpretant. Peirce's own explanation of the relationship is obscure enough to require an interpretant of its own, such as this gloss:

> The interpretant, the most innovative and distinctive feature of Peirce's account, is best thought of as the understanding that we have of the sign/ object relation. The importance of the interpretant for Peirce is that signification is not a simple dyadic relationship between sign and object: a sign signifies only in being interpreted.   (Atkin, 2006)

I won't try to match up my narrative triad with Peirce's semiotic one, but I do think his ideas about the importance of context and observer are essential to understanding fantasies such as McKillip's, in which knowledge is always relational.

And not just McKillip's. All the works I have mentioned involve similar kinds of concealment and revelation. I could go back through each example showing how Carroll, Eager, Jones, Hardinge, and Wilson variously set up perceptual barriers like those in McKillip's novel and how those barriers get integrated into new trajectories of action and modes of understanding. In each case, the occultation not only complicates characters' lives and generates narrative interest but also, by making things hidden, makes them mysterious and significant. Rather than multiplying textual examples, though, I will finish by going back to eclipses, which are a particularly dramatic form of occultation.

I was fortunate enough to see a total solar eclipse a few years ago, and it was a much more powerful experience than I expected. At the moment of totality, I became aware of two things. One was that I was not just seeing a flat image of two disks, but the movement of huge, three-dimensional objects through space, each of which was pulling powerfully on the other and on the earth I was standing on. It was an enormous dance: to apply Lakoff and Johnson's metaphor in reverse, we were seeing an argument between sun and moon. And, secondly, I realized that hiding the sun revealed it. As the last brilliant speck of sun disappeared behind the moon, the corona unfurled itself. I had seen pictures; I thought I knew what a corona was like. It was nothing like the pictures: it was eerie, like the Northern Lights, elegant in its imperfect symmetry, and vast—taking up much more of the sky than I imagined.

So occultation is also discovery. In astronomy, it results in new knowledge about comets and distant stars; in fiction, it allows everyday objects to reveal their mysteries, and ordinary characters to transform into ancient, powerful, sometimes tragic figures. The revelations don't just concern hidden things: the blocking object (which can be common sense, or received knowledge, or one's entire world view) is also transformed. To read in terms of occultation is to perceive doubleness and depth in simplicity. McKillip's choices of runic words, like *bread* and *tree*, are not accidental. They echo J. R. R. Tolkien's comment that, "It was in fairy-stories that I first divined the potency of the words, and the wonder of the things, such as stone, and wood, and iron; tree and grass; house and fire; bread and wine" (59). We don't know those things until we understand that they are occult, deceptive, and true in ways we can't imagine. Does the conflict model offer any such vision?

Our choice of model determines what we can do with that fiction afterward, when the book is closed and we look at the re-emerging world. I have offered three alternative metaphors for the engine that drives fiction. If those don't resonate, there are many more. If argument is a dance, as Lakoff and Johnson suggest, a story might be based on the exploration of missteps or stumbles. A metaphor from electronics might be interference, or noise. From sculpture, perhaps roughness or imbalance. Each of these offers new possibilities for interpretation, new things to look for in texts. I am talking about what we as readers can do with the text, rather than writers' choices in composing it. It is up to us to ask for, and praise when we find, more creative scripts, new ways to narrate justice and innovation and discovery, than the old standby of conflict. Scholars, reviewers, and readers often ask about a happy ending whether it is "earned." Did the characters work hard enough, suffer enough, display enough virtue to warrant their coming to what author Mary Hallock Foote, borrowing a metaphor from her engineer husband, called an "angle of repose"? I have never seen anyone ask whether the conflict itself was earned. What justified putting the characters through their misery? Was it simply that the plot needed interest? Did the writing need amping up with a little violence? Was the path of most resistance also the easiest to imagine?

There are many ways a story can earn its right to conflict. If working through the conflict results in uncovering injustice, I am all for it. If it nudges the reader toward greater understanding or deeper empathy, then, yes, the conflict had to be there. If conflict is part of the truth that the story testifies to, that truth can make it worth our while. But if the rationale is simply narrative interest, perhaps that is the lazy solution, especially if the result is habituating readers to ever-greater levels of cruelty and violence. The other kinds of plot complications I have been talking about are harder to set up and more perplexing to solve than most ordinary sorts of conflict. I suggest that readers seek them out and reward writers who opt for a more unexpected trajectory, for the narrative path that might turn out to be the "road to fair Elfland" glimpsed in the ballad of Thomas the Rhymer.

5

A Mitochondrial Theory of Literature

Fantasy and Intertextuality

Nike Sulway's story "The Karen Joy Fowler Book Club" (2015) sets the reader off on a complicated trail of sources and interactions. Sulway, a Tiptree Award winner for her 2013 novel *Rupetta*, immediately starts the chase with her title, a reference to Fowler's *The Jane Austen Book Club* (2004). Much of the charm and humor in Fowler's book has to do, in turn, with its characters' interactions with Austen's works; each chapter enacts— and critiques—a different Austen plot even as the characters are rereading and discussing those novels in the book club of the title.

Sulway likewise uses her fiction to set up a conversation with another writer. The story begins:

> Ten years ago, Clara had attended a creative writing workshop run by Karen Joy Fowler, and what Karen Joy told her was: We are living in a science fictional world. During the workshop, Karen Joy also kept saying, I am going to talk about endings, but not yet. But Karen Joy never did get around to talking about endings, and Clara left the workshop still feeling as if she was suspended within it, waiting for the second shoe to drop.

The fictional Karen Joy Fowler shares with her namesake the ability to unsettle with a wry comment that turns out to mean something entirely different from what we think. But Sulway's story takes a number of additional turns that link it not only to Fowler—and indirectly, through the title, to Jane Austen—but also to James Tiptree, Jr.

Though Sulway did indeed attend a writing workshop taught by Fowler ("Re: Bio"), her viewpoint character Clara and the rest of her book club turn out not to be human, though they have names, houses, gardens, and book clubs. They are the last rhinoceroses, living out a gradual extinction. The cause of that extinction is never named, but it is clearly us, since the real world exists as a distorted backdrop in the story. Human poaching and human indifference have already killed off Western black rhinos in real history and are on their way to doing in the other subspecies. The humor in Sulway's story is inextricably entwined with anger and deep sadness, and that is another link to Karen Joy Fowler, and particularly to a story called "What I Didn't See" (2002).

Fowler's story won a Nebula Award, outraging a number of fans by not really being science fiction. It is SF, though, or at least it is in conversation with science fiction, and the writer with whom it is having an intense and rather painful chat is Tiptree, whose classic "The Women Men Don't See" (1973) is echoed in the title. Tiptree's story involves a jungle, racism, aliens, and women who opt out of the patriarchal system. So does Fowler's—except that her continent is Africa rather than Meso-America, and her aliens are earthborn. They are mountain gorillas. The story is about an expedition to hunt them, with the oddly mixed motive of making the gorillas seem less formidable—and thus less likely to be slaughtered—by showing that even a woman hunter can bring one down. And that element suggests another link to Tiptree, or rather to the woman who was Tiptree's real-world self, and to Julie Phillips's biography *James Tiptree, Jr.: The Double Life of Alice B. Sheldon* (2007). Phillips starts her biography with an image from Sheldon's childhood:

In 1921 in the Belgian Congo, a six-year-old girl from Chicago with a pith helmet on her blond curls walks at the head of a line of native porters. Her mother walks next to her, holding a rifle and her daughter's hand.   (1)

Alice Bradley Sheldon's parents were explorers who brought their daughter along, perhaps with motives similar to those of the explorers in Fowler's story: to make the exotic seem less perilous and more imperiled. That didn't stop the group from killing: elephants, lions, and five gorillas (half the number they were licensed for). Phillips's biography includes a photo of Sheldon's mother Mary Bradley posed with native guides and a gun. Phillips points out that the very expedition on which the five gorillas were killed— along with the book Bradley wrote about it, *On the Gorilla Trail* (1922)—was a turning point in popular sentiment about the great apes, helping lead to the creation of wildlife preserves to protect gorillas and other species.

So Sulway's story invites us to read it alongside several other texts: a novel and short story by Karen Joy Fowler, a story by and a biography of Alice Sheldon, and Sheldon's mother's memoir. But that's not the full extent of it. The Fowler novel is also, obviously, immersed in the work of Jane Austen. The best way to read *The Jane Austen Book Club* is to intersperse its chapters with rereadings of the relevant Austen novels. Fowler's book can stand alone perfectly well, but where's the fun in that? The back-and-forth dialogue between texts is so much richer, more problematic, and more meaningful. And it doesn't just invoke Austen: through one of its characters, the book also invites us to read still more women SF writers: Connie Willis, Nancy Kress, and especially Ursula K. Le Guin.

When Fowler was interviewed in 2004 about "What I Didn't See," she mentioned some of its inspirations, which included not only Tiptree's "The Women Men Don't See" but also, she says,

> an essay by Donna Haraway which had a pretty startling assertion, . . . that in the early 1920s, a group was taken into the jungle by the man who ran the Natural History Museum in New York, and that his purpose was to have one of the women kill a gorilla. His thinking was that gorillas were increasingly seen as exciting and dangerous game, and that they were actually very gentle, and that if a woman killed one, the thrill would be gone. So his plan was to protect the gorillas by making killing them seem like something any girl could do. I was mesmerized (and appalled) by that, but then, a paragraph later, I was extremely startled to read that one of the women who had gone on this expedition, one of the two women he picked to play this role, was James Tiptree's mother. (Lawrence)

Near the end of Fowler's story, the narrator comments that after the killings and the disappearance of one of their members, the expeditioners were "All of us, completely beside ourselves" (185). So the Fowler story also looks not only backward to Sheldon's childhood and sideways to Haraway's feminist science but also (time-travel fashion) ahead to the Tiptree biography, published a couple of years later, and to her own novel about apes and humans, *We Are All Completely Beside Ourselves* (2013), which would not appear for nearly another decade.

I suggest thinking of all this as a social gathering of like-minded texts: a sort of club whose members are books. Picture them meeting together to gossip, share insights, and grumble together about how the world is ignoring or misinterpreting them. I would not push that metaphor too far—one could go a little crazy dressing up books in garden hats and giving them little plates of cookies and glasses of wine—but the idea of an all-book-club helps show how the internal references work in these stories.

The traditional rhetorical name for this practice is *allusion*, a term found in lists of literary devices right after *allegory*. The implication is that cross-textual connections are merely a way of fancying up a text. That is the way people generally thought of metaphor as well until George Lakoff and Mark Johnson told us that metaphor is not just an ornament to speech but a mode of thought, part of our mental equipment. Lakoff and Johnson's *Metaphors We Live By* gives me permission to do two things. One is to look for some fundamental, cognitive aspect of texts referring to other texts. The other is to try out further metaphors to describe the operation, since non-metaphoric terms like *reference, allusion,* and even Julia Kristeva's *intertextuality* are misleadingly abstract.

One component missing from those terms is the social function of literature: the way texts connect with people as well as with other texts. They shape and inspire us, and they depend on us to bring them to life. My metaphoric club-of-books doesn't seem to have any people in it, but those books aren't going to circulate themselves—and circulation is part of the point of intertextuality. Literary movements and revivals exist to keep texts in front of us, so that they can be referred to and otherwise remain in use. Likewise, the highest function of critics and scholars is to keep reminding people of the great books that are out there and to teach them how to see that greatness. We are half cheerleaders and half travel guides. Every work of literature that we think of as important has had its share of both. Without Melville to lead the cheers, we would not have seen Hawthorne as a dark genius. Modernist poetry needed Ezra Pound and I. A. Richards to guide readers toward comprehension and thence appreciation. So the club of books is also a club of book-lovers, which means my metaphor has collapsed into literality—but not entirely. Literal book clubs tend to be predominantly made up of women, as in *The Jane Austen Book Club*, in which the addition of one male member is initially looked on with suspicion. By contrast, the Critical Establishment Book Club tends to be mostly men. And men have an amazing ability to forget or undervalue women.

Joanna Russ's *How to Suppress Women's Writing* (1983) belongs in the club of books I've been talking about, since it is another way of talking about "The Women Men Don't See." Though her topic is women's literature in general, Russ is careful to call out writers such as Vonda N. McIntyre, Ursula K. Le Guin, Suzy McKee Charnas, Octavia E. Butler, Mary Shelley, and James Tiptree, Jr.: many of the mothers, along with Russ herself, of feminist fantasy and science fiction. In a witty and scathing survey modeled after (and thus conversing with) Virginia Woolf's *A Room of One's Own*, Russ lists all the ways women's literature can be dismissed or sidelined by the men's club that is the literary establishment. A couple of her points are most relevant here. First, the disappearance of women writers from literary history seems to operate in all times and places and frequently without even malicious intent: it is like a natural law. Surveying reading lists and anthologies, Russ finds

> that although the percentage of women included remains somewhere between 5 percent and 8 percent, the personnel change rather strikingly from book to book; Aphra Behn appears and vanishes, Anne Bradstreet is existent or nonexistent according to whom you read, Elizabeth Barrett Browning and Emily Brontë bob up and down like corks, Edith Wharton is part of English literature in 1968 and banished to the outer darkness in 1977—and yet there are always enough women for that 5 percent and never quite enough to get much past 8 percent. (79)

The second pertinent point is that social habits—the club bylaws, as it were—masquerade as aesthetic judgments. Male critics don't deliberately exclude women writers; they just don't see them, and they blame the book rather than the reader.

Russ imagines a distinguished literary Circle (her version of my Critical Establishment Men's Club) piously explaining their decisions:

> Of course we were fair-minded, and would have instantly let into the Circle . . . any who demonstrated Circular qualities, as long as they were just like ours.
> Somehow they were not.
> We did, actually, let a few in. (This made us feel generous.)
> Most, we did not. (This made us feel that we had high and important standards.)
> . . . how could we possibly let them in?
> They were clumsy.
> Their work was thin.
> It wasn't about the right things.
>
> (135)

Out of that list I especially want to point out the word "thin." It reveals much about reading. I will return to it.

Things are a little better now than they were when Russ's book came out, but not as much improved as we might hope. A recurring feature called "By the Book" appears near the front of each week's *New York Times Book Review*. In it, some writer is asked a set of questions that include "What books are on your night stand?" and "What other genres do you especially enjoy reading? And which do you avoid?" That last is an invitation to trash other people's taste, and the invitation is all too often taken up by the persons being interviewed, who are happy to declare themselves superior to romance, or science fiction, or young adult literature. Typically, women writers will list both men and women they are reading, or have been influenced by, or would like to invite to a dinner party. Equally typically, the men list men. Occasionally they will recall a token woman, maybe Austen. Russ's five to eight percent is overly optimistic here.

Sometimes the "By the Book" author will make a greater effort to reach outside the Circle or even comment on his own limitations. I was ready to be thoroughly miffed by this recent list from comics writer Alan Moore until I came to the last few names and his final statement:

> Pynchon; Coover; Neal Stephenson; Junot Díaz; Joe Hill; William Gibson; Bruce Sterling; Samuel R. Delany; Iain Sinclair; Brian Catling; Michael Moorcock...; Eimear McBride; the remarkable Steve Aylett for everything...; Laura Hird; Geoff Ryman; M. John Harrison; screenwriter Amy Jump . .?.?. Look, I can either go on forever or I can't go on. I'm already mortified by the pathetic lack of women writers represented and find myself starting to come up with wretched excuses and squirming evasions. Best we end this here.   (4)

If you are keeping score, that's three women to fourteen men, which is twice Russ's eight percent. Not bad. Few of the men interviewed are so self-aware.

The pattern continues despite the efforts of scholars and literary activists, and with no reference to the excellent work from contemporary writers who are female or transgender or nonbinary. Le Guin's essay "Disappearing Grandmothers" (2016), which updates Russ's book, notes that

> A science fiction anthology recently published in England contained no stories by women. A fuss was made. The men responsible for the selection apologised by saying they had invited a woman to contribute but it didn't work out, and then they just somehow didn't notice that all the stories were by men. Ever so sorry about that.   (90)

Le Guin, always aware of the power of words, deliberately uses the passive voice here: "A fuss was made." Who made it? Who should damn well keep making a fuss as long as it is (passive voice) required?

Because no woman writer is immune from this selective forgettery. Angela Carter also noticed the pattern. In an interview in *The Guardian* in 1984, she said, "It would be whingeing to say that men who are no better than I are very much more famous and very much richer, ... but it's amazing what the Old Boys' club does for itself" (Quoted in Wood 2016). According to her biographer Edmund Gordon, "When the boys listed the 'important British contemporary writers' ..., they'd include Kingsley Amis and Malcolm Bradbury, but omit Doris Lessing and Beryl Bainbridge. They certainly never included her—unless the boys were B. S. Johnson or Anthony Burgess, both of whom admired her work, and neither of whom were exactly mainstream" (Wood).

Besides making us gasp at the blindness of the literary community, these comments from Carter should remind us that the alternative book club—the one that includes her and Russ and Tiptree—also includes some alert men like Johnson and Burgess. The cluster of texts and writers I started with, moving outward from Sulway to Fowler and Tiptree and Le Guin, also includes Samuel R. Delany (who is cited by Russ) and Tiptree-Award-winners like Patrick Ness, Geoff Ryman, and John Kessel. Kessel won the award for "Stories for Men" (2002), which explicitly addresses male resistance to women's power. His novel *Pride and Prometheus* (2018) declares itself, via its title, to be in the same club as not only Jane Austen but also SF precursor Mary Shelley. (In the novel, Kessel matches up Mary Bennet, Austen's bluestocking middle daughter, and Victor Frankenstein, both of whom turn out to have been rather shabbily treated by their original authors.)

As has been mentioned, literary movements put books into circulation and keep them in the public eye. That is demonstrably the case with a male literary circle like the Inklings—Lewis, Tolkien, and their friends. Diana Pavlac Glyer's 2007 book on the Inklings, *The Company They Keep*, is subtitled *C. S. Lewis and J. R. R. Tolkien as Writers in Community*. As the subtitle suggests, it isn't so much a study of individual works as an examination of the way members of the group acted as what Glyer calls "resonators" for one another in light of the general hostility of the Men's Book Club of their day to fantasy, which was seen as trivial, inartistic, and, yes, thin. "Resonators," she explains, "function by showing interest in the text—they are enthusiastic about the project, they believe it is worth doing, and they are eager to see it brought to completion" (48). Despite denials by many of the Inklings and their commentators that they influenced one another, they made each other's work possible.

And they made frequent reference to one another: dedicating books to others in the group, reviewing their books, quoting them, alluding to one another's imagined worlds, and even transforming other Inklings into characters in their fiction (Glyer 2007, 188–200). Glyer points out, for instance, that the sonorous speech of Treebeard the Ent was a reference to Lewis's booming voice (173). The Inklings had set out to revive myth and reinvent romance in an era that was hostile to both. It is no wonder they relied on each other for praise, informed critique, and mutual enrichment. Glyer looks at the Inklings mostly as a writing group, but they were also a reading group, a book club, teaching one another how to read the stories they all loved in ever-richer ways. Tolkien's fantasy seems trivial if the reader perceives only a slice of the entire frame of reference. A cross-section of anything is going to look thin. Tolkien's work echoes the songs, stories, and imagined worlds of the pre-Shakespearean past, and it resonates with Lewis's literary scholarship and Owen Barfield's philosophy and the beliefs and experiences of the other Inklings. To see the Inklings in reference to one another is to see not thinness but depth and complexity.

This sort of writing community is poorly represented by linear terms like allusion and influence, and at this point I want to move away from the club metaphor for a while. Glyer's term "resonator" works because it brings in the whole metaphoric domain of music: the wood of a violin, the untouched sympathetic strings of a sitar, the sonorous space of a concert hall. But it is still a passive image: resonators only react. A few other metaphors have been offered for the ways our imaginations are interdependent. Mikhail Bakhtin, for instance, proposed the idea of a dialogue: within any given text there is more than one voice, whether quoted directly or indirectly or echoed unconsciously. Gilles Deleuze and Félix Guattari used a biological metaphor, the rhizome. A rhizome is technically just an underground stem, but the way Deleuze and Guattari use the term suggests something larger: the kind of underground mat of roots and filaments that links communities of plants and fungi. Forest biologists have discovered that what looks like a grouping of separate trees and undergrowth is really a nervelike network of inter-connections, without hierarchy and without boundaries: what has been termed the wood wide web. With this discovery, Robert Macfarlane explains in his book *Underland*, "the whole vision of a forest ecology shimmered and shifted—from a fierce free market to something more like a community with a socialist system of resource redistribution" (91). To illustrate the meta-phoric extensions of the image, Macfarlane cites Le Guin's *The Word for*

World Is Forest, which was published in 1976, well before biologists came up with the idea (105). Dialogism, rhizomes, and what Macfarlane calls the "social network" under the wood (91) are all useful metaphors for cultural studies and models of the imagination. They tell us a lot about how we think and speak and write, but they don't say much about how a specific allusion or intertextual gesture functions within a text. They don't fully reveal the richness that derives from community or the delight of following leads from one text to the next.

Le Guin has come up several times in this discussion and she is clearly a major node in the networks of feminist and fantastic literature. The most obviously intertextual of her novels is *Lavinia* (2008), which is intertwined with Vergil's *Aeneid* and therefore also in dialogue with the Iliad and Dante's *Divine Comedy*. Less obviously, the novel is a response to feminist reworkings of myth such as Margaret Atwood's *The Penelopiad* (2005) or Marion Zimmer Bradley's *The Firebrand* (1987). The way Le Guin under-cuts Aeneas's heroic trajectory and replaces it with a narrative of quiet endurance links the novel with Le Guin's essay "The Carrier-Bag Theory of Fiction" (1986) and with several of her works of sf and fantasy including *Always Coming Home* (1985) and *Voices* (2006). In that last novel, housekeeping—maintaining a household in the face of violence and igno-rance—*is* heroism. *Lavinia* also draws on a number of unnamed historical and archaeological sources that serve as correctives to Vergil's fanciful, Greek-influenced picture of early Italic life. The novel's "Afterword" credits a 1949 study by Bertha Tilly called *Vergil's Latium*, which is based, Le Guin says, on Tilly's walks through the region armed "with a keen mind, a sharp eye, and a Brownie camera" (275). All of these texts, from Homer's to Atwood's, are part of the club.

Vergil not only provides *Lavinia* with its basic plot and setting but also appears as a ghostly presence—referred to only as "the poet"—with whom the title character interacts in moments that transcend her ordinary time and place. Their conversations serve as commentary on both his poem and the novel within which they appear. *Allusion* doesn't cover this sort of intricate textual infolding, which is intended neither to retell the *Aeneid* nor to correct it but to show how it changes in response to different cultural assumptions. The whole poem is present in the novel, at least by implication, and so are the circumstances of its composition and its reception over the centuries. The *Aeneid* remains itself despite being surrounded by another text. The two texts exchange information and insights and alter one another, just as the characters do. T. S. Miller suggests that as a result of the two authors' joint efforts to create the character and her world, the setting of the novel becomes a fundamentally transactional landscape. In effect, the very fabric of Lavinia's curiously meta-fictive reality serves as a record of Le Guin's reading of the *Aeneid*, with its foundation in Vergil but its particular rendering in later readers like herself. (Miller 2010, 34)

So the novel has at least three separate textual levels and narrative trajectories—Vergil's epic, Le Guin's novelistic rendering of the life of one of Vergil's characters, and Le Guin's Tilly-influenced reading of Vergil— which are further complicated by the fact that Lavinia and Vergil, in their conversations, also contemplate each other's textualized existence.

Lavinia is a highly metafictional book, but I would suggest that we can think of it not only as meta- but also as mito-, that is, as mitochrondial, and unlike Sulway's fictional Karen Joy Fowler and endings, I have actually come to the point where I need to talk about mitochondria.

Mitochondria are structures within our cells. They are part of us and yet they are not. I first heard of them from another SF writer: Madeleine L'Engle. Here is how her character Charles Wallace explains them in the 1973 novel *A Wind in the Door*:

"Well, billions of years ago they probably swam into what eventually became our eukaryotic cells and they've just stayed there. They have their own DNA and RNA, which means they're quite separate from us. They have a symbiotic relationship to us, and the amazing thing is that we're completely dependent on them for our oxygen." (20)

Charles Wallace, who is a bit of a pedant at age six, needs glossing here. *Eukaryotic* means having cells with separate organelles such as nuclei, a description which covers pretty much all multicellular organisms; prokaryotic cells don't have those separate structures, and they include things like red blood cells and bacteria, which is what mitochondria seem to have been originally. L'Engle's description still matches current thinking, although biologists have added to the model. Basically, we aren't the integral selves we think we are, but rather colonies of commensals. Very early in evolutionary history, bigger cells swallowed the smaller ones whole without digesting them and thereby gained the ability to utilize energy, to grow, to diversify, and eventually to become everything from whales to field mice. Plants also made their own separate bargain with another kind of free-living organism that moved in to become chloroplasts, the organelles that allow for photosynthesis.

Mitochondria retain their own separate DNA, as Charles Wallace explains. That genetic minority report is part of the key to understanding evolutionary history, since mitochondrial DNA is close enough to some modern bacterial DNA to support the commensalism hypothesis. As the bacterial invaders settled in, they gave up some of the functions that allowed them to survive on their own in exchange for protection and food supply from the host cell, and so mitochondrial DNA is incomplete compared to the DNA of the nucleus. Mitochondria are also, like their hosts, subject to mutation and thus have their own genetic diseases. One of those diseases generates the plot of *A Wind in the Door*.

So a mitochondrion is a not-quite-living creature that is both separate from and part of the host cell. It provides energy that allows that host cell to function and in turn carries on its own life with the aid of the host. It communicates continually with the organism around it. It changes that larger organism even as it is changed by it. It has its own ancestry and purpose and yet shares needs and purposes with the host. If I have set up my description properly, it should begin to sound like the way one text can be embedded in another. The *Aeneid*, we could say, acts as an organelle within the cells of *Lavinia*. The novels of Jane Austen do mitochondrial work for *The Jane Austen Book Club*. They remain themselves and yet are transformed within the new setting.

For this metaphor to work, it must be both concrete and dynamic. The link between source domain (cell biology) and target domain (literature) has to show us things about the latter that might not otherwise be evident. Thinking in mitochondrial terms reminds us that a text that is drawn into a newer text is still alive, still working, still itself. The metaphor invites us to see how host and symbiote both benefit from the relationship. And it shows that a thing so familiar as to be ignorable—a cell, an allusion—is, in reality, much stranger and more complex than we realize. A simple act of reference is really a whole history of incorporation, negotiation, and synergy.

All of that suggests that we need to rethink both meaning and value in literature, since our perceptions of aesthetic quality and of significance depend upon the connections we are able to make with the text. Without those connections, any literary work is going to seem thin and anemic—and, by coincidence or maybe not, anemia is one symptom of mitochondrial disease. As I said before, movements and literary groupings such as the Inklings have always served as connection-makers, at least for the community of male writers and readers. Renaissance dramatists stole freely from one another. Romantic poets defended one another's practice and published together. Modernist novels like *The Great Gatsby* and *The Sun Also Rises* are significant partly because we read them as voices in a conversation that also includes Hemingway's self-justifying *A Moveable Feast* (1964) and Gertrude Stein's more acerbic *The Autobiography of Alice B. Toklas* (1933). We read such "great works" also in an echo chamber of publishers, editors, reviewers, scholars, and teachers telling us that this is what fiction should do, these are the themes that matter, these are the kinds of characters and actions we are interested in (which is to say, not women, people of color, or children). These works thicken one another. Each helps create resonances, invites contemplation of shared themes, and constructs the cultural and generic codes that allow us to read the others richly and actively.

So how do literary mitochondria work? Imagine you have just picked up a story and started reading it. If you are like me, you're waiting to be won over: "entertain me," you say to the story first, and then "convince me you matter." Sometimes the story is pre-sold: it is in a prestigious anthology or comes from an author you already know and trust. Other times you start out skeptical, looking for an excuse to put the work aside. The burden of proof is on the text to earn your time and emotional investment.

But maybe as you're reading the first couple of pages, you come across a link to something else that you recognize. Perhaps it's a story pattern. For instance, a little way into Helen Oyeyemi's *Boy, Snow, Bird* (2014) you suddenly realize that the abused heroine is a version of Snow White. Now, whatever else happens in the story, you are carried along by wanting to know how that strange scenario of female competition is going to work out this time around. The story isn't just the one you are being told by Oyeyemi's narrator but also a whole constellation of narratives including the Grimm version and the Disney version and the Anne Sexton version. By making the reference, Oyeyemi enters into a longstanding conversation and invokes all the agonies about gender, appearance, and aging that hover over that fairy tale. She's got you. And then she can go on to do surprising things with the structure of story and characters, bringing in new issues of work and race and community and psychology.

Snow White's story is a cellular dynamo that lives within the tissues of Oyeyemi's novel without being assimilated to it. It amplifies and energizes and gives the reader additional ways to care about the book. The relationship between the two texts is complex and ironic and ultimately beneficial to both.

Another way to call out to previous texts and invoke their significance is to create characters who represent important literary and historical themes. One of the main characters in *Boy, Snow, Bird* is an experimental psychologist who forces us to question the nature of gender—like Alice Sheldon. I don't know for sure that Oyeyemi deliberately based this character on James Tiptree (who shared Sheldon's biography in all but gender during the ten years that Sheldon used her pen name as a public persona) but since one of Oyeyemi's other novels was on the long list for the Tiptree Award, she is aware of the award's namesake. Intentional or not, the reference resonates with many of the novel's other themes and images. Tiptree stories like "The Psychologist Who Wouldn't Do Awful Things to Rats" (1976), which fictionalizes Sheldon's experience acquiring a Ph.D. in experimental psychology, constitute another mitochondrial strain, providing yet more power to the novel's cells.

Besides plot and character, there are many other ways of signaling affinity with previous texts: titles that are quotations from the Bible or Shakespeare, familiar settings, echoed phrases, and even apparent denials of reference like T. S. Eliot's "I am not Prince Hamlet, nor was meant to be," in "The Love Song of J. Alfred Prufrock" (1915). Male writers doing guy themes have it easier in this regard. They have direct access to most of myth, religion, and elite literature—in other words, they can stick to the kind of reference that hails other men and be rewarded for doing so. This network of references is so built into our ways of reading that female readers and even women writers have to unlearn the lesson that their own experience is less rich, less resonant, less significant than that of their male counterparts.

But the mitochondrial chain I've just been tracing goes from Madame D'Aulnoy and the other littérateuses of seventeenth-century French courts, to the young women who told "Snow White" to the Brothers Grimm, to Mary Shelley and others who used the shock value of the Gothic (one form of which is the literary fairy tale) to shake up assumptions about gender, and so on up to the present—and that is also a rich heritage and one to which women have generally been better attuned than men, since much of the cultural work of fairy tales is aimed at them.

One more fact about mitochondria can be metaphorically brought to bear on these questions of textual interdependence and literary value. When a new individual forms, mitochondrial DNA is retained not from sperm but only from the egg. It comes down from the mother—from the mothers—all the way back to what geneticists have nicknamed the Mitochondrial Eve. While we can't, simply by analogy, cancel out the influence of male writers on one another or on women (noting what Le Guin does with Vergil's epic) the mitochondrial metaphor does suggest that an all-male, or even what Russ reveals to be a 92- to 95-percent-male model of literary history, is seriously out of whack.

The James Tiptree, Jr. Literary Award (renamed the Otherwise Award in 2019) is a recurring thread in this discussion. One of the Award's main achievements has been to foster awareness of these kinds of mitochondrial connections. The Award, along with the community that has formed around it, not only hails new stories but also gives them a pedigree and a context, and thus new ways to read and value them. The mitochondrial genetic code is also a reading code.

Russ's book points to some of the mothers who have been erased from literary history. The obverse of that is that the men stay in, but for reasons we might not have noticed. Glyer's study shows how the lone-genius model of creativity misses many of the most important interactions that take place within groups of male writers—and she suggests reasons that both the writers themselves and their critics might deny the possibility of influence. Men generally like to think of themselves as integral selves rather than permeable assemblages or as parts of something else. Hemingway's fictio-nalized memoir *A Moveable Feast* is a great example of the masculine artist rewriting his own history to erase lines of influence, especially from his literary mother Gertrude Stein. Hemingway is only willing to acknowledge a sort of Oedipal relationship with literary fathers like Mark Twain. That is a standard (male) critical trope as well: it's the entire basis for Harold Bloom's theory of the Anxiety of Influence. It completely misses the possibility that influence might be both fun and feminine. We need those mitochondria. Without them we're stuck at the one-celled, beginning level.

At this point, I am working with two seemingly unconnected metaphors: the book club and the mitochondrion. It's going to take a little sleight of hand to put those together. But if you think about the family tree I have been tracing, it starts with Mary Shelley and Jane Austen (with roots and fungal threads in folk literature). They donate their mitochondria to another generation that includes forgotten or undervalued women writers like Mary Hallock Foote and Margaret Oliphant (both mentioned by Le Guin as examples of "Disappearing Grandmothers"). From them the DNA passes to early SF and utopian writers like Charlotte Perkins Gilman and Inez Haynes Gillmore and then on to C. L. Moore and Leigh Brackett and Leslie F. Stone. They pass the mitochondria on to Sheldon and Russ and Butler and Le Guin. The work of those writers inhabits and enlivens stories by Nalo

Hopkinson, Kelly Link, Karen Fowler. And that gets us back to Nike Sulway and other emerging writers, which is where I started.

This is both a genealogy and a long-functioning book club. The biology metaphor shows us how texts work within other texts; the club metaphor reminds us that the process is not automatic but involves choice and thought. One has to join a club.

In addition, a book club can also be thought of as another kind of cell: the covert kind that functions as a tool for resistance and revolution. I would propose that the James Tiptree Jr. Book Club, which is also the Ursula K. Le Guin Book Club, the Karen Joy Fowler Book Club, and so on, constitutes a set of interlocking cells, what one male SF writer once suspiciously termed the Secret Feminist Cabal. This, unfortunately, is a time for resistance: for secret cells and mutual support and active intervention in literary culture and the broader culture. Whenever a group of readers takes in a new book, that book becomes part of the collective DNA and a powerhouse for the cell, the conspiracy, the cabal. That is part of what Karen Joy Fowler is telling us in "What I Didn't See" and Nike Sulway tells us in "The Karen Joy Fowler Book Club." Whatever we call the process, whether mitochondria or allusion or something else like the Exhilaration of Influence, it can serve as a corollary to Russ's work, showing How Not to Suppress Women's Writing. It also reminds us to keep reading and praising fairy tales and science fiction by women—and the men who read those women—and to keep retracing the lines of descent that enrich and enliven their work.

6

Young Adult Dystopias
and Yin Adult Utopias

Utopian literature is where fantasy acknowledges politics. The premise of any utopia is that we could do things differently, plan better, throw out old ways of organizing society and replace them with something more rational—with results that, according to the writer's view of human nature, would either be splendid or disastrous. We call the former variety utopia, or, respecting Greek roots, eutopia: the good place. (Thomas More's coinage also suggests outopia, or "no place.") The latter outcome is dystopia: etymologically not the bad place, but the sick or damaged one. Both are rationally conceived societies, rather than naturally evolving ones. Less obviously, both are inherently fantastic, though the kind of fantasy involved is usually a matter of hypothetical technologies rather than overt impossibilities and magical transformations.

One reason utopia doesn't look much like fantasy is that its ground rules demand that the good place be achieved by human effort, through human institutions, rather than through divine intervention or magical means. Yet the world-building impulse—the effort to produce coherent, convincing counterfactual worlds as something more than mere backdrops—is the same in all branches of the larger family of fantastic literature, which includes science fiction as well. And science fiction and utopias are intertwined throughout the history of both genres: from Francis Bacon's gadget-filled *New Atlantis* (1626) to Jo Walton's reimagining of Plato's Republic in *The Just City* (2015). Many writers, like Walton, have explored multiple varieties of fantastic literature. SF and fantasy notables such as Samuel R. Delany, Joanna Russ, Octavia E. Butler, Kim Stanley Robinson, and Ursula K. Le Guin are largely responsible for the rebirth of the hopeful utopia after it was pronounced dead in the mid-twentieth century.

Utopia is the branch of fantastic literature with the greatest power—or at least the most overt ambition—to change collective behavior. It does so in two primary ways, starting from two different premises or (underlying those) two temperament-based world views: what philosopher Wilhelm Dilthey called *Weltanschauungen*. Premise one says that there is much wrong in the world and that we could do better: injustice and unhappiness arise from design errors in existing societies. Premise two says that those errors are part of human nature, and thus that any attempt to rectify them will inevitably make things worse. If you accept premise one, you believe that a better world is attainable; if you start from premise two, you believe that even trying for utopia will end in disaster. Within the realm of fiction, both premises are valid because both generate interesting and illuminating thought experiments. Dystopia has a narrative advantage over utopia in that it implicitly poses problems for characters—especially when narrative interest is equated with conflict. Tension and anxiety are built in; violence is probable. Utopias, though, are notoriously boring as fictions: things are good to start with and there is seemingly nowhere for the plot to go. I will get back to that "seemingly" in a bit.

Looking outside fiction to history, utopian social experiments always fail if the goal is a permanent, stable, and harmonious state. If the goal is something else, however, such as finding innovative solutions to social problems, some utopian communities have a much better record: Robert Owen's experiments at New Lanark and New Harmony, in the Old and New World respectively, left behind a number of reforms in labor, hygiene, education, and architecture. American democracy is arguably a utopian experiment, though one whose success is still being debated. On the other hand, some of the most appalling mass crimes of all time also had, or claimed, utopian ambitions: Nazi Germany, Stalinist Russia, Mao's Cultural Revolution. Those real-world events are not the same as the literary genre of utopia, but they inevitably color our response to fictional invented societies. Whether one takes the historical record as evidence pro or con depends on one's Weltanschauung as well as on the current state of the world: arguments about the literary merit of utopian and dystopian literature can never be purely aesthetic.

For the past century, dystopia has had the upper hand in literary debates. The most popular form of alternative social vision these days seems to be the young adult dystopia. Bookstore shelves are full of individual novels and series in which teenage protagonists try to fight their way out of nightmarish societies. The most popular example is Suzanne Collins's *Hunger Games* trilogy (2008), but the field also includes Veronica Roth's Divergent series, M. T. Anderson's *Feed* (2002), Scott Westerfeld's Pretties books, and many others. And in addition to having dystopias served up especially for them, teen readers frequently turn to works written for older readers: Orwell's *1984*, Huxley's *Brave New World*, Ray Bradbury's *Fahrenheit 451* (1979), and so on.

Children's literature scholar Michael Levy used to point out that "[o]f course young adult readers like dystopias. They live in dystopia." It's the same principle that worked in *Buffy the Vampire Slayer*: the idea that high school really is a hell-mouth. I would like to push Mike's insight a little further though. Adolescence is not only a time of mood swings, emotional drama, and arbitrary rules but also a time when many teens become aware of the best and the worst in the larger world around them: great ideas, cool gadgets, and an arc of history that may ultimately bend toward justice but seems to have a lot of detours into hypocrisy and injustice perpetrated by the very adults they have trusted.

The young heroes of YA dystopias live amid these contradictions. They are also uniquely positioned to do something about them: newly awakened to their own abilities but not yet slotted into adult roles. If, as Karl Mannheim theorized, utopia is the opposite of ideology, then emerging adults who are not yet accommodated to the ideologies that surround them are the perfect utopians.

The brain during adolescence is more adaptable than at any other time after infancy. Much of what popular culture blames on hormones is caused instead by changes in the cerebral cortex. The teenage brain is constantly forming new synapses and just as incessantly pruning away unused connections. Whatever society demands and rewards will be reinforced in the very structure of the brain; whatever is suppressed or ignored will be edited out. This period of neural plasticity is a form of liminality: that powerful, dangerous state of in-betweenness that is part of all transitions and rites of passage. The maturing individual doesn't yet know what doorway they are passing through, or what identity awaits on the other side.

And then there's sex. Part of adolescence is the discovery that we have been systematically lied to about adult sexual arrangements. Grown-up sexuality is a whole lot messier and more ambiguous than the version we offer to our children, if we tell them anything at all. Newly awakening desire coupled with anger over this deception is an almost irresistible push toward disruption. But sex is only one part of an even greater force: passion. No one hurts more deeply or longs more passionately than an adolescent. The fifteen-year-old Wallace Stevens, writing to his mother from camp, conveys this intensity perfectly in describing his brother's mandolin playing: "the keen, splattering tink-a-tink-tink-tink-tink-a-a-a" (Lensing 2018, 122). The

half-nonsensical phrase captures not only the sound of the instrument—
suggesting the kind of poet Stevens was to become—but also the feelings of
performer and listener. Keen and splattering indeed! Keen as a knife;
splattering like a grenade.

Adolescence is all about what isn't now but might yet be. A piece of
proverbial wisdom often attributed to Hannah Arendt (though it's probably
not hers) goes something like "Every civilization raises up its own barbarian
invaders." That line is usually invoked in order to reinforce a conservative
viewpoint. It associates the disruptive power of youth with destruction and
warns us to socialize our children as quickly and thoroughly as possible. Yet
sometimes civilizations need barbarian invaders. The young have less stake
in stability than do the old, so they need not accept the compromises on
which stability depends. When a civilization begins, as Robinson Jeffers put
it, to "[settle] in the mould of its vulgarity, heavily thickening to empire,"
who but the young can bring change? (Jeffers 2001).

Dystopian writing is a device for uncovering current tendencies that
threaten to become tools of oppression. It is a form of critique that comes
equipped with a number of narrative hooks, suitable for old adults as well as
young adults: desire, resentment of those in power, a pull toward justice,
an aptitude for violence, and the potential for renewal. Dystopias have given
us much of the language for understanding our contemporary nightmares:
Huxley's soma and Fordism; Orwell's Big Brother and Newspeak, Atwood's
handmaids and gender traitors.

In contrast, there is eutopia, the frequently-dismissed, never-vanishing,
hopeful side of the utopian imagination. Though the vision of a perfected
state goes back to Plato and acquired its name from Thomas More's satirical
novel in the sixteenth century, utopian writing and utopian thought really
had their heyday in the nineteenth century, particularly in America, where
the landscape was littered with religious colonies and socialist communes
and where, in 1888, Edward Bellamy's novel *Looking Backward* became a
bestseller, spawning scores of sequels and fictional rebuttals. People formed
Bellamyite societies, inspired by the novel's vision of a rational, gadget-filled,
egalitarian society that seemed the perfect answer to Gilded Age greed and
corruption. And those Bellamyite clubs evolved into the early Progressive
Movement, so *Looking Backward* fostered real change in the world,

And yet, as utopian scholar Tom Moylan puts it, "In the twentieth century,
utopian writing came upon hard times" (Moylan 1986, 8). What happened?
One thing is that people started to pay attention to the texts themselves, rather
than to the dreams they inspired. Those nineteenth-century novels are, almost

without exception, deadly. Only two things ever seem to happen in a utopia: the newcomers (there's always a newcomer) go on tours, and they get lectured to. They *exist* to be lectured to, like the lone woman character in any 1950s science fiction movie, and they have just about as much individuality and interior life.

And still the lectures are generally more interesting than the tours, because they at least involve change: lecturers can tell visitors how we got from your terrible reality to our pleasant, if bland existence. And now we don't have to change any more, because we are a perfect society and any change would necessarily be for the worse. And here is our school, and there is the communal dining hall, and see how green and pleasant our landscape is, and we would show you our hospitals but nobody ever gets sick here.

The most interesting thing about most of these novels is the thing the author doesn't intend you to notice: how coercive it all is. Just as utopias resist change, they also resist diversity. If you were to find yourself in the world of William Morris's *News from Nowhere* (1890) and you had a taste for, say Brutalist architecture rather than Craftman-style cottages, you would be out of luck—and probably subjected to some serious re-education. Many historical forces were at work in the twentieth century dictating against utopian writing, but the eclipse of the form was at least partly the fault of the writing itself. Yet in spite of boring plots and repressive visions, these utopian novels still have a certain charm: they at least remind us that there are other ways to do things. As writer China Miéville has observed, fantastic stories are "good to think with" (Miéville 2002, 46), and utopias, whether dark or light, are a branch of the fantastic. We need to think about how things might get worse, and we need to think about how they might be better.

Utopia has always had enemies on both the progressive and the conservative fronts. Conservatives see danger in overthrowing traditional practices and institutions, while progressives dismiss utopia as mere "wish fulfillment," as Marx called it, and as a distraction from the practical work of reform or revolution. But even within the circle of utopian speculation, any plan for society can go horribly wrong, and the more devoutly its creators believe in their own ideas, the greater the tendency for abuse. A case in point is Plato's Republic, in ill-repute as a practical plan after Dionysus, Tyrant of Syracuse, invited Plato to visit with "the purpose of disseminating the philosophical lifestyle," and mistakenly "expecting that he could expand it to the whole territory [...] without slaughter" (Araújo 2016, 154).

That is why another term for dystopia is anti-utopia: such societies aren't just places of misery and injustice—there are plenty of those in history—but of planned and systematic repression for our own good. An old piece of wisdom about utopias says that in order to succeed, they have to be either populated by saints or ruled by angels. Of those, it is the incorruptible angel you have to watch out for. The utopianisms of the nineteenth century spawned the totalitarianisms of the twentieth. The takeover of Marxism by the Bolsheviks led Yevgeny Zamyatin, in 1921, to create the first great dystopian novel, *We* (1972). Aldous Huxley's *Brave New World* (1932) was partly a reaction to the gung-ho utopianism of H. G. Wells's 1905 novel *A Modern Utopia*, along with Taylorized mass-production and the drug-fueled hedonism of 1920s Bright Young Things. And in 1953, Ray Bradbury's *Fahrenheit 451* showed the American democratic experiment being diverted into mindless entertainment and the book-burning paranoia of McCarthyism. Each of these nightmares can be traced back to someone's dream of a better world.

However, utopian scholars Frank E. Manuel and Fritzie P. Manuel suggest that it might work the other way as well: "If in the background of every utopia there is an anti-utopia, the existing world seen through the critical eyes of the utopia-composer, one might say conversely that in the background of many a dystopia there is a secret utopia." (Manuel and Manuel 1979, 6). Huxley provided an interesting example of just that re-reversal in his 1962 novel *Island*, which returns to a lot of the same ideas that made *Brave New World* alarming but reimagines them as social virtues.

In discussing the single-sex utopias of science fiction a few years ago, I described this trick of perspective through the metaphor of intaglio (Attebery 2002, 116). Intaglio is a form of low-relief carving, but in reverse. Where something like a cameo brooch shows a face as a flattened form of itself, an intaglio image takes the convex and makes it concave. A signet ring is a form of intaglio; the impression it makes in hot wax goes back to normal modeling. The striking thing about intaglio is that you can't always tell whether the image recedes or projects. Photograph a cameo and its intaglio inversion side by side and they will look identical except for the direction of the shadows. That seems to me to sum up the relation of utopia and anti-utopia: they are the same thing under different lighting. It also suggests that we need a fourth term to cover all structural possibilities: just as utopia generates anti-utopia, dystopia can reverse itself to become anti-dystopia. That is exactly what *Island* is: the intaglio version of *Brave New World*.

However, Huxley's new version has the same flaws as the Wells novel he was previously critiquing—blandness, hidden coercions, wooden mouthpiece characters—and so reversing the reversal doesn't really get us out of the utopian trap. Not until the 1970s did a profoundly different form of utopian writing emerge, largely in response to feminism.

Feminism and utopia are another natural pairing, like utopia and SF: in the nineteenth century many utopias attempted to free women from domestic drudgery, and in the second wave of feminism, everything from family structures to gendered bodies could be reconsidered and reconfigured. Part of that 1970s–1980s utopian revival included the republication of neglected older texts such as Charlotte Perkins Gilman's utopian *Herland* (1915) and Katherine Burdekin's dystopian *Swastika Night* (1937), both of which powerfully interrogate male privilege and the suppression of women as the root of injustice. But it was the other utopias of the 70s and 80s, the new ones, that took a more radical approach to the genre itself. Writers like Joanna Russ, Samuel R. Delany, Marge Piercy, and Ursula K. Le Guin were too good to fall back on the lecture/tour model. They knew how to tell stories, and they knew how to use those stories, as Miéville says, to think with. Tom Moylan gave this crop of novels a new name that breaks up the utopia/dystopia binary: he called them critical utopias. Here is Moylan's description:

> A central concern in the critical utopia is the awareness of the limitations of the utopian tradition, so that these texts reject utopia as blueprint while preserving it as dream. Furthermore, the novels dwell on the conflict between the originary world and the utopian society opposed to it so that the process of social change is more directly articulated. Finally, the novels focus on the continuing presence of difference and imperfection within utopian society itself and thus render more recognizable and dynamic alternatives. (Moylan 1986, 10–11)

I want to highlight a couple of important parts of that definition. First, Moylan, on behalf of this contemporary group of writers, rejects the idea that a utopia is necessarily just a social blueprint. He suggests we look more closely at the process of change represented in the narrative, and not merely at its results. Second, he sees utopia as being always in dialogue with the real world, the world of the reader. The full meaning of the text is not contained within the text: it also includes the circumstances of reading. Thinking in terms of sexual politics, for instance, these feminist utopias remind us that even if an imagined alternative is problematic, the existing system could hardly be worse for women. Pretty much any change (short of those depicted in *The Handmaid's Tale*) must be for the better. Any alternative challenges assumptions and norms: the tyranny of common sense.

And this takes me back to Wallace Stevens. Stevens, now the adult poet, sums up that tyranny in his 1937 poem "The Blue Guitar," inspired by Picasso's 1904 painting *The Old Guitarist*. The collective voice of common sense in that poem—simply called "they"—objects to the painting because it departs from reality: "They said, "You have a blue guitar,/You do not play things as they are" (Stevens 1972, 133).

The rest of the poem is basically a lengthy set of variations on "Why would I want to play things as they are?" By allowing the mind to play freely in the field of Things as They Aren't, we wind up at what the poem calls, "The swarm of thoughts, the swarm of dreams/ Of inaccessible Utopia" (146). Utopia is inaccessible only in the sense that you can't get there from here. But Stevens invites us to start somewhere other than the here-and-now: to arrive at imaginary shores we only have to set out from those same imagination-washed shores (145). Somewhat more prosaically, Fredric Jameson departs from Marxist orthodoxy to praise utopia for being "like those baroque sunbursts in which rays from another world suddenly break into this one" and thus reminding us "that other systems, other spaces, are still possible" (2009, 612). His claim applies to dystopia as well as utopia.

Despite these attempts to rehabilitate utopia, dystopia continues to get most of the acclaim and the sales, especially from younger readers. Lyman Tower Sargent's authoritative bibliography of utopian literature (2016)—available on his website at Penn State University, https://openpublishing.psu.edu/utopia/—offers some revealing statistics. My search for "young adult dystopia" produced an impressive 296 results, while keywords "young adult utopia" yielded only 14. The negatives outnumber the positives by more than twenty to one. Of the latter, one is a nineteenth-century work, a book by Lady Florence Dixie called *Gloriana; or, The Revolution of 1900*. Its 1890 publication date puts it in the post-Bellamy utopian boom and makes the retroactive label "young adult" questionable. The thirteen remaining works are described, without exception, as being "flawed utopias," and some of them, like Roth's Divergent books, are also grouped with the anti-utopias. The reverse is not the case: I found no dystopias characterized as "hopeful" or even "ambiguous," although some may arguably be so, even edging toward anti-dystopia.

So, even granting that dystopias are eye-catching, well suited to adolescent readers, and often very powerful, there is a shortage of young adult literature that gestures toward utopia. In contrast, some writing for younger readers does so, including three classics of children's literature. E. Nesbit's *The Story of the Amulet*, from 1906, includes a time-travel visit to a Fabian socialist utopia where H. G. Wells is memorialized as "The Great Reformer." William Pène du Bois's *The Twenty-One Balloons*, a Newbery Award winner in 1947, wittily combines the explorer/Lost World tale with a New Atlantis-style technological utopia. And L. Frank Baum in the later Oz books, especially *The Emerald City of Oz* in 1910, depicts his fairyland as a place of harmony where difference is not just tolerated but actively welcomed and celebrated. That is one of the reasons that Oz has long served, as Dee Michel's study *Friends of Dorothy* (2018) demonstrates, as a utopian refuge for all kinds of outsiders but especially gay men and boys.

In order to catch teenage readers, though, a young adult utopia has to up its game in a couple of ways. First, it must limit its claims: to give up the totalizing tendency that so easily becomes totalitarian and to be willing to get small. Second, it can follow the critical utopias of the 1970s and find new and better ways of telling stories.

Starting with that second point, there are several promising narrative strategies among Moylan's critical utopias and their successors. As noted in chapter 3 of this book, the standard model of fiction is based on equating narrative interest with conflict. but I think that is a category error. If, as I suggested in that chapter, motivated change over time is the only absolute requirement for a story, then utopian and dystopian fiction equally meet the criterion. In both, however, the motivation is societal rather than individual, which is one reason why even the better utopian plots fail to register on critics looking for individual tragedies or epiphanies in fiction. To find the narrative interest, we need alternative ways of describing sources of resist-ance in world and in story: friction, dissonance, stumbles in a dance, or even a disturbance in the Force. Thinking in terms like these can bring up suggestions of better ways to tell stories in utopia, and it might allow us to perceive aspects of social interaction and change that are otherwise invisible.

Trying to identify some of the narrative strategies that have been used with greater success in critical utopias, I came up with six basic story lines or tropes. Each involves some sort of resistance, dissonance, occultation, or whichever metaphor allows us to see how the trope generates the necessary tension and engagement. My names for these six are the Ambassador from

Utopia, the Misfit in Utopia, the Would-Be Immigrant, the Threat to Utopia, Building Utopia, and the Neverending Revolution.

The Ambassador from Utopia storyline actually goes back at least to the nineteenth century, with William Dean Howells's *A Traveler from Altruria* (serialized 1892–93). One advantage of this trope is that the writer doesn't have to imagine a whole society or to make it convincingly superior, only to imagine a viewpoint from which to observe our own all-too-flawed world. Joanna Russ came back to this concept in 1975 with her blockbuster *The Female Man*, in which a visitor from the all-female future world of Whileaway skewers pretty much every assumption about women and gender. Russ also offered other alternative futures in the same novel, including a dystopia in which women and men are at war. A good recent instance of the Ambassador trope is Andy Duncan's story, "An Agent of Utopia" (2018) which does its social commenting obliquely while the title character is engaged in intrigues involving Thomas More's severed head.

One of the most celebrated examples of the Misfit in Utopia is Ursula K. Le Guin's "The Ones Who Walk Away from Omelas" (1973). In this brief parable, those who walk away from that seemingly idyllic city are unwilling to stake their happiness on the unhappiness of another. On a larger scale, Samuel R. Delany's sprawling *Trouble on Triton*, from 1976, imagines a freewheeling society on one of Neptune's moons. The protagonist is unhappy in spite of being offered a rainbow array of gender identities and sexual options; his unhappiness ironically serves to validate the utopia because it becomes clear that he would not be happy anywhere, or if he were it would be at the expense of everyone else's happiness.

Le Guin gives us another Misfit, and an even more fully imagined utopian society, in her encyclopedic *Always Coming Home*, originally published in 1985. The people in that society, called the Kesh, "might be going to have lived a long, long time from now" (Le Guin 2019, 7) in a post-historical northern California. The Misfit in this case is a young woman called North Owl. Her unhappiness has to do partly with a broken family and an uncertain identity—her father is an outsider from the warlike Condor people—and partly from the usual turmoil of adolescence, including an inappropriate and unrequited crush that results in North Owl leaving home to seek out her father's tribe. Life among the Condor forces North Owl to grow up fast. The Condor part of the plot touches on another trope, the Threat to Utopia. Le Guin works out a convincing resolution to the threat that does not violate the Kesh's peaceful views: the Condor military empire is economically unsustainable. It collapses from hunger and infighting before the invasion can occur.

Both the threat and the immigrant story also show up in a work that strongly influenced Le Guin: Austin Tappan Wright's *Islandia* (1942). *Islandia* is one of the few genuine utopias to appear between the end of the nineteenth-century boom and the advent of the critical utopias of the 1970s. It imagines an egalitarian and Earth-friendly nation on a subcontinent somewhere in the southern hemisphere: the would-be immigrant to Islandia, John Lang, also brings with him the threat of American colonial and capitalist exploitation, which he must renounce before finding a place in the culture he has come to love.

Gilman's *Herland* similarly has a viewpoint character who must come to terms with being part of the threat to his adopted home. He is one of three male explorers who find their way into a non-patriarchal society; the fates of the three vary according to their ability to adapt to female rule. Of the three, only the narrator's friend Jeff settles permanently in Herland with his new partner Celis. Terry commits an act of rape and is forcibly expelled. Narrator Van and his Herlandian partner Ellador choose to accompany Terry back to "civilization" and thus become examples of the Ambassador trope. Alice Sheldon, using her pen name James Tiptree, Jr., retold the same basic story in her 1976 story "Houston, Houston, Do You Read?" In that instance of the trope, though, no male is deemed admissible: maleness itself is the threat. Even Tiptree's "good" male reveals his propensity for violence under the influence of an inhibition-lowering drug and must be killed for the sake of the future.

Kim Stanley Robinson, who has done much to keep the utopian flame alive, depicts a scaled-down utopia in his novel *Pacific Edge* (1990), which is the third of his "Three Californias" trilogy (the other volumes represent two different forms of dystopia). The plot-generating threat in *Pacific Edge* comes from within: it has to do with land developers but also with the personal flaws of everyone involved: Robinson's is not a utopia of saints but one of compromises and temporary fixes.

Jo Walton, as mentioned at the beginning of this chapter, offers an interesting perspective on utopian thought itself by going back to Plato in *The Just City* (2015) and its sequels *The Philosopher Kings* (2015) and *Necessity* (2016). That last includes threats both internal and external: the Republic, which has been implemented in the ancient Mediterranean and then time-shifted to another planet in the future, finds itself facing divisions among its citizens and outcasts while also confronting a set of non-human intruders.

All of these, and especially the first volume of Walton's trilogy, additionally depict societies-in-progress, the Building Utopia trope, which has the big advantage of coming into the story at a hopeful point—before anything that might go wrong has had a chance to. Robinson often uses this trope, for instance in his Red Mars trilogy (1992–96). In a variant of the Building Utopia trope, in Le Guin's short story "The Day Before the Revolution" (1974) the anarchist utopia of her novel *The Dispossessed* (also 1974) is as yet unbuilt. The story takes place as followers of the philosopher Odo are getting ready to depart their home world of Urras for the barren but potentially free moon of Anarres. The story, written after the novel, shows Odo as a dying woman, disabled by a stroke, thinking back on the struggles that have led to this point, even as those struggles are coming to fruition. Odo is the Moses who looks out at the promised land but cannot enter it. She has built the intellectual structure: others will have to implement it. A more ironic version of that scenario can be found in another story by Alice Sheldon, this time writing as Raccoona Sheldon. In Sheldon's "Your Faces, O My Sisters! Your Faces Filled of Light" (1976), we don't know whether the woman traveling the country heralding a soon-to-be-built utopia is visionary or delusional.

The Dispossessed is one of the most fully articulated and compelling of critical utopias. Its critical nature is signaled by the subtitle "An Ambiguous Utopia," as well as by the novel's dual structure. Matching the story's two worlds, there are two narrative threads, with alternating chapters leading up to and then following on from the journey of the protagonist Shevek from Anarres to Urras. Shevek is a physicist, so his discoveries about the double nature of time further compound and justify that structure: his story is both simultaneous and sequential. Further, Shevek faces resistance and willful obduracy from an academic establishment that is not supposed to be possible in an Odonian system. His scientific breakthrough necessitates a social breakthrough as well: the revolution on Anarres has grown stagnant and needs to be renewed and refought. That constitutes a Threat. The story of Shevek's companions and their Syndicate of Initiative is an unusual version of Building Utopia. Without meaning to he has become a Misfit in Utopia and then an Ambassador from it. And at the very end of the novel, we don't know whether Shevek will be readmitted to the closed society of Anarres, so he is a would-be Immigrant. Thus, Le Guin incorporates all the storytelling tropes while avoiding all the traps. The novel compellingly demonstrates that there can be other ways of living and being than Things as They Are, but that those alternatives will never be complete. They will always need work. The utopian revolution never ends; otherwise it ceases to be utopia.

These six narrative strategies could work just as well for young adult readers as for adults. I would love to see a shelf of critically utopian novels aimed at readers in their teens and early twenties: the stage when reading the right book can set you on a whole new path in life. As of now, though, there is no publishing niche for such books. Dystopias take up all the shelf space, all the oxygen in the room. Though stories can be good to think with, they can also prevent certain kinds of thought, such as the idea that the world could be remade in a good way. Ray Bradbury said once in regard to *Fahrenheit 451* (1959) that, "There is more than one way to burn a book. And the world is full of people running about with lit matches" (1979, 176). If all utopias go bad, or if we can see only the flaws, then we are likely to stop thinking about trying to make positive changes.

If one were to write a utopia for young adults, the tropes I have been describing could make it an engaging story. But a utopia needs to do more than take us on an exciting narrative ride: it requires substantive world-building as well as competent storytelling. As has been mentioned, eutopias have to limit their claims in order not to revert to the dystopian side. That need goes back to what Moylan says about critical utopias, that they must "focus on the continuing presence of difference and imperfection within utopian society itself" and so critique their own premises. Beyond that, utopian fiction also needs to set aside grand claims and go for smaller victories. A successful utopia might differ from the historical world in only one or two key ways. It might last for just a single lifetime, or a single year. It can be as small as a village, or a single institution, or even a family.

Le Guin, who thought a lot about what she was doing in her utopian fiction, made a distinction between big, ambitious utopias and more modest, low-key ones using the Taoist contrast between hot, masculine yang and cool, feminine yin. "[F]rom Plato on," she says in her 1982 talk "A Non-Euclidean View of California as a Cold Place to Be," "utopia has been the big yang motorcycle trip. Bright, dry, clear, strong, firm, active, aggressive, lineal, progressive, creative, expanding, advancing, and hot" (Le Guin 1983, 713). So what would the contrary be like? "It would be dark, wet, obscure, weak, yielding, passive, participatory, circular, cyclical, peaceful, nurturant, retreating, contracting, and cold" (714). Furthermore, as Le Guin says, (i)f utopia is a place that does not exist, then surely (as Lao Tzu would say) the way to get there is by the way that is not a way. And in the same vein, the nature of the utopia I am trying to describe is such that if it is to come, it must exist already.   (717)

Her society of the Kesh is decidedly yin, even down to the already-existing part. In constructing it, Le Guin drew on indigenous societies, peoples who have managed not to mess up their environment for millennia and whose happiness depends less on material goods than on what anthropologist Victor Turner termed *communitas*: community as an organizing principle and goal. The Kesh live lightly, live small, live richly. They are immersed in relationship and ritual, which, along with humor, help them cope with the misunderstandings and petty jealousies that are part of living in utopia without being saints.

With regard to families as potential small-scale utopias, in an essay called "All Happy Families," Le Guin takes issue with the famous opening of *Anna Karenina*, in which Tolstoy asserts that all happy families are alike.

Those happy families he speaks of so confidently in order to dismiss them as all alike—where were they? Were they very much commoner in the nineteenth century? Did he know numerous happy families among the Russian nobility, or middle class, or peasantry, all alike?...Did he know one family, one single family, that could over a substantial period of time, as a whole and in each of its component members, honestly be called happy?   (Le Guin 2004, 35)

Exactly the same could be said of utopias: they might not function for a substantial span of time; they might not succeed as a whole, and they might have constituents who are unhappy. Yet they do function, at least as instructive contrasts to the world we live in.

A limited, or yin, utopia doesn't have to last forever or cover the whole earth. It needn't address every form of social ill or injustice. It just has to be enough different from Things as They Are that we are forced to pause and reflect on why they are that way. So just how small can a utopia be and still count? In Joshua Kotin's book *Utopias of One*, he discusses various writers who constructed their own solitary visions: Henry Thoreau, W. E. B. Dubois, and—here he is, back again—Wallace Stevens. Unlike all other utopias, says Kotin, utopias of one do not fail. However, their success comes at a cost: they cannot serve as models for readers hoping to perfect their own lives or remake their communities. Utopias of one are exclusive—and, in most cases, inimitable. (2)

A utopia of one would be, as Kotin suggests, the absolute limiting case. In a utopia of one, everyone is always in agreement, like a choir of one singing "in unison." Kotin's final chapter pulls back from that solipsistic extreme, going back to what the chapter title calls "Utopias of Two." Since the reader is always there, one can argue, the textual utopia was never truly solitary—indeed, that might be the dividing line in Stevens' poetry, between poems where the writer's self-expression and the reader's comprehension meet and those where communication breaks down, where the language is too private to break into. I would stop there as well, with groups of two, on the grounds that utopia is fundamentally a social construct, like a family or an institution or a folk group.

Folklorist Elliott Oring makes a case for considering the dyad to be "the absolute minimum organization of enduring relations in society" (1984,19). Pairs of siblings, friends, spouses, and so on can have all the markers of a folk group, including shared sayings, jokes, nicknames, beliefs, and a sense of difference from the rest of the world. Individuals have none of those things: although Jay Mechling notes that folklore can be *performed* alone (Mechling 2006, 435), it isn't generated alone and it doesn't acquire meaning until shared. Likewise, talking to oneself is not utopia.

So we need at least a pair of individuals; what else? We need a profound change from Things as They Are: a social transformation of some sort. Our family must represent a different way of being a family: more equal, more cooperative, more inventive. Our couple must share a viewpoint that changes the world. Our village or school or church must develop its own profoundly new ways of worship or teaching or governance. But it needn't do so for very long. Utopia can be a moment—providing it is a moment of life-changing, world-altering vision.

I play cello in a semi-professional orchestra. Its members are students, faculty, community members with day jobs: the usual mixed lot. Some are better players than others. Some are quiet while others tell jokes. We vary in age, sex, occupation, place of origin. But there are moments when none of that matters. In the middle of a performance, when we are all engaged in the same task of translating notes on paper into sounds first imagined by Dvořák or Copeland, something transformative happens. We focus. We listen. We watch the conductor—at least out of the corners of our eyes—and the concertmaster and our stand partners. And we stop being individuals and become an effective unit: a superorganism. Some evolutionary biologists think that music evolved as a way to get groups thinking in parallel or unison: it's the closest thing to telepathy. I would say that in those moments, we are a utopia, one made of disparate individuals brought together by pitch and rhythm. It doesn't last long—not always even a whole piece or movement of a piece—but it doesn't have to. We know it; the audience knows it.

And that is why utopian literature exists: to help us identify and value such moments of harmony. We need to know how to string such moments together into stories: stories of utopian emigrés or immigrants, stories of building or reconstructing the mechanism of society in better ways. And we especially need to offer such stories to our young people, who have the passion and the plasticity to make change happen. Utopias require the social equivalent of neuroplasticity.

It may seem weird to be talking about a literature that doesn't exist—actually it is a very structuralist move, to say, "The options are either this or not-this, and it doesn't much matter whether not-this can be found in the world." The missing half of the binary, my not-this, is the young adult anti-dystopia. As Le Guin said of yin utopia, perhaps it can only be reached by the path that is not a path, and that is not an impossible paradox if we are already there. Utopias for young readers do exist. They are out there, but they will not be recognized as such until we are willing to see utopia in small communities, even as small as a pair of like-minded individuals, and to find the moments of harmony that could be models of the good place.

And so a shift in vision is all that is needed to turn at least some of the YA dystopias into utopias-in-between-the-lines. Instead of looking for all the instances of terrible-ness, we can read books that are already out there for their eutopian potential. One example is Alaya Dawn Johnson's *The Summer Prince* (2013). Set in a high-tech, post-disaster future Brazil, Johnson's tale has all the earmarks of a dystopia. The giant arcology called Palmares Tres is divided spatially and economically—the wealthy on top, workers at the bottom—and rigidly controlled by its female elders. Information is withheld, hypocrisy is rife, and access to the city and its privileges is tightly controlled by the Aunties. Furthermore, the whole system depends, as in "The Ones Who Walk Away from Omelas," on a single sacrificial victim, not, in this case, an abused child but the Prince of the title.

Like any good dystopia, this has a trio of rebels: June, an emerging artist from an aristocratic family; her oldest friend Gil; and the chosen Prince in their year, Enki, who comes from the lowest stratum of the city. They form a rebel alliance and a love triangle, but the outcome of neither is what one would expect from the Hunger Games or *Star Wars*. The central romantic relationship is between Gil and Enki (the names signal Johnson's deliberate invoking of the Gilgamesh/Enkidu bond), and Enki embraces his sacrificial role as a way to engineer lasting change. Rather than overthrowing the regime, the adolescent heroes renew and reform Tres Palmares with the aid of the intelligent city itself. Their triad is both a small, yin utopia and the seed of a greater transformation. Perhaps because there is a utopia hidden within the dystopia, Sargent's database, though it lists *The Summer Prince*, does not place it in either category. Science fiction writer Nisi Shawl notes the exciting potential of the novel's imagined technologies and also notes that Palmares Tres is more racially inclusive than any existing society. She ends her essay on the novel with the comment that despite its problems, "I long for Palmares Tres. I long for this future, a site of hope and frustration, joy and tumult and striving and change."

Shawl implies that we can choose to emphasize the hope rather than the warning: to work our way through a dystopia to find its anti-dystopian twin. If the reader wishes it so, utopia is already there, presenting itself as science fiction, fantasy, even dystopia—all the modes that are not explicitly eutopian but that, by departing from things-as-they-are, serve as models of instruction and schemas for interaction. Perhaps, then, the true utopian condition is the act of reading and the reader's subsequent transformation. We may be the utopia we seek.

7

Gender and Fantasy

Employing Fairy Tales

A significant chunk of the work of fantasy has to do with its being employed as a road map for journeys of growth and searches for identity. Modern fantasy inherits that job from the traditional fairy tale, which served the same function even before therapists started inviting patients to turn to myths and tales for personal insight and release from trauma. Though the process of identification with fairy-tale heroes and victims is a complex one, and ill-served by the distortions of writers such as Bruno Bettelheim, narrative therapy based in traditional fantastic literature is well established in professional practice (e.g., Silverman 2004, Runberg et al. 1993) as well as pop psychology. Long before Freud or Jung, people were using tales for solace, guidance, and a chance to vent otherwise inexpressible emotions. That comfort or release is, however, not equally available to all, and over the past century the personal and artistic use of fairy tales in particular, as opposed to myth and other collective oral narratives, has become mostly women's prerogative. The question whether men read or write fairy tales is an odd one. It wouldn't have occurred to readers of Hans Christian Andersen or Charles Perrault. Yet since the mid-twentieth century, the fairy tale has become a major form of artistic expression, self-examination, and political activism for women, while male writers and consumers are often made to feel like interlopers when they venture into the realm of the wonder tale. This imbalance puzzles me, as a lifelong devotee of fairy tale, and I set out a few years ago to explore how it came about and what sorts of strategies male writers employ to establish their own claim on the tales. This exploration eventually led to a 2018 article in the journal *Marvels and Tales*, which I will draw on in this chapter, but I won't reproduce the article here. Articles prove theses; they have to make it look as if writers already know what they think and are simply laying out the case for their conclusions. As the text gets refined and edited, points are clarified and contradictions and digressions excised. But reality is not clear, and history does not have a single trajectory until some writer gives it one. So, if the reader will indulge me,

I will go back over the process by which my thinking on this topic developed over time, and turn the argument into a sort of detective story. It represents a long journey I didn't even know I was taking until well along the way. There were many scenes of discovery on the path: a mix of "aha!" and "duh" moments that I will try to label as I go.

A bit of a warning up front: talking about men and fairy tales is a hazardous business, because it looks like you are following the footsteps of chest-thumpers in the men's rights movement—think of Robert Bly mis-reading the tale of Iron Hans, whom he called "Iron John" and transformed from a nightmarish killer to a tutelary wild man (Zipes 1992, 16). I am not going to use traditional stories to reassert male privilege or to counsel going primitive. My reading of gender is based in feminism, which allows us to see not only girls and women but also men and boys as varied and vulnerable individuals. And so I start my story with feminist takes on the Disney canon of animated tales—which, if we are thinking in terms of a detective story, might be considered the initial crime to be solved.

Kay F. Stone's 1975 essay "Things Walt Disney Never Told Us," along with Karen Rowe's "Feminism and Fairy Tales" from 1979, encouraged women readers to question the lessons taught by the passive heroines of animated movies from *Snow White* to *Sleeping Beauty*. The anti-feminist work performed by those versions of the tales was both odious and obvious once pointed out. But the taming of fairy-tale women didn't start with Disney. Scholarship on the Grimms, such as Jack Zipes's *Fairy Tales and the Art of Subversion* (1983) and Maria Tatar's *The Hard Facts of the Grimms' Fairy Tales* (1987), has demonstrated how their editorial changes gradually selected against strong women characters, upped the level of violence, and turned previously active female heroes into good, quiet, or even dead models of German femininity. Later publishers followed the Grimms' lead, favoring mute, domestic heroines of the sort we know from Disney films. The silencing of female characters extended beyond editors and adapters. A few years after Rowe and Stone's initial accusations, folk-lorist Torborg Lundell did some sleuthing among the seemingly objective descriptions in standard indexes of folklore. What she found was that the same action performed by male and female characters would be summarized completely differently. For instance, there is a Norwegian tale known as "Mestermø," "The Mastermaid." The title character is a confident magic worker who outwits her troll captor and rescues and wins a fairly useless prince. The tale category to which "Mestermø" belongs is labeled in the Aarne-Thompson type index, "The Girl as Helper in the Hero's Flight"

(Lundell 1986, 153). In composing their type names, Antti Aarne and Stith Thompson, though not deliberately distorting the record, didn't even seem to perceive that the girl might *be* the hero.

And so another aspect of the rediscovery of women in tales was gathering together tales that could testify against the misogyny of Disney and the Grimms. Collections such as Ethel Johnston Phelps's *Tatterhood and Other Tales* (1978) and Angela Carter's *The Virago Book of Fairy Tales* (1990) bore witness to the clever, determined girls who had always been part of the oral tradition. For every Sleeping Beauty there was a Mastermaid, a Kate Crackernuts, a Mollie Whuppie—giant-killers, self-rescuers, girls who get by on their wits rather than their beauty, older female characters who guide young women rather than suppressing them. Further scholarship, especially Linda Dégh's *Folktales and Society* (1989) and Marina Warner's *From the Beast to the Blonde* (1994) has shown that the traditional image of a woman narrator, the eponymous Mother Goose, isn't wrong. Both women and men tell tales in most cultures, though not always the same tales or to the same audiences. And women raconteurs, not surprisingly, favor female leads.

About the same time that these traditions were being revived in print, writers such as Jane Yolen and Angela Carter began to compose original narratives that re-engineered some of the more oppressive tales such as Perrault's "Sleeping Beauty' and "Bluebeard" into stories of endurance and even triumph. Carter's poetic and disturbing collection *The Bloody Chamber* came out in 1979; Yolen's humorous children's book *Sleeping Ugly* in 1981. As different as those two books are, both do the same work of reclaiming and transforming tales that had been used to keep young women in line. Put those together with Anne Sexton's and Sylvia Plath's poetic self-explorations, Dégh's contextual study of a woman storyteller in Hungary, Zipes's and Tatar's investigations of the Grimms's work, and the psychoanalytic turn championed by Bettelheim and other less problematic commentators, and you have the conditions for a creative and scholarly gold rush with regard to women and fairy tales.

So where do men come into that—and where did I? In the latter case, basically by reaping the benefits. During the feminist heyday of the 1970s, I was a student with an interest in folklore. I was excited by the rediscoveries, which reinforced memories of the strong female characters I had come across scattered throughout Andrew Lang's multicolored fairy books— which I didn't know at the time were more Nora Lang's work than her husband's. I loved the many subversive takes on familiar tales that began to appear in fantasy: Robin McKinley's *Beauty* (1978), Tanith Lee's *Red as*

Blood (1983), the stories and poems in Ellen Datlow and Terri Windling's *Snow White, Blood Red* (1993), and the novelized tales that Windling commissioned for her Fairy Tale series. Some of my own favorites include Susan Palwick's "Ever After" (1987), which imagines Cinderella as a vampire being inducted by her "fairy" godmother, Kelly Link's "Travels with the Snow Queen" (1997), which riffs on Hans Christian Andersen's "The Snow Queen" (1845), itself a boldly female-centric coming-into-power story; and Delia Sherman's 1995 poem, "Snow White to the Prince," in which the final stanza completely reimagines the tale's family dynamic. "Do you think I did not know her," Sherman's Snow White asks, and explains,

> Of course I took her poisoned gifts. I wanted
> To feel her hands combing out my hair,
> To let her lace me up, to take an apple
> From her hand, a smile from her lips,
> As when I was a child.
>
> (Sherman 1995, 41)

The whole cluster of original work and revisionist history reinforced my convictions about the aesthetic, as well as social, benefits of feminism and helped steer my own work toward explorations of gender as well as genre.

And that leads to the next development in my mystery story. In 1999, I offered a course at Hollins University called "Gender and Fantasy: Men, Women, and Dragons," starting from the vague idea that dragons might be a destabilizing third term in the gender equation. The course didn't include only women writers and female characters. Robert Munsch's *The Paper Bag Princess* (1980) was a popular entry in the subvert-Disney effort, and going back further, Kenneth Grahame's "The Reluctant Dragon" (1898) is a remarkable dismantling of conventional masculinity. Ursula K. Le Guin's *A Wizard of Earthsea* (1968) has a male hero and assumes a patriarchal society of wizards, but by the time Le Guin returned to Earthsea with *Tehanu* (1990), both hero and society are called into question, and her dragons enact many of the changes in concepts of gender over the span of time during which the stories appeared.

The second time I taught the course, I had a student who wanted to investigate therapeutic uses of fairy tales. What the student discovered is that there is a sizeable literature, primary and secondary, concerning girls and fairy tales. The many, many stories in which a female hero is threatened with incest or rape and triumphs over abuse are called upon to help patients get past their own traumas and rewrite the scenarios of their lives. This use of the stories is reinforced by comments from women writers: notably Terri Windling's powerful testimony about the saving power of fairy tales in her own life, which can be found in the introduction to her anthology *The Armless Maiden* (1995). As Windling says,

> what's important about these stories, from the point of view of any of us who have gone through the deep dark woods in childhood ourselves, is not the expectation of ending "Happily Ever After." Rather, it's the way that ending is achieved, through the process of transformation. (15)

With all this in mind, my student went looking for fairy tales about abused boys, and their potential usefulness in treatment. And found nothing. Where, we wondered, are the stories about male Cinderellas, Snow Whites confronting jealous stepfathers, or boy Donkeyskins who must flee from incestuous mothers or fathers? There seemed to be no stories for helping boys, as those stories are used for girls. Or, if there are, they are obscure, and no one has been motivated to seek them out. My student and I did find a few motifs involving physical and psychological mistreatment of boy heroes, but no acknowledgment in folk tradition that males might be victims of sexual abuse, and at least by the early 2000s there were no comparable books or articles focusing on male patients.

At this point, you might be raising doubts, as I was, about the reliability of bibliotherapy, or thinking about Freud's dismissal of his patients' reports of abuse, or pondering the reasons for cultural blindness about boys as victims. With regard to the mystery at hand, though, these are red herrings, and sorting through them demands kinds of expertise I can't claim. Sticking to my field of narrative, I was struck by the asymmetry of the evidence. There was so much about women and fairy tales, so little about men. Part of the reason is that men for so long have been treated as the norm, the default case. Without the intervention of feminism and its interrogation of femininity, it is almost impossible to see masculinity as equally constructed, equally problematic. Men and boys were so long the universal example that Bettelheim is able to say, with complete and clueless sincerity, that

> [t]he fate of these heroes convinces the child that [though] he may feel outcast and abandoned in the world..., like them...he will be guided step by step, and given help when it is needed. Today, even more than in past times, the child needs the reassurance offered by the image of the isolated

man who nevertheless is capable of achieving meaningful and rewarding relations with the world around him. (1977, 11)

Those "isolated men," one must remember, include Bettelheim's own chief examples of Snow White, Red Riding Hood, and Cinderella. Women are ill-served by the universalizing of masculinity, but so, in many cases, are men, and especially in cases where the universal standard gives neither guidance nor comfort.

All of that sat simmering in the back of my mind while I worked on other research, including a book on gender in science fiction. As part of that project I was reading feminist critiques of science and semiotic studies of gendered identity and meaning. I also encountered the emerging field of masculinity studies: particularly the work of Michael Kimmel and R. W. Connell. Connell introduced the concept of hegemonic masculinity, which looks at the way power is allocated or withheld according to an individual's conformance with socially approved gender roles. What this means for boys is that the ideal of mastery is continually dangled in front of them but its confident exercise is forever deferred. Connell, Kimmel, and their followers demystify male privilege and reveal rifts in masculine identity. They show how masculinity depends on suppressing anything feminine in the self—and then erasing the evidence of that suppression.

All of that opens the door to a whole new level of textual detective work, especially in reference to seemingly simple texts like fairy tales. And so, a few years ago, it finally dawned on me that I could go back to the questions that came up in my "Men, Women, and Dragons" course, and especially the imbalance revealed by my student's project. I conceived a conference paper on masculinity and fairy tales. As one does, I sent in an abstract, assuming that I would have examples and something to say about them by the time the conference rolled around. I really didn't know what I was going to find, although I had a few examples in mind, a few suspects to interrogate: Appalachian Jack Tales; the Norwegian "Askelad," sometimes called a male Cinderella story; Neil Gaiman's "Troll Bridge" (1993), which puts a modern spin on another Norwegian tale; Maurice Sendak's visual accompaniments to the Grimms' collection; the void that is the Prince in any classic Disney cartoon.

As I started looking for models and sources, I came across the work of Kate Bernheimer, and especially her paired anthologies about writers responding to traditional tales. The first, *Mirror, Mirror on the Wall: Women Writers Explore Their Favorite Fairy Tales* (1998), was widely praised for bringing together testimony from writers such as Margaret Atwood and A. S. Byatt on the importance of fairy tales in their development. Then, when Bernheimer proposed a second installment dealing with men and fairy tales, she was told outright, "No one will be interested in what men have to say about fairy tales" (Bernheimer 2007, 5). It took her several years to assemble contributions and convince a publisher to issue *Brothers and Beasts: An Anthology of Men on Fairy Tales* (2007). The consensus among the contributors, which included Neil Gaiman, Jack Zipes, and Gregory Maguire, was that of course some boys find themselves in fairy tales, but they have to go against significant social pressure to do so. Novelist Christopher Barzak articulates this feeling in his entry:

> [R]ecalling the friends of my youth, I remember being aware at a young age that, among the boys I was friends with, none of them read very much. And they especially didn't read fairy tales. Watching the Disney versions was okay when we were small, but even those became off-limits the closer we drew to our teenage years.   (Barzak 2007 27–8)

In other words, boys who do read the tales are the marked case: not the norm—reversing the usual social dynamic. And it still isn't clear which tales male readers might find most meaningful.

Kate Bernheimer took the warnings against looking at men and fairy tales as a challenge, and so did I. This is the moment in a detective story when someone cautions the detective to stop looking: whatever you are being warned against is exactly the thing you should be investigating. But where should one start the probe?

I knew what I didn't want to spend time on: canonical treatments by male writers of the same female characters that Sexton and Carter had dealt with so much more subtly. Basically, that means I didn't want to touch Donald Barthelme or Robert Coover. I thoroughly dislike Barthelme's *Snow White* (1967), and besides, Cristina Bacchilega's *Postmodern Fairy Tales* (1997) already does an excellent job of analyzing their cultural work. Nor did I want to focus on fictions that look at the same cluster of female-oriented tales indirectly, taking minor characters like the rat coachman of Cinderella as points of view. That, unfortunately, leaves out interesting work by the likes of Gregory Maguire, David Henry Wilson, and Philip Pullman. Another regrettable cut was Randall Jarrell's many responses to fairy tale, including his translations from the Grimms and his original tales such as *The Animal Family* (1965). I didn't want to give up Jarrell, especially his poem "The

Black Swan," (Jarrell 1969) but that one didn't fit the profile I was compiling in my detective work, since it's about sisters, one of whom is or seems to be a swan. Yet, because in mysteries the ignored clue is often the key to a solution, it is worth contemplating the layering of identities in the poem, in which the male poet uses a female voice that transforms into that of a swan. Jarrell's poem ends with a dreamlike collage in which the sights and sounds of the marsh invade the speaker's bedroom. As the categories of swan and human, wild and tame, sky and water, all blur and transform, the speaker takes comfort from the caressing black wing of the swan that is both sister and self. It's a beautiful, terrifying poem, and I suspect that it was at the back of my mind in formulating my ultimate account of fairy-tale masculinity, in which, as I will explain, swans were to play a prominent role.

Armed with lists compiled from Heidi Anne Heiner's *SurLaLune Fairy Tales* website (https://www.surlalunefairytales.com), a treasure trove of modern and traditional fairy-tale texts; with Bernheimer's anthologies; and with the contents of the Datlow and Windling collections along with correspondence with Ellen Datlow, I started gathering novels and volumes of stories. One thing I discovered—this is one of the "duh" moments mentioned at the beginning, since it took me a long time to realize it—is that there is significant overlap between queerness (in several senses) and love for fairy tale. Christopher Barzak, whose essay I quoted from earlier, discusses that link. There are several volumes of invented or adapted fairy stories that represent gay lives and identities, including Peter Cashorali's *Fairy Tales: Traditional Stories Retold for Gay Men* (1995), Lawrence Schimel's *The Drag Queen of Elfland* (1997), Steve Berman's *Red Caps: New Fairy Tales for Out of the Ordinary Readers* (2014), and, fortuitously appearing while I was compiling my archive, Michael Cunningham's *A Wild Swan and Other Tales* (2015).

So I had a pretty substantial stack of evidence to work through, using my patented method of surrounding myself with a lot of material and sifting through it, feeling—"looking" suggests something too deliberate—for patterns. A number of patterns offered themselves: a pervasive sense of going against the cultural grain, identification with secondary characters such as Cinderella's rat coachman, and glimpses of unorthodox desire in earlier stories that become central motivators in later ones. Eventually I settled on a threefold model of alternative masculinities, and I turned my attention to a cluster of tales that fit those models. These were not necessarily the kinds of stories I had expected to find, and I wasn't sure at that point how my proposed three kinds of masculinity might relate to one another or to theoretical concepts such as Connell's hegemonic masculinity. I'll come back to those questions later on: that will be the moment of assembling the suspects in the parlor for a grand reveal. For now, I'll just say I had a positive response to the conference talk and was encouraged to write a more formal article on the topic. So that meant getting a lot more systematic in my sleuthing.

I sent a version of the talk to the journal *Marvels & Tales* and had it sent back for revision. Readers wanted me to say a lot more about masculinity studies and folklore, and less about feminism and literature. That was fine: I was happy not to have to rehash old arguments about Disney and the fairy-tale canon, although I have done some of that here. I was even happier to be steered toward sources I hadn't been aware of, such as Jeana Jorgensen's 2012 dissertation *Gender and the Body in Classical European Fairy Tales*, which looks at the way male and female bodies are described in terms of beauty and vulnerability. I didn't know Lewis Seifert's *Fairy Tales, Sexuality, and Gender in France, 1690–1715* (1996). And I was especially fascinated by James M. Taggart's 1997 study of storytelling in two communities, one in the Old World and one in the New, titled *The Bear and His Sons: Masculinity in Spanish and Mexican Folktales*. None of the sources I was directed toward really changed my ideas, but they challenged me to ground them more carefully and place them in academic context. It's always good for a detective to be called to account for hasty conclusions or careless fieldwork. As a journal editor myself, I'm fully aware of the lazy habits senior scholars get into. People tend to listen to us without calling us into account. We issue proclamations about the meanings of things and fall back on older research to back us up. We need peer reviewers and blind readings, even though those will occasionally produce odd results, such as a contributor being instructed to read their own work.

As I mentioned, the first version of my article was (rightly) bounced by readers. Every detective faces setbacks. I reframed the argument, retooled the rhetoric, shored up my sources, and came up with something that I think makes its case much more strongly. I was still questioned on some of my findings, which meant another round of footnotes and refining of claims. Again, all to the good, because, among other things, reviewers' strong responses mean that there is something at stake in fairy tales. Tales tell us who we are, including what our gendered identities might be. The cultural significance of circulating and refashioning tales is not merely their personal use: it has to do with the way society is organized and power allocated.

So what were the patterns I detected, and how did I lay out my case? As I said before, I sensed at least three versions of masculinity in these retellings. Literary renderings of any of these three tend to draw from more than one tale type, plus variants within the types, so that I ended up looking at a half dozen diverse groups of source texts. Some of these I expected I would be examining: "Jack and the Beanstalk," "The Brave Little Tailor." Others I would not have predicted: "Bluebeard" and "Rumpelstiltskin." I thought I might find retellings of "Puss in Boots" or "Aladdin," or "The Ashlad," but I did not. I ended up naming the three patterns the Little Man, the Monster Bridegroom, and the Erotic Swan. Each pits its protagonist against some version of hegemonic masculinity; each evades or transforms or demolishes that powerful imagined male ideal.

So let me introduce my suspects. First up, the Little Man. I just mentioned one of his models, "The Brave Little Tailor," a story that might not be familiar to everyone, even though it did get the Disney treatment in a 1938 cartoon short with Mickey Mouse in the lead. The English version reconstructed by Joseph Jacobs is titled "A Dozen at One Blow," and it starts like this:

> A little tailor was sitting cross-legged at his bench and was stitching away as busy as could be when a woman came up the street calling out: "Home-made jam, home-made jam!"
>
> So the tailor called out to her: "Come here, my good woman, and give me a quarter of a pound."
>
> And when she had poured it out for him he spread it on some bread and butter and laid it aside for his lunch. But, in the summer-time, the flies commenced to collect around the bread and jam.
>
> When the tailor noticed this, he raised his leather strap and brought it down upon the crowd of flies and killed twelve of them straightway. He was mighty proud of that. So he made himself a shoulder-sash, on which he stitched the letters: A Dozen at One Blow.
>
> When he looked down upon this he thought to himself: "A man who could do such things ought not to stay at home; he ought to go out to conquer the world." (Jacobs 1916)

Several elements in this are worth pointing out. First, the hero is a grown man, not a boy, but he is always described as undersized. And he is neither a peasant lad nor a prince but a working man. He performs a less-than-heroic deed, killing flies, and then boasts about it, which might be expected to get him in trouble when he ventures out into the world to repeat the task with giants instead of flies. Instead, his ingenuity, courage, and ability to lie with a straight face win him a royal bride and half a kingdom.

The tailor doesn't have a name in the tale, but it could well be Jack—the generic underdog hero of British and American traditional tales (cf. McCarthy et al. 1994). All the Jacks are versions of the Little Man, including the one known as the Giant Killer and the one who climbs the beanstalk. In the James Lapine/Stephen Sondheim musical *Into the Woods*, originally produced in 1986, Jack acts out an adolescent rite of passage, and the songs he sings point to the sexual dimensions of his adventure. "There are Giants in the sky," he proclaims on returning to earth, including "A big tall terrible lady Giant [who] draws you close/ To her Giant breast,/ And you know things now/ that you never knew before . . ."

Lapine and Sondheim incorporate psychoanalytic readings throughout their musical—there's a good bit of Bly and Bettelheim—even while they critique and undercut some of those readings. In this case, they start with the Oedipal reading of Jack as man-child, the beanstalk as phallic dream, and the male and female giants as father-ogre and mother-object-of-desire, respectively. And then they complicate things by having the woman giant come back, looking for revenge for her husband's murder—but that's another story.

As I was collecting contemporary versions of the Little Man, it began to strike me that there was another, very different version of the same basic configuration: another small workingman who goes up against the rich and powerful, with a sometime ally in the form of a female figure who is attached to the richer, older, bigger male. In this case, the Little Man's trade is not tailoring but spinning, and his name is Rumpelstiltskin. Rumpelstiltskin is not a sympathetic figure as Jack and the Tailor are, but modern writers tend to reverse that evaluation, noting that the dwarf makes a bargain in good faith and that his primary motivation seems to be desire for a child. In contrast, the King in the story is greedy and ready to execute his bride if she can't produce the gold, and yet we are asked to consider their marriage a happy ending.

All versions of the Little Man involve his coming up against male power. To counter the might of giants and the wealth of kings, all he has on his side is misdirection and a kind of psychological judo that uses his opponents' strengths against them—plus, if he works his charm, collusion from the giant's wife. As Cunningham comments,

Jack climbs up the beanstalk, the giant's wife lets him in, Jack steals the giant's gold, Jack comes back a second time, and giant's wife lets him in again—she once again admits the young man who robbed her husband. What's going on in that marriage?   (Cunningham 2015)

All of this works for Jack, but not for Rumpelstiltskin, who ends up tearing himself in half with rage and frustration. As a matter of fact, one of the modern retellings I found was Kevin Brockmeier's "A Day in the Life of Half of Rumpelstiltskin," which follows his riven halves past the end of the traditional tale. Another revision was Cunningham's, one of the stories in *A Wild Swan*, and it was in Cunningham's title that I found the link between the two tale types: he calls his version of Rumpelstiltskin "Little Man." In that story, he brings out the pathos of being excluded from the biological route to parenthood, "so readily available to any drunk and barmaid who link up for three minutes in one of the darker corners of any dank and scrofulous pub" (Cunningham 2015, 60). Further, the narrator says, "[i]magine reaching the point at which you want a child more than you can remember wanting anything else," but then points out that: "Adoption agencies are reluctant about doctors and lawyers, if they're single and over forty. So go ahead. Apply to adopt an infant as a two-hundred-year-old gnome" (60). That is an illustrative example, I think, of the way modern writers use the queering properties of fairy tale: its ability to make the familiar strange and the strange relatable. Jane Yolen makes a convincing case that Rumpelstiltskin is an expression of antisemitism (Yolen 2000, 107). Cunningham makes an equally compelling case that it might be about gay fatherhood.

My second version of non-hegemonic masculinity is what I have called the Monster Bridegroom. That title suggests "Beauty and the Beast," which is indeed one of the traditional tale types I had in mind (Aarne-Thompson-Uther type 425C). It's a version of the Cupid and Psyche story (ATU 425B) as well as one of a number of tales about animal bridegrooms, such as "Bearskin" and "East o' the Sun and West o' the Moon." "Beauty and the Beast," best known in a version by Perrault's contemporary Jeanne-Marie Leprince de Beaumont, is a story pattern that has been particularly useful to female writers investigating the belief that true love can tame an abusive partner—a belief that definitely falls in the "don't try this at home, kids" category. But the male writers I looked at find a slightly different meaning in the story, especially when we put the Beast figure together with another menacing Bridegroom: Bluebeard.

Bluebeard is a monster of a different sort from the Beast and comes from an entirely separate family of tales (ATU types 312 for "Bluebeard" and "The Tiger Bridegroom"; 311 for "Fitcher's Bird"; and 955 for "The Robber Bridegroom"). Bluebeard is, as the Grandmother says in Neil Jordan and Angela Carter's 1984 film *The Company of Wolves*, one of those who is "hairy on the inside." Rich and handsome, he is also a serial seducer and murderer of young women. In Perrault's version of the story, his violence is excused on the grounds that his brides keep disobeying his order not to open the secret room, the Bloody Chamber from which Carter takes the title of her collection. As Marina Warner says:

> In 'Bluebeard', the initial weight of the story swings the listener or reader's sympathies toward the husband who instructs his young wife, and presents his request for her obedience as reasonable and the terror she experiences when she realizes her fate as a suitable punishment, a warning against trespass. (243)

Some of that sympathy comes through in Bela Bartok's operatic version, *Bluebeard's Castle* (1918), in which the castle is a double of Bluebeard himself and the curious wife an interloper who violates the privacy of his soul.

However, Michael Mejia, in his contribution to the Bernheimer anthology, challenges this reading. Mejia ends his essay, which looks at both Perrault and Bartok, by defining himself against the image of the blue-bearded bully: "I am not Bluebeard. I am no murderous lothario . . . I am no sociopath, no misanthrope, no tragic beast who exits the woods only long enough to lure a bride back to his weeping castle . . . " (Mejia 2007, 132–3). Yet, he is not sure where that leaves him: "Am I, then, the little bride in this story?" (133).

If the Little Man stories are about challenging hegemonic masculinity through trickery and theft, Monster Bridegroom stories are about refusing to become the male master, the brute. That isn't always easy. There is no alternative version of maleness in Perrault's "Bluebeard." Angela Carter adds a sympathetic male in "The Bloody Chamber," but makes him helpless, a blind piano tuner. (In Carter's version, it's the protagonist's mother who comes riding to the rescue, pistols blazing.) Other traditional versions of the story, such as the Grimms' "Fitcher's Bird" and the English "Mr Fox" add in brothers or kinsmen to come to the bride's assistance. These variants have none of that blaming-the-bride-for-her-own-abuse that we get from

Perrault—and even from commentators like Bettelheim. However, if we are looking for non-hegemonic masculinity in the story, we get only a generalized picture of family; the brothers are not characterized and there is no alternative suitor.

One of the texts I looked at, though, does bring in a significant male figure who might be a partial answer to Meijia's question about where to find himself in the story. Gregory Frost's *Fitcher's Brides* (2002)—written for Windling's Fairy Tale Series—departs from Grimm by introducing a lover for one of the three brides of the villainous preacher Fitcher. Retellers who don't want to identify with Bluebeard or the Beast can use fairy tale's tendency to double and triple characters and incidents. They can split the male role. In a way, "Beauty and the Beast" (from yet another ATU tale type, number 425) already does so, if we think of the Beast and his transformed self as different possible ways of being a man. One of the most famous retellings of the story, Jean Cocteau's 1946 film *La Belle et la Bête*, adds an additional character named Avenant, a suitor of Beauty's and another chance to feature star Jean Marais. Avenant is the Beast's foil: impressive on the outside but lacking the Beast's capacity for selfless love. At the end, the transformed Beast takes on Avenant's form, and Cocteau uses every cinematic trick to cast a glamor on his leading man and real-life lover, who positively glows on the screen.

And that element in the story brings me to my third alternative version of masculinity, but first I'm going to offer a brief flashback, a detour through the early Disney fairy tales that helped me solve my case. I have mentioned the blankness of the male leads in those movies. Their unsatisfactoriness was acknowledged by the studio artists, who kept the Prince figure offscreen as much as possible because they couldn't figure out how to make him move. Animator Frank Thomas explains in his study of Disney animation that "[w]hen a pretty girl or a handsome prince are presented romantically, they must be conceived as 'straight' and drawn realistically and carefully" (Thomas and Johnston 1981, 326). What Thomas means by "straight" here is realistic, not caricatured, but other meanings of the term are relevant. To be realistic is also to be careful, guarded, even closeted, lest the figure on screen reveals truths about masculine behavior and desire that social norms deny.

The Disney Prince is just one example of the form of gender coding I think of as subtractive masculinity. To be eligible for the social benefits of patriarchy, men must give up any traits that might be labeled feminine, because masculinity is defined primarily by not being womanly and secondarily by not being effeminate, which is the same phobia at one remove (that is, fear of not being sufficiently not-womanly). This means, especially in Anglo-American culture, that a man should not dance, cry, gesture, nurture, empathize, or show any sort of vulnerability. All of those and more are subtracted from the range of possible expressions. No wonder it was hard to make romantic male figures interesting, visually or narratively.

But, as in the case of Cocteau's film, the bargain changes when same-sex attraction is added to the mix. If men can be desired by women (reversing the cinematic gaze uncovered by Laura Mulvey in her classic essay "Visual Pleasure and Narrative Cinema," 1975) but also desirable to other men, they might also be allowed to demonstrate all the other things subtractive masculinity denies, such as physical grace. At least they can if they are swans, rather than humans.

The title story of Cunningham's collection is "The Wild Swan," a version of which is found in Grimm but best known in Hans Christian Andersen's literary retelling. In the story, six or eleven or twelve brothers (depending on the variant of ATU type 451) are transformed by a vengeful stepmother into swans, and their lone sister must gather nettles and weave them into shirts to restore them to human form. If we focus on the sister's heroism, this story fits in with other Andersen tales with strong female figures, such as "The Snow Queen," but I am looking at the brothers and what they have meant to later writers.

Andersen's biographer Jackie Wullschlager notes that "Swans were part of Andersen's private mythology, recurring in his letters as symbols of mystery and grandeur even before he began writing fairy tales" (2000, 189). Besides "The Wild Swans," he wrote a sort of hymn to the beauty and power of the birds in "The Ugly Duckling":

> The duckling had never seen anything so beautiful. They were swans, and uttering a peculiar cry they spread out their magnificent broad wings and flew away from the cold regions to warmer lands and open seas. They mounted so high, so very high, and the ugly little duckling became strangely uneasy... Oh, he could not forget those beautiful birds, those happy birds ...   (Andersen 1945, 79)

It has been an open secret among Andersen scholars that his sexuality was ambiguous, and the swan was a stand-in for a dancer with whom he was obsessed, Harald Scharff. Both "The Wild Swans" and "The Ugly Duckling" can be read as attempts to express desires that could not be acknowledged more openly: no wonder the Duckling feels "strangely uneasy" as he gazes at the swans.

My reading of the Erotic Swan figure, like my other two non-hegemonic models of masculinity, fuses several source texts together: Cocteau's biography and filmography; a couple of Andersen's tales; Cunningham's retelling of one of those tales; an echo from Randall Jarrell's "The Black Swan," with its shape-shifting, masculine-voiced swan maidens; and the black and white swans in conventional productions of Tchaikovsky's *Swan Lake*. And that last leads us to the most dramatic version of the Erotic Swan. In Matthew Bourne's 1995 production of *Swan Lake*, the choreographer chose not to employ the usual troupe of female swans in tutus. Instead, he drew on Tchaikovsky's own life and that of his inspiration Ludwig of Bavaria (the so-called Swan-King) to create a tale in which the swans are danced by men. They are (like real-life swans) powerful and dangerous as well as beautiful, a dynamic that is very much in the spirit of Andersen's tale and is brought to the surface in Cunningham's retelling as well. At the end of Cunningham's version, the brother whose shirt was unfinished and so ends up with one wing, becomes a fetishized object of desire for women with "some Leda fantasy" (Cunningham 2015, 11). He describes himself as "ninety percent thriving muscled man-flesh and ten percent glorious blindingly white angel wing" (11).

Bourne's swans are featured as the happy ending of Stephen Daldry's fairy-tale-structured film *Billy Elliot* (2000), which rounds out a whole chain of gay male artists working against social norms to construct a version of masculinity that doesn't depend on denial of grace, beauty, strength, and vulnerability. The enduring popularity of *Billy Elliot* as a stage musical as well as movie suggests the value of the Erotic Swan as a missing male paradigm: a story in which nonconforming or abused boys can find themselves and through which they can free themselves.

In the end, then, I found a triple solution to my mystery. Each of the three figures challenges hegemonic masculinity in a different way: the Little Man shows how to outwit the Giant and steal his treasures, though he doesn't always get the girl or obtain a desired child; the Monster Bridegroom serves as an emblem of what not to become, though invited to by society; and the Erotic Swan is a utopian possibility of reclaiming some of what is lost in the masculine models offered by Western culture.

I don't know if I have solved the case correctly; I'm sure my threefold solution is not the only valid one. I can think of a number of other configurations for manhood in tales, traditional and retold. There is the old soldier, for instance, who chooses not the youngest but the oldest bride in Andersen's "The Twelve Dancing Princesses"; and Death's godson; and Hans My Hedgehog who is grouped with the animal/monster bridegrooms but who has a whole life history of his own before marrying—to say nothing of Asian and African tales and the Native American and other indigenous literatures, each of which codifies gender in different and often paradoxical ways. Yet because traditional tales are ever-unexpected and irreducibly weird, in their queerness they offer alternatives to whatever dominant, hegemonic model is offered to young listeners and readers, boys and girls alike. The real solution to the mystery is something each reader must try afresh, putting the clues together into an individual, social, regendered or genderless self.

8

The Politics of Fantasy

In 1991, I spoke to the International Conference on the Fantastic in the Arts about "The Politics (if Any) of Fantasy." Since that time both fantasy and politics have changed: the former mostly for the better, the latter mostly for the worse. In 1991, fantasy came in four flavors: the classic work of Tolkien and other Inklings; newer inventive and ambitious fiction by the likes of Gene Wolfe and Patricia McKillip; a heritage of excellent writing for children by Lloyd Alexander, Susan Cooper, and many others; and a growing body of formulaic fantasy adventure with little symbolic weight or philosophical import. Now, three decades later, fantasy is all those things enriched and amended by the presence of more writers of color and the viewpoints of non-European traditions. It is produced—and occasionally acknowledged as such—by writers with mainstream credentials. It has also grown beyond print fiction, with an explosion of fantasy in media such as film, television, comics, and games. And politics—well, that requires a new paragraph.

Politics in the twenty-first century challenges the idealistic claim made by Theodore Parker and echoed by Martin Luther King, Jr., that "the arc of the moral universe . . . bends toward justice." From the micro to the macro level, justice is being undermined by authoritarianism, hypocrisy, and threatened or overt violence. Internet trolls and fascist regimes—overlapping categories— eat away at civility and work at corrupting or overturning democratic institutions. Tabloid journalism does the work of propaganda. Money is deemed political speech; corporations are classified as people and yet have none of the restraints or obligations that let people live in harmony. The old political categories of right and left have traded roles and swapped DNA. Fear and mistrust drive out political goodwill as bad money drives out good.

And yet there is also resistance, and there is still reform. In secular societies, at least, the small commonwealth that is the family is a bit more equitable, less rule-bound, and more adaptable to different needs and desires—and found families often serve where biological ones fail. Indigenous peoples are fighting back, with or without the support of the courts, for their contracted rights and cultural autonomy. The melting-pot model of society has given way to other, less homogenizing metaphors. Dominant cultural myths such as the westward course of empire or the inevitability of proletarian revolution have been challenged, with other narratives offered as historical master plots. And one source of those myths and metaphors is fantastic literature.

Because fantasy cannot exist outside of society, the politics of the primary world will inevitably be reflected in the secondary worlds of fantasy. In turn, the narrative structures of fantasy, which offer a chance to rewrite common wisdom and unconsidered habit, tug at the world outside the fiction. Of the many and wide-ranging forms of the fantastic, the most overtly political, as mentioned in chapter 6, is utopia, both in its optimistic eutopian phases and in the depressive dystopian parts of its cycle. Yet, as I observed in 1991, there are many ways to be political and the message offered by any particular imagined society might differ according to one's situation. Though the talk and its printed record are inextricably entwined in the events and attitudes of the day, I still stand by my reading of the genre's potential as political action and reflection even as I temper, update, and redirect my earlier statements.

Fantasy may look like it's outside of politics. In comparison with many other genres, including its close relatives science fiction and utopia, fantasy seems to sail above the winds of political change. It isn't real, so it needn't concern itself with real-world conflicts. What have dragons to do with votes and back-room deals, or elves with colonialism or propaganda? And yet fantasy writers and readers are swayed by the same political currents as anyone else, and the invention and reception of imaginary worlds are shaped by the same political anxieties and hopes as any human activity. It's just that the mechanisms by which those dreams and fears are translated into narrative are different from those that produce satire or fictional exposé. Likewise, the political uses of fantasy are not so direct or transparent as those by which *Uncle Tom's Cabin* nudged the United States toward civil war.

When fantasy depicts politics directly, it tends to fall back on ancient conflicts and causes, like restoring the monarchy to Tolkien's Middle-earth or refighting the Wars of the Roses in George R. R. Martin's Song of Ice and Fire. Was Tolkien promoting monarchism? Is Martin suggesting assassination as a political strategy—or necromancy? Such readings are not so much wrong as irrelevant. The more directly a fantasy transcribes real-world conflicts, the more likely is it to fall into the pedestrian mode that Ursula K. Le Guin skewers in her essay on fantasy stylistics, "From Elfland to Poughkeepsie" (1973; Le Guin 1989). In place of wonder, we get elves and wizards talking strategy as they stroll through palace corridors like characters in Aaron Sorkin's *The West Wing* (1999–2006). It can be done, but why bother?

Fantasy can certainly include political maneuvering and power struggles in its mix of ingredients, because fantasy novels are the hybrid offspring of nineteenth-century realism and traditional oral forms such as the wonder tale and the supernatural legend. Anything can go into the baggy monster that is the novel. As Kathryn Hume points out in *Fantasy and Mimesis* (1984), fantasy is not so much the opposite of realism as a complementary mode. Most individual fantasy texts overlay the marvelous and the real, including real-world power dynamics. Yet there are many things fantasy does better than represent political deals, and many genres that are better suited to exploring those sorts of arrangements, especially their economic underpinnings. The Washington roman a clef, the dystopian satire, and even the beast fable—think of *Animal Farm*—all work well as devices for thinking about the practical side of politics. Fantasy does not. That is not one of its affordances, to use the term invented by James G. Gibson to describe the aptness of a device's design to its uses. A steam engine can be used in a timepiece—there is a charming steam clock in Vancouver, B. C., though it uses steam power only to rewind the weights—but there are more appropriate technologies for the purpose, and the might of the engine is largely wasted.

But politics is more than governments and party affiliations. To get at some of the ways fantasy works more effectively as a means of exploring politics, it is helpful to turn to compound terms: environmental politics, gender politics, racial politics. Each of these suggests that power can be consolidated and exercised outside of formal organizations. Each offers different ways to group people by their beliefs and identities, and each invites us to look for narratives of the sort that fantasy can generate. In those narratives, power moves in and through other mechanisms than government: first, for instance, through speech or the suppression of speech; second, through unconsciously adopted constraints on action; and, third, through the construction and invocation of collective narratives. These are some of the primary operations of hegemony, the means for a political system to naturalize itself and shift the burden of enforcement onto the populace. I'll get back to those three mechanisms later in the chapter, but first I need to address the perception—the starting-point of my 1991 talk—that fantasy might be aligned with repressive and reactionary politics.

This association is something that had never occurred to me until a conversation I had long after I began reading Tolkien in the mid-1960s. My generation then had a reputation for being innovative and socially conscious: we were not yet the fearful and greedy Baby Boomers of current caricature. Reading Tolkien was a rite of passage into a state of utopian hopefulness and ecological awareness. It is not coincidental that the first Earth Day in 1970 closely followed the Tolkien boom, which reinforced the lessons of Rachel Carson's *Silent Spring* (1962) and Paul Ehrlich's *The Population Bomb* (1968) and resonated with protests against U.S. involvement in Vietnam and the worldwide turbulence of 1968.

But Baby Boomers were never a uniform group, and the cohort holding the sentiments I just described were always part of a mix that included unreconstructed racists, war-supporting jingoists, and embryonic stock-market manipulators. Undoubtedly many of them also read and enjoyed fantasy as much as we tree-huggers did. But what did they take from Tolkien?

My first inklings (so to speak) of other possible responses came with the conversation mentioned above, a meeting with literature students in Rome, where I gave a series of lectures at the Centro di Studi Americani in 1988. Fantasy, the students told me, was associated with the far right, while science fiction was seen as belonging to the left. Science fiction and fantasy scholar Salvatore Proietti informs me that this is no longer so much the case, but that it certainly had been so at the time of my visit, and the memory lingers:

> On right-wing politics and fantasy in Italy, a short answer could simply be that the newer generations of readers have moved on. Still, from the mid-1970s through the 1990s Tolkien (and his epigones) were crucial inspirations for far-right subcultures [and] the association between right-wing politics and fantasy lingers in the generalist literary establishment. In some circles, Left readings of Tolkien seem to have become as dogmatic as the reactionary ones—the far right in the past, part of the far left now, seem to feel the need to postulate some sort of Tillyard-esque monolithic "Tolkienian world-picture," whether Tory-conservative or pacifist-antiNazi. (Proietti)

If the far right was finding validation in Tolkien, that meant that they saw his story-world as supporting authoritarian regimes, suppression of dissent, conspiratorial beliefs, and the demonization of the racial or cultural Other.

My surprise at this association was genuine, if a bit naive. I was aware that Marxist critics of science fiction such as Darko Suvin were not fond of fantasy, which had demonstrated neither the satirical bite of dystopias nor

the Blochian logic of the extrapolated but realistic future societies of
SF. Rosemary Jackson, in her *Fantasy: The Literature of Subversion* (1981),
dismissed Tolkien and the whole category of the "marvellous"; for her, it did
not qualify as either fantastic or subversive. The Italian conversation took
place before China Miéville arrived on the scene with his subversive versions
of fantasy fiction and his critique of fantastic world-building in the 2002
issue of *Historical Materialism*. José B. Monleón had not yet published
A Specter is Haunting Europe: A Sociohistorical Approach to the Fantastic
(1990). So it was only after my visit to Rome that I began to perceive that
Tolkien's appeal for young, idealistic Americans might not extend to radical
British or European readers, who had more direct knowledge of entrenched
privileges and aging aristocracies.

Maria Sachiko Cecire identifies both the appeal of Tolkien's vision and its
hidden agendas in her book *Reinchanted: The Rise of Children's Fantasy
Literature in the Twentieth Century* (2019). Looking at a particular cultural
use of the fantastic medievalism deriving from Tolkien and his friends
and imitators, she describes the opening ceremony of the 2012 London
Olympics thus:

> a pseudo-historical arc that identifies Britain's origins in a dreamlike
> medievalist past of cheerful peasant farmers, maypole dancing, and cricket
> greens—all set against the mythological (and yet real-world) mound of
> Glastonbury Tor. This harmonious national "childhood" is emphasized as
> such by clusters of actual children who surround the arena in ambiguously
> premodern garb to count down to the start of the games . . . The ceremony,
> titled "Isles of Wonder," brands Britain for international and home audi-
> ences as a mystical land that is at once ancient and eternally young.
> According to the ceremony's logic, children's fantasy is one of Britain's
> most important exports and gifts to the world, nearly as pervasive as the
> empire that the show manages to almost omit, but more universally
> beloved and (presumably) benign.   (Cecire 2019, 19–20)

This pageant sums up a particular nostalgia for what never was: the magical
Britain that was the product of the imaginations of Tolkien and C. S. Lewis
and later J. K. Rowling, Kevin Crossley-Holland, Susan Cooper, Diana
Wynne Jones, and Philip Pullman. All of these except Rowling were associated with the University of Oxford, and Jones and Cooper have written
about attending Tolkien's and Lewis's lectures there. Hence, Cecire refers to
a particular branch of fantasy as the Oxford School.

Cecire invites us to see in the works of these writers another sort of pageant: not merely an entertainment but a ritual embodying faith in a national myth of magic and innocence, located in a past that can only be reached through imaginative reconstruction. It is not the historical past, because that is messy and violent and full of deep injustices. Rather it is a past associated with childhood because childhood is likewise rewritten by adults as a pristine space of innocence—here Cecire borrows from children's literature scholar Jacqueline Rose, whose *The Case of Peter Pan* (1989) asserted that the primary audience for children's literature (including those who write it) is adults who need children to perform the innocence that they themselves lack. Perry Nodelman sees this move as a sort of colonization of childhood by adults (Nodelman 1992, 29), akin to the imposing of categories such as "primitive" on non-Western societies who are thus expected to enact the childhood of the species. Cecire also draws upon Helen Young's *Race and Popular Fantasy Literature: Habits of Whiteness* (2015) and Ebony Elizabeth Thomas's *The Dark Fantastic* (2019), both of which demonstrate the way racial otherness is used to fuel tension in classic works of fantasy and to generate sympathy for the fair-skinned heroes. As Thomas says, "The traditional purpose of darkness in the fantastic is to disturb, to unsettle, to cause unrest. This primal fear of darkness and Dark Others is so deeply rooted in Western myth that it is nearly impossible to find its origin" (19). Because fantasy renders primal forces concrete and local, the narrative result is that, as Thomas reminds us, "Darkness is personified, embodied, and most assuredly racialized" (Thomas 2019, 20).

Popular journalism and fan conversations—never particularly good with subtleties—have turned this re-evaluation into a "Tolkien was a racist" meme, which is not the claim any of these critics make. They know that a text's politics often differ from an author's, and that the uses of that text can take a different direction yet again. Rather than locating racism in the writer or even his creation, they are talking about the roots of Tolkien's vision. Medieval literature is racist; European cultures and their derivatives around the world are racist; folk culture is, if not uniformly racist, at least prone to assigning to outsider groups undesirable characteristics and the villain role in narratives such as the blood-libel legend, used then and now to stir up antisemitic violence. It is impossible to incorporate these sources into a fantasy world without also bringing in the negative aspects. One can only, as a newer generation of writers has done, confront that racist heritage directly and seek to alter it for the better.

The situation is oddly parallel to another that I have discussed before with respect to science fiction. My sense then was that the sexist past of science fiction was precisely what made it so useful for writers who sought to challenge norms and expectations about gender: since gender was already so markedly there in the genre (and so odiously, for the most part), it was available as something to be investigated, undercut, or revised. Similarly, race is inescapable in fantasy and in what John Clute, in the *Encyclopedia of Fantasy* (1997), calls its taproot texts. The dark Other is part of the structure of meaning in European legends, tales, romances, and epics. Ergo, the possibility of redrawing the maps and inverting the hierarchies is also built in. Tolkien's method of working backward from medieval texts to the imaginary past that they posit can also be a method of challenging the narrative. The reconstructed Middle-earth of *The Lord of the Rings* is what Tom Shippey calls an "asterisk reality"—comparable to the vocabulary of vanished languages like Proto-Indo-European (Shippey 1983, 15). All such word forms are conventionally marked with asterisks to indicate that they are hypothetical. Philologists (like Tolkien in his scholarly capacity) take later written evidence and run it through an elaborate wayback machine that reverses linguistic changes and fills in gaps in one branch of a language family with survivals in another. Because language reflects and shapes world views, reconstructing words entails reconstructing worlds. And from that act comes fantasy's original sin and the possibility of its redemption.

Much has been written about various science-fictional challenges to older norms of racism, gender bias, and Eurocentrism. Feminist critical fictions by writers such as Suzy McKee Charnas and Joanna Russ have been followed up and challenged in turn by Afrofuturist and Indigenous Futurist writers. It is a little harder to make fantasy work as political critique or utopian vision. A lost Golden Age hardly seems like a practical goal to work toward, especially when it must be administered by angelic figures such as Gandalf or deities like Lewis's Aslan. Nostalgia for what never was is a dubious source of political energy. But the best twenty-first-century fantasy replaces nostalgia with subversion, and theme-park medievalism with an array of alternative pasts. Just as historians have revisited the classical, medieval, and early modern worlds and found that women and people of color were there all along, active, aware, and resisting like fury, contemporary fantasy offers worlds built from materials previously obscured by master narratives such as Great Man history and imperial triumphalism, Even as boy heroes and white saviors continue to be written, they find themselves competing with other, more compelling fantasies of self-discovery and social transformation.

Rather than name all the wonderful, subversive writers and texts that make up this reconfigured genre, I will go back to the three narrative patterns introduced earlier—involving enforced silences, characters' self-limitations, and revision of collective narratives—and trace each through a handful of representative examples. The first of these patterns, the silencing of women or other oppressed people, is a theme that pervades literatures of all sorts, of course, but it can be particularly poignant in fantasy, in which speech and writing have magical potency. To be forbidden to speak in public is one thing; to be prevented from uttering spells, invoking the mythical past through storytelling, or communing with higher powers is quite another. Many traditional tales involve voluntary or involuntary self-silencing, as when the sister of the enchanted swans in the Grimm tale of "The Six Swans," (ATU type 451) undertakes to disenchant her brothers by gathering nettles and weaving them into shirts, all without uttering a sound even when her royal husband orders her execution at the stake. The tale of Philomela, in Ovid's *Metamorphoses*, makes explicit the link between silencing and sexual violence. Raped by her brother-in-law (another king), and rendered mute by having her tongue cut out, Philomela conveys her story through a different kind of text, a tapestry depicting the attack, that stirs her sister Procne to take revenge on her behalf. Both are eventually turned into birds, nightingale and swallow respectively, making the story into an interesting mirror image of the German tale. One starts, the other ends, with transformations into birds.

Such stories were rarely, if ever, read as political until the abuse of women began to be seen in terms of a patriarchal system and an entire class of subjugated people rather than as a private affair between spouses or even as the legitimate prerogative of husbands. Yet the political implications were there from the beginning. It is no coincidence that the man in such stories is typically a king, the woman the closest and most vulnerable of his subjects.

Many modern fantasies follow up on these oral models, starting perhaps with the inarticulate wind-up doll Olympia in E. T. A. Hoffmann's "The Sand-Man" (published in German in 1817) and wandering through such variations as Hans Christian Anderson's voiceless "The Little Mermaid (1837) and James Thurber's Princess Saralinda, in *The 13 Clocks* (1950), who is allowed by her magician uncle to say only, "I wish him well" to the hero. More explicitly political interpretations of such silencing begin to appear after feminism's Second Wave popularized the aphorism that "The personal is political." Ursula K. Le Guin's work is a particularly revealing example, because her early fantasies predate her coming to understand and embrace feminist principles. *A Wizard of Earthsea* (1968) resembles the work of the Oxford school of fantasy in that it creates a fantasy world by weaving together many traditional motifs and tropes without challenging their implicit politics: in it, men are wizards, women weak and wicked witches. Between the writing of that novel and the fourth book in the series, *Tehanu* (1990), Le Guin was castigated by feminist critics for her unthinking acceptance of such conventions, and, after a brief period of defensiveness, set about to complicate and redirect her own magical universe—brilliantly without contradicting anything that she had set up in the original formulation. *Tehanu's* female hero, Tenar, who had earlier refused to take up a wizard's speech-related powers and had instead retired to a quiet life as a farm wife, comes in middle age to realize how much she has given up in the way of autonomy. By not learning to speak the True Speech through which wizards perform their magic, Tenar has also made herself vulnerable to abuse by men, including her own son, who assumes his right to take over the family farm that she has managed capably after her husband's death. More focused and malevolent silencing comes from the male community of wizards, and especially from one called Aspen, who abuses his power to enslave Tenar's will and especially to prevent her from speaking. He taunts her: "But first, maybe she wants to say something. She has so much to say. Women always do" (Le Guin 1990, 222). Earlier, the ex-archmage Ged had explained the source of such resentment of women: "If your strength is only the other's weakness, you live in fear" (198).

But Earthsea was never the protected white space of Oxford fantasy. Le Guin had to fight to have her hero represented in cover art as the brown-skinned man he is. In Earthsea, only the barbarian invaders are pale. And the cultural traditions from which Le Guin drew include those of the Native Americans her father A. L. Kroeber worked with, as well as the Pacific Island societies whose systems of magic and mana were studied by Bronislaw Malinowsky. Le Guin helped transform the story-space of fantasy into something more global, more inclusive, and better able to challenge power structures and cultural norms.

After *Tehanu*, Le Guin continued to explore the continuum of silence and speech, sometimes offering a Taoist endorsement of stillness as the necessary matrix for speech and at other times following up on Ged's insight about self-hatred turned outward as a motive for silencing others. The centerpiece of her Annals of the Western Shore is titled, appropriately, *Voices* (2006). It comes between *Gifts* (2004) and *Powers* (2007), each of which focuses on misuses of magic, but the magic in *Voices* is that of testimony rather than mastery and is thus harder to deploy for ill. The politics in the novel are particularly fraught: the protagonist Memer lives in an occupied city, and the occupiers are attempting to smash the culture of the enslaved people of Ansul by burning their writings and banning references to their history and beliefs. Memer is a key part of the resistance because she is keeper of a hidden library and because she can reach the Oracle. This Oracle speaks through the books but is not embodied in any one sacred text; rather it seems to represent voices from the past and the collective voice of the culture insofar as the right reader brings those to life. In one key scene, Memer speaks oracularly, reading words to a crowd in such a way as to spark revolution; later, the book she has read from turns out to be a simple volume of animal fables for children. The power is not in the book itself nor in the reader alone: it is in the combination of text, performer, and situation. When those align, "There is a god in every leaf; you hold what is sacred in your open hand" (Le Guin 2006, 341).

Written during wartime (the invasion and occupation of Iraq, with all of its complex alliances and murky justifications), *Voices* can be read as a political parable about religious fundamentalism and colonial aggression, but its message is not a direct one. The parable is as simple and opaque as the utterances of the oracle; what it means depends on the reader and the context, as those bring the text to life. Some messages are clear: knowing the past is better than being ignorant; wisdom isn't contained in any one volume; war may be justified but it is never just, because the vulnerable will always suffer the most (Memer herself is the child of rape by one of the invaders); suppression of knowledge will fail in the long run, but that run can be long and painful indeed. Even the valorization of books and reading isn't total or unambiguous. One of the main characters is a traveling poet and performer, and his unwritten texts are just as powerful as the library's volumes. I think Le Guin meant us to hear the pun in that character's name: Orrec, which is an echo of Oracle. Books are speech of a different sort, and, like any speakers, they depend on silence and a willing listener. All of that is wrapped up in the fantasy but it is also plain truth about the world we live in; the fantasy only heightens the contrasts and brings out the patterns more clearly.

I used the term "story-space" to indicate the impact Le Guin had on the fantasy genre: as mentioned in my introduction, that is my approximate translation of M. M. Bakhtin's awkward coinage "chronotope." For Bakhtin, a chronotope is not merely a setting: a time and place, as the roots of the term indicate. It is also a set of narrative possibilities: within the space defined by the words of the story, some events are likely or even requisite, while others cannot be conceived of. Some kinds of characters belong; others are incompatible. Time will manifest in a particular way, as will time's corollary, causality. The story-space of fantasy changes as the genre changes, but it always looks back to an imagined past, whether the imaginary medieval Britain called up by Arthurian romances, the pre-industrial crafts-man's paradise William Morris imagined, or the alchemists' mystical Egypt—Ægypt, as John Crowley calls it in the four-volume historical meta-fantasy with that title. Tolkien's asterisk Middle-earth is a variation on the same theme. It is the history we imagine, reconstructed from the fragments of earlier imagined pasts. But not everyone feels welcome in that particular past, nor desires to pay its political toll.

One of the most exciting trends in recent fantasy has been the opening up of other pasts, especially by writers whose experiences are grounded in other identities than Oxford White male privilege. Telling new stories is one answer to the silence imposed on colonized and oppressed peoples. Ebony Elizabeth Thomas notes that it is relatively easy to insert racial others into the alternate histories and alternative story-worlds of fan fictions and comic book multiverses (Thomas 2019, 156). Samuel R. Delany's Nevèrÿon stories of the 1970s to 1980s took the barbarian exoticism of pulp fantasy—the story-worlds of Robert E. Howard and C. L. Moore and Fritz Leiber—and added layers of archaeological revisionism and semiotic ambiguity. The resulting chronotope allowed him to explore issues of race, power, and desire from his own perspective as a gay Black intellectual while still spinning swords-and-sorcery adventures. The city name Nevèrÿon is another version of No Place (the primary literal translation of More's Utopia) or, as Leiber's Ffard and Grey Mouser stories call their world, Nehwon; a mirror-written Nowhen. Delany's fantasy world is a Zone of the sort theorized by Brian McHale, following up on Michel Foucault's concept of the heterotopia. Roger Luckhurst describes such Zones as "weird topologies that produce anomalies, destroy category and dissolve or reconstitute identities" (Luckhurst 2011, 23). Zones are the spatial equiva-lent of Donna Haraway's cyborg (Haraway 1985): potentially liberatory in their monstrous illegitimacy. They have been explored in fiction by the Strugatsky brothers (Roadside Picnic, originally published in Russian in 1972) and Jeff VanderMeer (Annihilation, 2015) among others. Delany's Trouble on Triton (1976) which locates such a Zone on one of the moons of Neptune, is subtitled An Ambiguous Heterotopia, signaling his engagement not only with Foucault but also with Le Guin, who had not long before subtitled *The Dispossessed* "An Ambiguous Utopia" (1974). A Zone is not so much a place as an eerie, impossible merging of places, like the cobbling together of widely separated spaces through cinematic editing. By not being resolvable to a single locale in time or space, such fictional Zones allow for possibilities that realist narrative denies. Those possibilities include not only previously unheard voices but also new kinds of actions and identities—plot lines that are also avenues toward the claiming of strength and self-determination. Constraints internalized by the central characters fall away as they discover previously unimagined powers.

One writer who has taken up Delany's task of opening a queer and racially complex fantasy story-space is Kai Ashante Wilson. In two novellas and a set of related short stories, Wilson takes us to an apparently Mediterranean, maybe Roman-era world of fountained courtyards and beast-haunted wilderness. Like Delany, Wilson deliberately mingles linguistic and cultural codes to create a Zone that combines past, present, and a bit of future. Both *A Taste of Honey* (2016) and *Sorcerer of the Wildeeps* (2015) incorporate the kind of highly advanced technology that Arthur C. Clarke famously proclaimed indistinguishable from magic. Here is what Wilson says about the setting of his fantasies:

> The author Stephen Carter uses a phrase in one of his books, "African America"—note the missing final *n*—to signify the collective knowledge and opinions of black America; for example, "African America took a dim view of the new president's policies..." Ever since I first read that phrase it's fermented in my imagination. I kept picturing a literal continent, some mythological homeland where all the various and fraught streams of African American heritage were intrinsic and accounted for. My first novel(la)—*obviously!*—would have to be set there. And naturally this African America would be a place where all our many varieties of English could be heard everyday, all smashed together side-by-side: the exquisitely formal, the ludic and colorfully hood, the South American and Carribean inflections... [ellipses in original]   (Stuart 2015)

Within this hybrid, Janus-facing space, Wilson constructs narratives of multiple possibilities. Aqib, the protagonist of *A Taste of Honey*, lives two contrasting lives. One of them (but it isn't entirely certain which) is real, the other unrealized but fully spun out in the narrative.

Aqib is both privileged and oppressed. As an aristocrat with semi-divine parentage, he takes his privileges for granted but is keenly aware of restrictions on his behavior. The narrator frequently comments on what he can and can't do: he can go anywhere in the city unmolested, but he can't marry whoever he wishes. He can't speak his mind. He has an intuitive understanding with animals but fails to perceive the feelings of servants. He has particular trouble with the codes of masculinity: "manhood's ways had often tripped him up, and his errors provoked harsh correction" (Wilson 2016, 11). When a visiting warrior rouses Aqib's desire, he has trouble understanding his own emotions and falls back on the rules: "No!" he thinks, "Men *cannot* kiss!" (19). He is enforcing his own bonds.

Not until two of the ascended beings or gods come to visit does Aqib's extraordinary talent with animals (a sign of his divine ancestry) come to fruition, and even then he denies his own magical abilities until the god orders him to call a bird to himself:

> At her finger's touch, the world's richness and vividity doubled; it trebled and redoubled again. Aqib's perception expanded into a whole other dimension. Bees' buzzing, locust-chatter, the birds singing: no longer was this empty noise. It was lyric'd music, song with words. (37–8)

Aqib has learned from his culture to limit himself rather than exercise either his talent or his capacity to love. He is similarly clueless about science, mathematics, and even writing, all coded by his culture as feminine skills. Much of the story, and many of the hardships he experiences, have to do with breaking out of these self-limitations. A common fantasy story-structure, part of its heritage of story-spaces, is this coming-into-power of previously dismissed characters. The trope has extra resonance when the character belongs to one of the groups who have been dismissed in history, and the dismissal extends to their own sense of self-worth.

A similarly self-restricted character is at the heart of Nalo Hopkinson's *The Chaos* (2012). Set in a contemporary Toronto, Hopkinson's story gradually transforms its location into a fantastic story-space in which Sojourner Smith, or Scotch, as she calls herself, can finally face her fears and accept her own strengths. By the end, the story-world is a blend of magical and real, like Wilson's African America but in reverse—American Africa—since the base level is contemporary North America with an overlay of West African-based legendry. At the beginning of the novel, Scotch's problems seem to be largely of her own making: she is a (mostly) ordinary teenager struggling with emerging sexuality, guilt over having gotten her brother jailed, resentment at having been victimized by white peers at a previous school, and inability to communicate with her parents. There are only a few indications that something more profound is happening to Scotch. She sees small floating creatures that she calls Horseless Head Men, but believes them to be hallucinations; sticky black patches have started to erupt on her skin; she is treating them with an ointment from a folk healer. By the end, as a wave of unpredictability spreads around the world, her floating Head Men have been joined by many other fantastic creatures (a phoenix, Baba Yaga, a Jamaican Rolling Calf), she has been transformed physically, and she emerges unscathed from a volcano that has suddenly appeared in Lake Ontario. The veneer of ordinariness cracks to reveal a society full of structural injustices having to do with gender, sexuality, race, disability, and divergent thought: the Chaos of the title is in some ways simply an unveiling of those inequities and even a righting of some of the wrongs. Scotch's brother Rich reminds her that she has unknowingly benefited from the racial bias that ranks light-skinned Blacks above dark-skinned, especially if they have money. In jail, he says, "They told me I was rich, that I had it easy. Some of those guys could barely read. Couple of them told me they'd never tasted a vegetable that wasn't out of a can.... They can't walk into a store without security following them everywhere" (Hopkinson 2012, 50). Even though Scotch dislikes being taken for something other than Black, she accepts her privileges, and the system that generates them, until the black markings spread and eventually make a new, darker skin. Kristen Shaw suggests that Scotch's body is itself a story-space of a sort—a colonized territory that ultimately overthrows rule-by-discourse: "Scotch's experience during the Chaos operates as a metaphor for the ways black women's bodies are captured by various disciplinary lenses" (447).

Though the magical outbreak is in many ways destructive and cannot be reduced to a set of object lessons, Scotch's initial symptoms make sense as manifestations of the emotions she can't allow herself to express and thoughts she censors from her own consciousness. As Amandine H. Faucheux, in "Race and Sexuality in Nalo Hopkinson's Oeuvre," says of the novel, "Scotch's chaotic adventure throughout the book is a very literal representation of racial ostracization and of the experiences of people of color with racism and colorism" (Faucheux 2017, 568). Only when the Chaos makes Canada into a Zone of cultural contact and unpredictability does Scotch begin to speak and act in a way that expresses her own powerful and multiple nature. She can become the character she needs to be once the story-space allows it. And the change is not simply maturation or psychological integration: it is political, just as her new identity is, by virtue of its previous suppression, political.

The heterotopic story-spaces of *A Taste of Honey* and *The Chaos* represent linguistic as well as narrative experiments. In the interview quoted above, Wilson highlights his deliberate use of archaisms and contrasting dialects, through which "all our many varieties of English could be heard everyday, all smashed together side-by-side." This is his answer to the silencing of outsiders and outcasts. Similarly, Hopkinson invokes multiple language modes and communities in a technique she has called "code-sliding." More radical than the code-shifting through which speakers of stigmatized dialects adjust their speech to fit dominant cultures, code-sliding alters language and thereby changes the social circumstance within which it functions: "I'm fascinated with the notion of breaking an imposed language apart and remixing it. To speak in the hacked language is not just to speak in an accent or a creole; to say the words aloud is an act of referencing history and claiming space" (Hopkinson "Code-Sliding"). By bringing in multiple varieties of English and narrative traditions from Caribbean folklore, Hopkinson creates story-worlds in which her characters can try out different identities and replace the powerless versions of themselves that they have internalized, just as Wilson offers his characters linguistic and narrative codes through which they can reach out to distant and imagined pasts and even to an evolved humanity in the future.

Both Wilson and Hopkinson have been grouped with Afrofuturism, which is generally considered a branch of science fiction rather than fantasy. In both cases, their disruptive stylistic choices of language befit narrative strategies that resist genre-typing. Their work can be read as fantasy, science fantasy, science fiction, or magical realism, depending on which of their stories we pick up and which plot strands we wish to follow. The same is true of many other Afrofuturist fantasists: Delany, Octavia Butler, Nnedi Okorafor, Andrea Hairston, Karen Lord, N. K. Jemisin, Tade Thompson. Because both future and past can be used as political counters, both must be continually reinvestigated and reimagined: re-storied. The relative proportion of past to future, or fantasy to science fiction, depends on which the author is more interested in reclaiming. For some groups, the past is relatively stable and accessible but their place in the future must be fought for. Writers from those groups are often more interested in looking forward than looking back, and so they employ science-fictional tropes rather than proposing fantasy alternatives to a mythic Britain or Middle-earth. For others, large chunks of the past have been cut off by colonization or erased from popular memory, and so these writers might employ fantasy settings to restore what has been lost. But writers go where they need to, and genres continually shift and recombine.

Right now, one of the most useful narrative strategies seems to be retelling a familiar story in such a way that its boundaries are redefined and its applications expanded. This is fantasy's third response to cultural hegemony: the exposure and recomposition of metanarratives, which are story patterns that are not only collective but also coercive. Metanarratives force individual stories into their molds and, indeed, allow us to perceive those stories only insofar as they do fit the formula. One of the most effective examples of subverted metanarrative is Zen Cho's *Sorcerer to the Crown* (2015). In it, Cho lays claim to a fictional territory that is as familiar and as carefully guarded as the Oxford school's fantastic Middle Ages: namely, an imagined English Regency community that derives from Jane Austen's satirical novels, softened and romanticized by generations of acolytes. The fictional Regency is even more circumscribed than the medieval fantasy-scape: in it, servants are barely noticed, fortunes are made mysteriously in the colonies, war is an inconvenience except for the eligible officers it conveniently houses near the village, and no people of color exist. As a story-world, the Regency offers a limited array of characters and a handful of plots having to do with matchmaking and the transfer of wealth from unpleasant aunts and greedy cousins to deserving heroines. It requires very little alteration to turn Regency romance into Regency fantasy: enchant a few heirlooms, add magical talent to the list of feminine accomplishments, replace local curates with visiting wizards. An early and effective example is the epistolary novel *Sorcery and Cecilia* (1988), created as a correspondence game by Patricia Wrede and Caroline Stevermer.

Zen Cho's fantasy employs all of the conventional elements, including a poor but plucky heroine and a dark brooding hero who begin in misunderstanding and end as unbeatable allies and a satisfying love match. From page 1, however, the social implications of these conventions and the story-space they generate are challenged not only by the intrusion of magic but also by acknowledgment of racial and cultural difference and the exploitative colonial system that funds English society. We meet the hero Zacharias as a young slave boy on display before the members of the Royal Society of Unnatural Philosophers: he is there to demonstrate that Black people are capable of wielding magic—the scene is reminiscent of real-life challenges faced by artists such as Phyllis Wheatley and of the social experimentation conducted on the hero of M. T. Anderson's historical novel *The Astonishing*

Life of Octavian Nothing Traitor to the Nation (2007). This being a romance, Zacharias passes his magical test and grows up to become not merely a magician but his mentor's successor as Sorcerer Royal. A few chapters later, Zacharias meets his match in resourceful orphan Prunella Gentleman, whose surname ironically identifies her as belonging to a higher class than her current circumstances indicate: she is in danger of falling from pupil to servant at Mrs. Daubeney's School for Gentlewitches.

Even as Cho follows the conventions of the form, she introduces elements that transform it into something more pointed. Prunella is not as obviously racially marked as Zacharias, but he notices that she "was light enough for exertion to lend her cheeks a brilliant colour, but that she was not of wholly European extraction was clear from the warm hue of her skin and the profusion of dark curls tumbling over the back of her drab brown dress." Her late mother's identity as a royal Indian sorceress is not revealed until midway through the book, but various clues indicate an affinity with the Malay island nation of Janda Baik, which has sent a delegation to England. Janda Baik is also the home of powerful witches such as Mak Genggang, whose spells reach halfway around the world. Thus we have magicians of African and Asian descent interacting with the paler inhabitants of Regency London, and an acknowledgment of the dependence of English economy on colonial exploitation. With regard to the latter, English magic turns out to be a limited resource derived from Fairyland: "As Fairy was the source of Britain's magic, so it must be the source of its difficulties," thinks Zacharias, as he plans a visit to ensure the continued flow of magical power from Fairyland to mundane Britain. These two manifestations of colonialism turn out to be connected: the witches of Janda Baik are responsible for the breakdown of the arrangement with the Fairy Court, and behind their discontent is the same sexism and racism that hinder Zacharias's attempts at reform and threaten Prunella's status as a gentlewoman. Mak Genggan, having traveled via Fairyland to England, declares her interest to be "the fate of *my* nation, which your King seeks to bully."

The intricate plot works itself out, female magic is valorized, the racial interlopers make their way into the heart of English society, and the sovereignty of Janda Baik is upheld: all of this in the guise of a slightly tweaked Georgette Heyer romance. What Zen Cho does in this novel is similar to what many other fantasists are doing: retelling a familiar story in such a way that its political underpinnings are both revealed and subverted. The many retold fairy tales, legends, and myths of modern fantasy offer a way not only to revisit the past but to question assumptions about the way it has been narrated. History is not the (vanished, irretrievable) actual past but a story we tell ourselves about the past, and, like all stories, it has been told with a particular slant and purpose. Those can be challenged. The most effective way to challenge cultural narratives is not to avoid them but to reinscribe them. The discipline of history, like science, undergoes periodic transformations as new kinds of evidence are brought forward, new modes of analysis developed, and new questions asked. The same epistemic shift is occurring in fantasy, which is, among other things, the history of what people have thought the world to be. The fantastic past is now stretched to include all the asterisk realities, not only cosy English parlors and magical medieval villages and castles but also scenes and characters from African, Asian, Arabic, North American, Pacific Island, and Australian traditional narratives.

But does any of this change the real world? Do fantasies, no matter how sneaky or subversive, have any impact on political systems or the beliefs that uphold them? There is no question that stories are powerful political tools. Political scientist Mark McBeth points out that there are at least two kinds of political narratives:

> contemporary politics is constructed as battles between (often self-proclaimed) heroic figures and villains.... Narratives in politics too often create dichotomous worlds of right and wrong, with the result being the bitter polarization that we see today in US politics. It would be impossible (since humans make meaning through narratives) and undesirable to eliminate narratives in politics. However, democratic governance requires narratives that allow for some bridging between groups.
>
> (McBeth 2017, 7)

The fantasies I have been discussing in this chapter are of the bridging sort. They transplant motifs and characters from one cultural framework into another; creolize languages, and place non-European traditions on the same footing as the Oxford School's imagined history. And, if read carefully and critically, they encourage healthy skepticism about other sorts of fabricated narratives.

Shippey's description of Tolkien's method can be shifted into the present to describe the sorts of conspiracy-spreading and reality-denying that make social media into a political weapon. Folk narratives can be wonderful things—literally, full of wonders that fuel the imaginations of fantasy writers and engage readers. However, there is a darker side to folklore. Folk legend includes not only stories of the fairy folk but also slanderous belief-stories about outsiders. An infamous example is the blood-libel legend, mentioned earlier in the chapter, which is usually aimed at Jews but can also be directed toward Romany, Mexicans, and others. It too is found in medieval texts like those Tolkien mined to construct Middle-earth: Chaucer's Prioress told it to the Canterbury pilgrims; the ballad of "Sir Hugh" recounts it. And it comes around again every time someone wants to encourage violence against the Other. Folklorist Bill Ellis, who studied satanic cult legends in the 1970s and 80s, offers a nuanced view of such narratives. He quotes William H. Friedland's definition of myth as "a set of ideas which can be utilized as a basis for action" and includes contemporary urban legends in the same category, which means, he says, that "the legend is always fundamentally political in its impact" (Ellis 2018, 400).

Ellis concludes that "the surprisingly strong power of belief in the face of authoritative fact remains a valid focus for folkloristic research" (402). Such research involves tracing strands of communication, observing the dynamics of folk groups, and analyzing the narrative elements that compel belief against the evidence of authorities or the senses. In sum, understanding the power of fake news requires it to be contextualized, and fantasy offers a different way of contextualizing. If legend is political, then repurposed legend in fantasy form is also political. Just as science fiction estranges scientific knowledge and thereby enables important new perspectives on it, fantasy estranges the past and especially narratives about past wishes, fears, and the inherited story-worlds that give them power and a "local habitation." Telling fantastic tales is not a replacement for action in the real world, but the telling can give us glimpses behind the ballot and the barricade, to understand how stories fuel action and form identities. And once we understand, we have the power to change our stories, our story-spaces, and ourselves.

9

Timor mortis conturbat me

Fantasy and Fear

Throughout this book I have been investigating two fundamental questions about fantasy: how does it mean anything, since it can't claim to represent the world as it is; and what does it do, which is to say, what do we bring back from the narrated world into our lives? The primary answer to both questions has to do with the nature of storytelling, which has its own intrinsic value and meaning. Other answers follow from that: we depend on narratives to tell us who we are, put the world in order, and offer scripts for dealing with all that is strange and baffling. This chapter is about fantasy and the unknown: we fear what we don't know and, of those unknowns, most fear whatever seems most unlike ourselves. Fantasy, however, offers ways to absorb that fear and transmute it into something useful. There is a political dimension to all of this, though that might not be immediately obvious.

The folk tale called "The Story of a Boy Who Went Forth to Learn Fear" in the Grimms' collection has a more colorful title in the Southern U.S.: "The Boy That Never Seen a Fraid" (Roberts 1988, 35). In either version it tells about a boy who has never learned to tremble at ghosts or corpses or midnight monsters. Since he is completely ignorant of fear, he passes a number of tests of courage, gaining the usual fortune and marrying a king's daughter. At the end, he still wants to know what it is to be afraid, so his clever bride pours a bucket of icy water squirming with minnows down his back, which teaches him how to shudder. The story can be told as one of simple foolishness or true bravery, but the point is that this lad is missing something important. Fearlessness, the story suggests, is like color-blindness or tone-deafness: it cuts you off from some of the richness of the world.

Philosopher Søren Kierkegaard, a connoisseur of fear, writes about the same tale in his book *The Concept of Anxiety* (published in Danish in 1844). You might expect it to show up instead in Kierkegaard's *Fear and Trembling* (published in Danish in 1843), since the boy in the story eventually masters the trembling part, if not the fear, but the chief narrative example in the latter book is Abraham's attempted sacrifice of Isaac in Genesis.

Kierkegaard's choice of different parables in these two essays allows him to distinguish between fear, on the one hand, and anxiety or dread, on the other. This distinction illuminates a general truth about storytelling itself, especially fantasy storytelling. Fear, Kierkegaard says, is focused on a specific outcome; as when one stands on a cliff's edge and fears falling. Anxiety is unfocused because it involves freedom, or as Kierkegaard puts it, "the possibility of possibility" (Kierkegaard 1980, 42). In the Garden of Eden, says Kierkegaard, Adam starts in the simple anxiety of ignorance—he knows neither desire nor death—but moves to the higher anxiety of freedom once he is forbidden to eat from the forbidden tree of the knowledge of good and evil. Prohibition opens the door to possibility, and thus to dread, to fear that has no immediate object and no limit. That is why animals feel fear but not dread.

What I find especially interesting here is the connection Kierkegaard makes between the nonlocalized form of fear he calls dread and the imagination, especially imagination that takes narrative form. Kierkegaard regularly turns to stories to illustrate his points, and it is no accident that the story he has chosen to exemplify dread (in Danish, *angest*), is a folk tale, a magical tale in which ghosts and animated corpses exist on the same narrative plane as naive youths and wriggling minnows. The boy of the story might not learn fear, but the listener does. And, more importantly, the storyteller's audience learns that something can be done about fear: something can be done with it. Fear is not the end of the story but its engine.

Fantasy and horror are close kin. Both ask us to imagine strange beings and impossible acts. Both include genuinely scary scenes: Shelob's lair in *The Lord of the Rings* could easily be grafted into a story by H. P. Lovecraft (maybe with a shift of language toward the purple). The difference between the two genres is partly structural: Lovecraft would likely end the story there, with his characters facing the monster's dripping fangs, or else cut away to a hopelessly mad Samwise drowning memory in some dark Hobbiton pub. Tolkien, though, has his heroes go on to face even greater terrors and ultimately to defeat them. Similar elements can be found in most fantasy, from the Dementors of Harry Potter to the wicked witches in *The Wonderful Wizard of Oz*. Those last are surprising, because L. Frank Baum announced his intention, in an introduction to *The Wizard*, to write a fairy tale in the mode of Grimm and Andersen and yet to avoid the "horrible and blood-curdling incident[s]" that characterize their stories. His was to be a "modernized fairy tale, in which the wonderment and joy are retained and the heart-aches and nightmares are left out" (Baum 1983, 2). The book is, of course, full of ache and angst, and the 1939 movie version even more so, but the Witch is melted, the Wizard unmasked, and Dorothy returned to home and family, with all due joy in the end and wonderment throughout.

But Baum was right about traditional fairy tales. They are frequently terrifying: full of murder, monsters, and mayhem. Literary fairy tales written by the German Romantics imitate those aspects but don't always supply the resolution. E. T. A. Hoffmann's "The Sandman," for instance, presents the reader with a series of increasingly disturbing images of deceptions and dismemberments. It is no wonder that Freud used Hoffmann's tale as his type-case of the Uncanny, another affect related to Kierkegaard's dread. Writers like Edgar Allan Poe and Mary Shelley drew upon the German model to invent the tale of terror. Missing from these Gothic literary tales is the turn that transforms terror into wonder. J. R. R. Tolkien calls this turn the eucatastrophe, the good catastrophe, the "sudden and miraculous grace" that takes us from despair to joy ("On Fairy-stories" 1966, 68). For Tolkien, eucatastrophic uplift was an essential part of the fairy story, which was his model for fantasy. Unlike the verbal formula of "happily ever after," which he considered to be merely a framing device that "does not deceive anybody" (83), the fairy tale's eucatastrophe had all of the theological implications invoked by his word "grace."

Poe was one of the first theorists of horror as well as one of its pioneering practitioners, just as Tolkien was for fantasy. His essay "The Philosophy of Composition," in which he almost successfully disguises the motivations behind his own writing, lays out a principle for the short story that essentially rules out anything like Tolkien's eucatastrophe. In planning a story, he says, he begins by selecting a single effect.

> Having chosen a novel, first, and secondly a vivid effect, I consider whether it can best be wrought by incident or tone—whether by ordinary incidents and peculiar tone, or the converse, or by peculiarity both of incident and tone—afterward looking about me (or rather within) for such combinations of event, or tone, as shall best aid me in the construction of the effect.
>
> (Poe 1846/2011, 163)

Working backward from this final effect, everything that does not contribute is eliminated. Everything that does is doubled and redoubled. Furthermore, the kind of effect that Poe has in mind is an emotional one. Using his own poem "The Raven" to illustrate, he claims to have selected every detail—sounds, images, incidents—to guide the reader into an exquisite state of melancholy.

A typical fairy tale shatters Poe's rule. It takes the listener from curiosity to fear to despair to joy—not just one effect but several in succession. Revealingly, the common term for Poe's kind of tale is "horror," which names its emotional endgame. Is any other fictional genre named for an affective state? We don't go into a bookstore looking for the bemusement section, or the melancholia. (We might find "humor," but that names cause rather than effect.) Poe's successors have followed him in singling out the emotional whammy as the defining characteristic of their form. H. P. Lovecraft begins his examination of "Supernatural Horror in Literature" with the claim that "The oldest and strongest emotion of mankind is fear, and the oldest and strongest kind of fear is fear of the unknown." Like Poe, Lovecraft looks for stories that invoke such fear without the distraction of other emotions or other aims.

> We may say, as a general thing, that a weird story whose intent is to teach or produce a social effect, or one in which the horrors are finally explained away by natural means, is not a genuine tale of cosmic fear [. . .]. The one test of the really weird is simply this—whether or not there be excited in the reader a profound sense of dread, and of contact with unknown spheres and powers; a subtle attitude of awed listening, as if for the beating of black wings or the scratching of outside shapes and entities on the known universe's utmost rim.   (Lovecraft 2009)

"Why?" we might ask. If there's no teaching, no "social effect," then what is the purpose of making the reader feel *any* emotion, no matter how intense? I think the answer lies in Lovecraft's rapturous prose, which testifies that the horror lies not in the story but in the universe. It is the most real thing in the universe. Lovecraft is clearly in love with it.

Stephen King too emphasizes affect in his discussion of his chosen mode. He jokes about his own ambitions in a passage from his book *Danse Macabre*:

> I recognize terror as the finest emotion (used to almost quintessential effect in Robert Wise's film *The Haunting*, where, as in "The Monkey's Paw," we are never allowed to see what is behind the door), and so I will try to terrorize the reader. But if I find I cannot terrify him/her, I will try to horrify; and if I find I cannot horrify, I'll go for the gross-out. I'm not proud.   (King 1983, 37)

Behind the joking is a serious ambition that has to do with coming to terms with the terror, the visceral horror, and the involuntary disgust with which we meet, respectively, the cosmos, violence, and aspects of bodily existence that we deny and disguise. That last is what Julia Kristeva called the abject. Those are all powerful topics, worth exploring. But to my mind, horror as a genre fails to give us narrative paths beyond those emotional reactions. It summons them up and then leaves its characters—our representatives— immobilized by shock or despair or madness.

I speak as one who has no feeling for horror in literature or film. I don't get it; I'm the worst person to talk about its nuances and aesthetic achievements. But my impressions are corroborated by John Clute's evaluation, in *The Encyclopedia of Fantasy*, of the difference between fantasy and horror:

> This Story-driven urge to comedic completion also distinguishes full fantasy from its siblings, Supernatural Fictions and Horror, whose plots often terminate—shockingly—before any resolution can be achieved.... supernatural fictions and horror stories which pass through their natural habitats into the transformed world of healing tend to be thought of as fantasies (or Dark Fantasies). When supernatural fictions or horror stories become fantasies, they become stories which can be completed.
>
> (Clute 1997, "Fantasy")

Clute significantly separates dark fantasy from horror, though they share most of their bone-chilling effects. Again, the difference is structural, and therefore functional. What horror does is different from what fantasy does: the genres perform different work.

In a review of two particularly well-wrought horror novels, Clute suggests what that genre's cultural work might entail:

> In that realm of Fantastika called Horror we find ourselves, at the beginning of the tale, walking the surface of the world in a state of high anxiety until, in the blinking of an eye, we are given the truth inside. [...] our lives (great Horror stories tell us) are false. Hell is not being able to forget this.
>
> (Clute 2009, 320–1)

If Clute is right—and the three practitioners I have cited support his claim— then horror is fantasy truncated, cut off before the dynamics of story can redeem world, characters, and the reader's sense of order. The affect of horror functions to change the reader's world view by unmasking a deeper, more terrible reality. It is a form with strongly Gnostic sympathies. Beauty, love, justice all fall away as illusion fails and dark truth is revealed.

But something very different happens when the same sorts of terror come, not at the end of a story, but in the middle. I've mentioned fairy tale, and Tolkien's richly embroidered variations on it, but the story I want to introduce at this point is modeled, not on Märchen, but on a related oral form, the Icelandic saga, with additional influences from medieval romance and Jacobean revenge tragedy. It is E. R. Eddison's 1922 novel *The Worm Ouroboros.*

Near the beginning of Eddison's exuberantly eccentric tale, the Witch King Gorice accepts a challenge to single combat with Demon Lord Goldry Bluszco—it might not be obvious that Demons are the good guys and Witches the bad. There are some exceptions among the Witches but Gorice is not one of them: he is arrogant and tyrannical and he intends to cheat his way to victory over Lord Goldry in their wrestling match. Goldry, however, lifts the King off the ground—there are echoes of the myth of Hercules's wrestling match with the apparently unkillable giant Antaeus— and hurls him to his death.

It is up to the host of the tournament, ruler of a small realm allied with neither the Witches nor the Demons, to offer lamentations for the king's demise. He begins,

> I that in heill was, and gladness
> Am troublet now with great sickness
>> And feblit with infirmitie:
>> *Timor mortis conturbat me.*
>>>> (Eddison 1922/1967, 42)

And for ten more verses, the Red Foliot mourns, not the Witch King alone, but all of humanity, doomed to die. A note in the back of the book identifies the lament as an excerpt from the fifteenth-century Scots poet William Dunbar. The poem is "Lament for the Makaris," or Makers, or poets, and it goes on to pay tribute to Chaucer and Gower and a host of lesser-known poets of the day. At the end of each quatrain is a Latin phrase taken from the Catholic *Office of the Dead* that translates approximately as "Fear of death confounds me." Eddison's choice of poem is apt. *Timor mortis* is exactly what the scene is about. We have barely met the Witch king, but he seems unstoppable, until he isn't. Death stops him.

But the lines, and the scene, aren't really about death itself, but about the fear of death—*timor mortis*, rather than simple *mortem*—and about what comes of that fear, which is the working out of the whole novel's plot. What does the fear of death do? I gave the standard translation earlier, it *confounds* us. But that is not quite what the Latin says. It *conturbs* us, a word that briefly entered English but didn't make the final cut. We do still have its cousins, and they carry some of the meanings: fear of mortality *disturbs*, it *perturbs*, plus whatever is contained in the prefix *con-*, which we hear in the first translation choice, *confounds*. Without going farther down the etymological rabbit hole, I will just say that when we are conturbed we are deranged, roiled up so deeply and completely as not to be able to go on with other things. That is what *timor mortis* does to us. If Eddison had put the poem, and the scene that inspires it, at the end of his novel, our affective state would match that of the characters, and it would be a work of horror. But it comes, instead, just as *The Worm Ouroboros* is getting started. The whole novel, I would say, is about *not* being conturbed by the fear of death, or about overcoming that confounding to go on to further action.

In the chapter that follows Red Foliot's lament, the lords of Witchland drink and squabble and amuse themselves with gambling and song. They are attempting to distance themselves from death: whistling past the graveyard. Far away in the Witch capital, Gorice's heir wakes to power. Unlike his predecessor, Gorice XII is "a most crafty warlock, full of guiles and wiles, who by the might of his egromancy and the sword of Witchland shall exceed all earthly powers" (51). *Egromancy* is the same as *necromancy*, working magic through control of the dead. We also learn that Gorice XII has his predecessor's memories. The implication is that the kings of Witchland are all incarnations of a single evil spirit, a being that denies and evades death.

In contrast, the Demons welcome peril. At the end of the novel, when they have defeated the Witch king and attained what promises to be lasting peace, they ask the gods for a boon, and what they request is that their enemies be brought back:

"Would they might give us our good gift, that should be youth for ever, and war; and unwaning strength and skill in arms. Would they might but give us our great enemies alive and whole again. For better it were we should run hazard again of utter destruction, than thus live out our lives like cattle fattening for the slaughter, or like silly garden plants." (504)

So Eddison gives us two responses to the fear of death. One is to hold on to continuing existence, as it were, for dear life. The other, to which he gives his narrative blessing, is to seek out mortal danger as the thing that gives life its savor. Oddly, both responses are symbolized in the Worm Ouroboros that gives the novel its title: the serpent with its tail in its mouth, emblem of eternity. Two approaches to death, two visions of eternity—one that denies change and the other that welcomes it as part of a larger cycle.

A recent work that looks very different from Eddison's turns out to convey a similar message about *timor mortis*. Nnedi Okorafor's 2010 fantasy even puts the question in its title, *Who Fears Death*, which is also the translation from the Igbo language of the protagonist's name: Onyewonsu. The epigraph from Congolese rebel leader Patrice Lumumba asks it slightly differently: "Dear friends, are you afraid of death?" Where Eddison looked to the European past, Okorafor looks to an African future, in which magic has returned and European colonizers have disappeared but ethnic strife continues. Onyewonsu is a child of rape, an outcast marked by her light skin and bushy hair. Okorafor says that the book was generated by a newspaper story about weaponized rape in the Sudan (Okorafor 2010, 387), but it could reflect many other instances around the world of hatred and violence triggered by fear of the Other. In *Who Fears Death*, Onyewonsu's father is a powerful magician from the dominant tribe, who wants to instill fear of death into his daughter to make her weak. But in the end, it is the father Dain whose attempts to kill her bring about his own end. Onyewonsu is willing to die, and so she lives. A shapeshifter, her first transformation is into a vulture, a carrion-eater, and part of the lesson she learns from that transformation is that death is necessary and even productive.

One of the things Okorafor brings to fantasy is a wealth of traditions and beliefs from her Nigerian parents' culture. Her characters and her stories are not locked into a Western mindset in which death and darkness are on one side of an absolute moral divide, separated off from light and life. A number of other writers have likewise nudged fantasy away from the Battle Between Good and Evil, using the genre's resources to offer alternative models of the world. Ursula K. Le Guin's Earthsea, for instance, draws on both Asian philosophy—especially Taoism—and Native American animism to erase those sorts of boundaries. Marlon James, in *Black Leopard Red Wolf* (2019), bases his fantasy world, as Nnedi Okorafor does, in African tradition, which is such a wide-ranging category that his story resembles Okorafor's only in its un-Western moral ambiguity. And Australian writer Patricia Wrightson frequently (and controversially) borrowed characters and ways of seeing from Aboriginal myth to connect modern white Australians to their adopted (or stolen) land.

Wrightson has been in eclipse lately. Her use of Aboriginal traditions seemed forward-thinking and narratively clever in the 1970s but now has the taint of colonial privilege, no matter how much care she took to respect her sources and to acknowledge the tragedies that resulted from European invasion. Those problems are most evident in her grandest effort, the trilogy called The Song of Wirrun. *A Little Fear* (1983) rests more lightly on Aboriginal lore, partly because it isn't a world-spanning heroic epic but the account of a domestic struggle. The struggle pits elderly Mrs Tucker, who has just checked herself out of a nursing home to take up residence in a rural cottage left her by her brother, against the Nijimbin, a supernatural being based in Aboriginal tradition. The Nijimbin considers the place his own. At first Mrs Tucker is unaware of the magical creature that torments her hens and draws ants into the house and lures her dog into an untethered boat to float away downstream. Hence, one of the fears referred to in the title is her fear that she is going mad. But the Nijimbin goes too far. First, Mrs Tucker's dog Hector trees it, and though she can't see it directly, it drops its small stone axe at her feet:

> And the first thing she thought was that the axe was real. It was here in her hands.... And there was one thing a silly old woman who was going off her head could not possibly do: she could not climb a stringybark tree, drop a stone axe, and rush down the tree again to pick it up. (Wrightson 1983, 76)

Then the Nijimbin enlists the help of a larger, wilder creature, a Hairy Man, which, unlike the Nijimbin, is visible to Mrs Tucker:

> It looked at her. Its eyes were dark and heavily browed. It did not look old but its eyes were as old as a lizard's. Mrs Tucker's old-blue eyes gazed back. Something—a sense of pity or of fellowship—flowed between them. Then the hairy thing put out a long arm and brushed her aside. (90)

It seems to be a stalemate: determined old woman against sly and stubborn Nijimbin. But Mrs Tucker makes the decision to concede.

She writes to her daughter, revealing where she has gone. "She had always known," says the narrator, "that the old thing was part of the land itself, and she could not fight a war against the land" (105). If the Nijimbin were really the source of her fear, we would conclude that she has lost her fight. But the struggle has given her back "the dignity of independence in her own home; the right to risk breaking her leg in a fall from a stepladder; the freedom to choose her own undershirts and her own company" (109). It doesn't matter that she concedes the cottage to the being she calls "old mischief" (109). She has been changed by the encounter, and she is no longer afraid of dying alone, no longer conturbed by fear of the unknown or the inevitable.

I go back and forth about how I feel about the book, and not only because of its now-obvious cultural appropriation. I want Mrs Tucker's stubborn courage to be rewarded; I want the embodied spirit of nature to reclaim its ancient property. I also go back and forth about the meaning of the title. Does Wrightson mean that the Nijimbin is just a little fear, unlike greater and deadlier spirits that Mrs Tucker might have encountered? Or does the title signify that "a little fear" is a necessary part of living fully, a trace ingredient that gives the zest to the recipe? A little fear may be a prophylactic against the great fear, so that Mrs Tucker can move forward with the life she has left.

But it was never death that Mrs Tucker feared most. It was loss: of family, of friends, of her own faculties, of self-determination. Death lurks in the story, but in the end, the death of the body is just a stand-in for a broad range of emotional and philosophical dangers. Looking at *mortis* without the *timor*, death turns out to be a pretty interesting thing, what Peter Pan calls "an awfully big adventure." And that is true regardless of one's belief or disbelief in an afterlife—or at least so says much fantasy.

A curious thing about symbols is that they can reverse directions. The source domain of a metaphor can suddenly seem like the target domain instead—the thing meant becomes the vector of meaning. I noticed this first when thinking about Freud and the ubiquitous sexual metaphors in *The Interpretation of Dreams*. Whether you dream about a potted plant or an omnibus, it's about sex, says Freud. My own take on this is not that everything is about sex but that sex is about everything. It is part of how we understand existence. We impose our bodies on the world. We grasp or comprehend with metaphoric hands, we arrive at an understanding on metaphoric feet. Mark Johnson explores the wide range of conceptual schemas derived from the bodily experience of maintaining one's balance, from aesthetics to mathematics (1987, 97–8). Near and far, inside and outside, are metaphors so ubiquitous that we don't even realize we are using our bodies to map the universe. So sex, such a powerful attractor of our imaginations, becomes the way we understand everything from gravity to the Big Bang.

Like the "little death" that means orgasm, so the big one, death itself, can become the source domain for a host of metaphors and symbols. We can see this in T. S. Eliot's 1930 poem "Marina" (which rests on Shakespeare's fantasy *Pericles*). After the opening, Eliot begins to list groups (of people, presumably) defined by surreal images and actions such as "Those who sharpen the tooth of the dog" (105), each of which, the poem explains, means Death. If we take Eliot at face value, pretty much everything comes down to death—the word in the poem is always set off by itself on a new line—but the interest in this passage is in whatever precedes the clanging repetitions: from the dog's tooth to the hummingbird's glory. So perhaps we should read the "meaning" verb with its arrow reversed. We interpret all those things through our awareness of death and its inevitability. Furthermore, Eliot doesn't stop there—by the time he wrote "Marina" he was well out of what we can call his horror phase and into elusively transcendent narratives, culminating in the "Four Quartets" of the late 1930s and early 40s. So the death omens in the poem are all blown away by

> A breath of pine, and the woodsong fog
> By this grace dissolved in place

As in Shakespeare, Pericles's and Marina's story goes on through death to mystery and reconciliation, like any good fantasy, though it takes work and trust to get there at last.

If fear of death isn't the end-*ing* of a fantasy, or a fairy tale, then it's not the end, either; that is, it's not the goal, the purpose, the rationale of the story. What, then, is its function? As I suggested in chapter one, the best way to approach function is often through structure. *Timor mortis* can crop up at various points in the narrative. We see it at the climax of Wrightson's tale, and at the beginning, in Eddison's. Memorably scary scenes in other fantasies come at various points along the way. For instance, the journey through a series of caves in the middle of Alan Garner's *The Weirdstone of Brisingamen* (1960) was sheer torture to a mildly claustrophobic reader like me. I have already mentioned the Wicked Witch who casts a shadow over Dorothy's first moments in Oz. Another unforgettable scene involves the barely controlled panic with which Gerald and Mabel face magically animated dummies—the Ugly-Wuglies—as the action ramps up toward the end of E. Nesbit's *The Enchanted Castle* (1907). Then there is the unnamed evil conjured by the young, overconfident Ged at the end of the first sequence of Ursula K. Le Guin's *A Wizard of Earthsea* (1968)—we will come back to that. In Tolkien, we have not only the spider Shelob but also, much earlier in the story, the incredibly tense episode of hiding from the Nazgul who has come to the Shire seeking "Baggins."

At each of these moments, the characters are very nearly, but not quite, conturbed by fear. Each anxiety-raising scene is a reminder that the happy ending to come is not inevitable: there is another unwritten story in which the outcome is horrific. These are story nodes, potential branching-off points. They are points at which the story points toward possibilities, or, qua Kierkegaard, possibilities of possibility, that will never become narrative realities, and yet that contribute to the shape and meaning of the actual narrative. Part of the reader's job is to look a little way down those other, unexplored paths, which Umberto Eco called "inferential walks" (Eco 1979, 214).

Even though such nodes can occur in many parts of a story, they don't occur randomly. In the fairy-tale structure outlined by Vladimir Propp, there are at least three segments where characters are likely to confront particularly fearsome things. First, there is the moment near the beginning where either "an interdiction is addressed to the hero" (and always violated) or "the villain makes an attempt at reconnaissance" (Propp 1968, 26–8). The visit from the Nazgul is a textbook instance of the latter. Ged's willful reading of a forbidden spell is a good example of the former. In either case, hackles are raised and fear functions like a starter gun in a race: characters take your marks, get set, go!

Second, there is a point in fairy tales where the hero "is tested, interrogated, attacked, etc., which prepares the way for his receiving either a magical agent or helper" (39). George MacDonald's fantasies provide several such moments of testing, such as the scene in which Curdie, in *The Princess and Curdie*, must trust the old lady in the tower enough to thrust his hand into a heap of burning roses:

> Curdie dared not stop to think. It was much too terrible to think about. He rushed to the fire, and thrust both his hands right into the middle of the heap of flaming roses, and his arms halfway up to the elbows. . . . He held the pain as if it were a thing that would kill him if he let it go—as indeed it would have done. He was in terrible fear lest it should conquer him.
>
> (MacDonald 1883, 80)

Yet Curdie doesn't draw back, and the resulting magical gift is an ability to feel the true nature of anyone whose hand he touches. He has passed the test of pain, and the greater ordeal of fear.

A third fairy-tale segment that can generate fear is the optional coda in which a false hero steps forward to claim the reward that belongs to the hero (Propp 1968, 60), who at that point is imprisoned or slaving in a kitchen. Everything could slip away just before the happy ending: the stepsister will get away with cutting off her toe to fit Cinderella's shoe and the troll princess will win the enchanted prince away from the heroine of "East o' the Sun and West o' the Moon." But a more terrifying possibility is that the double *is* the real hero and the protagonist the imposter. Doppelgangers are always uncanny, and the greatest fear, according to fairy tales, is not of death but of the expunged, denied, exiled parts of the self. Carl Jung named these parts of the self the Shadow, and the purest example of a Jungian Shadow in fantasy literature is Ged's shadow in Ursula K. Le Guin's *A Wizard of Earthsea*.

Le Guin said later that she didn't have Jung in mind; hadn't read him; was surprised to find that she had so neatly reinvented his archetype (Le Guin 1976, 44). Here is Le Guin's paraphrase of Jung in an early essay examining the sources of her own imagination: "Unadmitted to consciousness, the shadow is projected outward, onto others. There's nothing wrong with me—it's *them*. I'm not a monster, other people are monsters" (Le Guin 1989, 59–60). Eventually she was to come back to Jung in a more skeptical frame of mind, making note of his sexism and racism, but for a time, he helped her address some of the patterns her unconscious tended to generate.

In Jung and in Le Guin, the Other can transform from enemy to source of strength and self-knowledge, but only if one is willing to look on the Shadow and be changed by it. Her character Cob, from the third Earthsea book, *The Farthest Shore* (1973), is a failed wizard, unable to allow that transformation. He sees death as something to be evaded, and so he opens a hole in the universe that keeps him suspended between life and death and also threatens to destroy the Balance of all of Earthsea. *Timor mortis* conturbs not only Cob but also his entire world. It is up to Ged to confront the Other—not Cob, who is pitiable in his denial, but death itself, as a part of life and a part of the self.

This act, through which Ged intends to sacrifice his life and does indeed sacrifice his powers, is forecast in *A Wizard of Earthsea*. Having accidentally unleashed a dangerous shadow-being and chased it across the world, Ged finally discovers how to tame it. To do so he must face it and name it. The name he gives it is his own. It is his own shadow, the shadow of his pride and power: what other name could it have? As the narrator says, "Ged had neither lost nor won but, naming the shadow of his death with his own name, had made himself whole: a man: who, knowing his whole true self, cannot be used or possessed by any power other than himself, and whose life therefore is lived for life's sake and never in the service of ruin, or pain, or hatred, or the dark" (Le Guin 1968, 203).

Facing the Shadow is a little more complicated than naming it. We always hear that advice: face your fears. Even Le Guin uses the expression in "The Child and the Shadow." We children, she says, must learn from fairy tales to

> see ourselves and the shadow we cast. For we can face our own shadow; we can learn to control it and to be guided by it; so that when we grow into our strength and responsibility as adults in society, we will be less inclined, perhaps, either to give up in despair or to deny what we see, when we must face the evil that is done in the world, and the injustices and grief and suffering that we all must bear, and the final shadow at the end of it all.
>
> (Le Guin 1989, 66)

But the Shadow in *A Wizard* has no face. For most of the book it is a formless darkness, a rift in the universe rather than a coherent being.

Artist Charles Vess tells about an exchange with Le Guin when he was working on illustrations for Earthsea: "I had this drawing, and the shadow creature obviously had a head and arms," he says. "Ursula responded, 'Well, it's a little too human-like.'" She told him that the Shadow was inspired by taking a look through a microscope at something "'very creepy, dark'... moving across the slide. "That became her shadow," he says (Moher, 2018). That something was probably a tardigrade, Le Guin told Vess: one of those tiny, blobby, bearlike creatures that haunt microsopes and our imaginations. But half-glimpsed and transmuted in Le Guin's imagination, the Shadow was neither bearish nor humanoid—just unformed and terrifying in its unbeing. Ged's job is to give it form.

Similarly, in C. S. Lewis's most complex novel, *Till We Have Faces*, the main character Orual has to confront the Other that she fears and rejects: in this case the gods. Since the book is a retelling of Apuleius's story of Cupid and Psyche, a major plot point is that the god of love visits his bride unseen. When Psyche lights a lamp to make sure he is not the monster that her sister Orual says he is, either he or his mother casts her out. By trying to put a face on her husband, Psyche has broken the rules and must go through a set of ordeals to try to win him back.

This god's mother is not the beautiful Aphrodite of Greek poetry but a cruel devouring entity Orual's people call Ungit. Even that name is somehow formless, not so much a name as an auditory place-marker for a word that can't be spoken. Ungit's statue is likewise formless, only vaguely human-shaped and with only the suggestion of a face showing up when blood is poured over the stone in sacrifice. Here is Lewis's—or Orual's—description:

> she was very uneven, lumpy and furrowed, so that, as when we gaze into a fire, you could always see some face or other. She was now more rugged than ever because of all the blood they had poured over her in the night. In the little clots and chains of it I made out a face; a fancy at one moment, but then, once you had seen it, not to be evaded. A face such as you might see in a loaf, swollen, brooding, infinitely female. (Lewis 1956, 270)

Setting aside Lewis's general problems with women and sexuality, this description gets at the terror inspired by that which is at once too human and not human enough: Freud's Uncanny. Orual will never be reconciled with Ungit until Ungit acquires a face, which can only happen when Orual realizes that the female figure she loathes is herself.

The novel's title comes from a line in the book: "How can they [the gods] meet us face to face till we have faces?" (294). But that question can be turned around: "till they have faces." Like other metaphors, this one contains another with its direction reversed. Lewis wants us to read the story primarily as a Christian allegory, with the sisters Psyche and Orual representing different aspects of the soul and the god of love as an emblem of the Christian God. Yet the story has its own dynamic that doesn't entirely fit Lewis's theology. Ungit or Venus is more truly faceless than Orual is, and her son Amor is a narrative absence through most of the plot. Not until Orual confronts the gods in a mock trial, issuing her complaint about their unfair treatment of herself and her people, do they reveal themselves to her by revealing her to herself. To face the gods, the story tells us, is to lend them our own faces.

The fear of death and the Other will continue to confound, derange, or conturb until we learn to recognize that death is part of life and the Other dangerous only so long as we deny that it is also us. We remain caught in a cycle of horror and revulsion until we can finish the story, rather than terminating it before it can be resolved. We can trace the effects of that narrative short circuit outside of fantasy, in the real world. We see people being guided by fear: building walls, stockpiling weapons, voting for tyrants, demonizing outsiders, and cutting themselves off from the larger community. I don't think any story—even the most fully realized fantasy—can turn all this around and save us from ourselves, but I also think we have no hope of finding our way out of the maze without stories to tell us we can do so. Fantasy does not end with *"Timor mortis* conturbat me," but goes on to show how embracing the other might redeem us. "Ged reached out his hand," says *A Wizard of Earthsea*, "and took hold of his shadow, of the black self that reached out to him. Light and darkness met, and joined, and were one" (Le Guin 1968, 201).

Like the boy in the folk tale, we sometimes have to learn inner truths through their outer effects: like a shivery mass of minnows or a story that raises what the Scots call a grue. We learn from fantastic tales not to be overwhelmed by death and its grues, nor to let them govern us, but to give fear a name and a face and a place in our lives. *Timor mortis* will not conturb us if we can learn to use it. Instead, it can teach us to keep going to the end of the story, to connect with the other, and to transform dread into compassion.

10

How Fantasy Means and What It Does

Some Propositions

Here, without anecdotes or close analysis of examples, is what I have been saying throughout the book—the answer key at the back of the book, as it were. The numbering corresponds to chapters and sequence in those chapters.

1.1 Fantasy borrows one kind of truth from its mythic sources. To say that is simply to transfer the burden of understanding from the modern genre to the rituals, narratives, and world views of traditional cultures.

1.2 In riddles, the literal truth of what they are saying is somehow blocked, for instance by self-contradiction, and so we are forced to shift into thinking metaphorically. A similar thing happens in fantasy.

1.3 A third kind of truth in fantasy is structural: though the imagined world and its story are unbelievable in themselves, their component parts and the way those are articulated tell us something valid about the real world.

1.4 The invented world and the story are not two separate things but a single working mechanism. The world is a world in which such a story can happen; the story is the sequence of events that the world calls into being. This relationship between story and world is what M. M. Bakhtin called a *chronotope*.

1.5 Surface realism, which capably reproduces social interactions and psychological traits, often hides underlying causes and disruptions that the fantastic can reveal.

1.6 Fantasy has both a vocabulary and a syntax. The vocabulary largely consists of motifs from oral literatures, but those have been reworked in writing and recirculated as what Maria Nikolejeva calls *fantasemes*. The syntax is likewise borrowed, and likewise significantly reconstructed, from the structures of traditional narrative.

1.7 Just as the novel is capacious and acquisitive, assimilating letters and histories and many other textual types, fantasy can incorporate into itself virtually any kind of realist discourse such as social satire and stream of consciousness. However, such discourse is always made strange by its fantastic framing: it is defamiliarized or estranged, with all the cognitive and political implications those terms have in critical theory.

2.1 Even the most realistic kinds of fiction may disguise magical thinking and fairy-tale structuring. This is not a flaw but a precondition for generating the illusion of the real.

2.2 The difference between realism and fantasy is largely a matter of figure and ground: what we are invited to pay attention to versus what we are expected to ignore or take for granted. The latter, in realist fiction, includes formulaic patterning of events and character types.

2.3 All literature is genre: genres are codes for generating texts and making sense of them.

2.4 Hierarchies of genre are social and political constructs. No genre is inherently better or worse than any other, though they lend them-selves to different uses and appeal to different audiences.

2.5 We tend to classify as realistic what is actually only familiar.

2.6 The disturbing and shocking are not more real than the comforting and the inspirational. In narrative, all these effects are products of selection and arrangement.

2.7 Realism and fantasy are not ends of a single scale but two different properties of narrative. One particular story might be both more realistic and more fantastic than another.

2.8 One of the most important functions of genre is the way successful writers and memorable texts serve as authorizing instances for later writers. A story such as *Huckleberry Finn* told American writers they could write in colloquial language about familiar experiences. William Faulkner made the South available for literature. This pro-cess is the same for realistic and fantastic fictions, though the prod-ucts may look very different.

2.9 Genres must be continually renewed through the inclusion of new experiences and perspectives. As writers imitate the forms and tech-niques of their authorizing texts, they also change those forms and techniques. In their innovations, they end up serving as authorizers for other writers in turn.

2.10   The fantastic is the default form of narrative, with realism a later innovation and metafictional frame-breaking an even more recent combination of the two. All are games that writers and readers enter into willingly, learning the rules as they go.

2.11   Wishing is part of reality; the way a story deals with it determines which generic pile the story goes into.

2.12   Story-worlds have a larger existence than the texts in which they are introduced. Every reader has a different Oz or Middle-earth or Baker Street. Some readers use those story-worlds as personal retreats, others turn them into playgrounds for socializing, and still others use them to construct new imagined spaces of their own. In this regard, too, realistic fiction is no different from fantasy.

3.1   When fantasy reframes traditional myths, it invokes the world views embedded in those myths. As populations migrate and interact, their mythic systems confront one another, sometimes violently, yet the narrative logic of the fairy tale seeks reconciliation and harmony.

3.2   In modern cities, different groups are thrown into close proximity that requires economic exchanges and encourages social interactions between individuals from those groups. Each interaction and exchange is also a negotiation among beliefs and among scripts for behavior.

3.3   The saving grace for disparate populations may be the fact that no one constituency is a solid majority. In many cases, social minorities are also cognitive minorities, using Peter Berger's term, and so such minorities can only prevail by forming alliances and accepting differences of belief. A number of contemporary fantasies depict that process.

3.4   Acceptance of others' world views requires acknowledging that knowledge is situated: we know the world from one position and perspective and yet from other viewpoints, things might seem quite different. Fantasy is particularly good at demonstrating that situatedness.

3.5   Fantasy scenarios of the past, especially heroic battles between good and evil, are giving way to other narrative patterns, including the ironic "nobody is a good guy any more" and the more hopeful "we have to live together so let's work out an arrangement where nobody wins or loses."

3.6   In much contemporary fantasy, two other epistemological models interact with the mythic: one is science and the other is history. Both work against absolutism and intolerance, though it is hard to resist the appeal of certainty and the assurance of the sacred.

3.7 Fantasies set in worlds where different knowledges compete offer new forms of narrative resolution that are congruent with the shape of real-world justice. One of those patterns for resolution is the vulnerable, messy, mixed neighborhood that is so often a target for ideological purists and ethnic cleansers. Such neighborhoods show up in many contemporary fantasies.

3.8 One of the strongest counters to intolerance is the kind of radical hospitality that characterizes many traditional cultures, especially those in hostile environments. Fantasies such as Ursula K. Le Guin's Annals of the Western Shore and Laurie Marks's Elemental Logic series foreground hospitality as a narrative principle and a force for transformation—and an alternative to a model of narrative based on conflict.

4.1 Many critical schools and prescriptions for writers emphasize conflict as the basis for narrative interest. The claim is that there is no story without conflict, and yet the only essential element for narrative is motivated change over time.

4.2 There are many ways to motivate such change and make readers care about it. These include fidelity to historical models, psychological insights, redemptive journeys, and uncovering of mysteries. Casting all of these as forms of conflict invites us to choose sides and to anticipate that some characters or groups will defeat others.

4.3 Except in the case of stories of argument or actual combat, conflict is only a metaphor for the kinds of interactions involved, and it is not necessarily the aptest metaphor.

4.4 The kinds of complications, frustrations, and anticipations that keep us engaged in stories might better be represented metaphorically by calling them something other than conflict. Some alternative metaphors include dissonance, friction, resistance, and occultation.

4.5 Each alternative metaphor also implies a different script for dealing with problems and with problematic people. The conflict script locks us into scripts of opposition. Others may be better for steering us toward compromise, reconciliation, and mutual discovery.

4.6 Many of the stories that are cited as instances of conflict actually better illustrate some of these other metaphors for narrative energy. This is particularly true for the innovative fantasies of writers such as China Miéville, Diana Wynne Jones, Frances Hardinge, and Patricia McKillip.

5.1 A story's meaning and significance are functions of the text's connections outside itself. Some of those connections will be with the reader's own experience; others with the reader's knowledge of the story's historical and geographical setting; still others with the interpretive codes built into the text.

5.2 We learn to interpret texts from other texts: they give us the codes and much of the other knowledge we need.

5.3 A reading without sufficient connections will always be thin and unsatisfactory. That might not be the fault of the text but of the reader's experience.

5.4 We have been taught to make certain kinds of connections with the Bible, with classical myth, with Renaissance drama, with Romantic poetry, and so on. Because those links are mostly to male writers, they teach us (including women) to read as men.

5.5 We have not been taught to look for chains of association from outside the circle of privileged men: for instance, to indigenous texts, to oral narratives like fairy tales, to less-prestigious genres such as letters and stories for children, and to texts by women.

5.6 Critical tradition teaches us to see connections between texts in terms of influence or allusion. These terms imply that such connections involve either passive acquiescence to the literary past or decorative reference to it.

5.7 Better metaphors for literary connectedness include Diana Pavlac Glyer's *resonators* (developed to describe the way C. S. Lewis, J. R. R. Tolkien, and the rest of their circle contributed to one another's work), Deleuze and Guattari's biologically inaccurate but richly suggestive *rhizome*, and Bakhtin's *dialogism*.

5.8 To the above set of metaphors for connectedness, we can add another biological one: mitochondria. Mitochondria are organelles, parts of cells derived from what were once free-living organisms that eventually lost the ability to live outside the host. The resulting relationship between the two organisms is beneficial to both.

5.9 The features of mitochondria that make them relevant to discussions of literature include their production of energy for the host, their maintaining a genetic heritage different from the host's nuclear DNA, and their transmission strictly down the maternal line. Just as we can trace human ancestry back to a hypothetical mitochondrial Eve, we can trace a line of women's literature despite omissions from and deliberate erasures of the historical record.

5.10 Like mitochondria, texts that have been incorporated into newer texts are still alive and still working on behalf of themselves and the new host. Any act of reference is really a whole history of incorporation, negotiation, and synergy.

5.11 The story "The Women Men Don't See" by Alice Sheldon can be used as a reading guide for a whole host of texts. Its title, for instance, invites us to seek out lives and testimony of women and men excluded from literary establishments and power structures, and to look for linkages among their lived and narrated experiences. It invites us to see and to value other literatures than the ones we have been taught to care about.

6.1 Another undervalued chain of literary transmission is utopian and dystopian fiction. Just as the critical establishment prefers texts by men, it elevates representations of the real over works of the imagination.

6.2 One problem with realism is that it offers no way out of what Wallace Stevens called "things as they are." Of the literatures of "things as they aren't," the most overtly political is utopia, including its positive, or eutopian, and its negative, or dystopian, versions.

6.3 Utopian world-building is essentially the same as fantasy's except that its ground rules require that it be the product of purely human, non-magical efforts. Most utopian writers have also created other forms of fantasy (including science fiction); significant examples include Jonathan Swift, William Morris, Edward Bellamy, H. G. Wells, Mary Shelley, Ray Bradbury, Samuel R. Delany, Joanna Russ, Ursula K. Le Guin, and Kim Stanley Robinson.

6.4 The utopian impulse can be expressed through social experimentation and reform movements as well as literature, but the genre of utopian fiction is a form of narrative art and should be read for literary value as well as for philosophical speculation and political applications.

6.5 Of the two major branches of utopian storytelling, dystopia has a better reputation than eutopia, partly because of the critical belief that conflict is the same as narrative interest—and partly because many of the earlier eutopias were not very well written.

6.6 The resurgence of eutopias in the 1970s, most of them based in feminist and ecological speculation, also involved a re-engineering of the utopian storytelling techniques to produce what Tom Moylan calls the *critical utopia*. Key elements in this reinvented genre are acknowledgment of difference and imperfection within the imagined society and an emphasis on utopia as an ongoing process rather than a finished state.

6.7 In the 21st century, dystopias written for a young adult audience have brought renewed attention to the genre. There are a number of reasons that the form and the audience suit one another: teenage rebellion and idealism, the plasticity of the adolescent brain, the repressive aspects of educational institutions, and the appeal of heroic rebel figures. Many of those factors could work equally well in service to utopian visions.

6.8 The relationship between negative and positive utopias is more complex than just "good place equals bad story" and "bad place, good story." Every dystopia is also the ghost of a potentially positive utopia, a eutopia-gone-astray. Thus, another name for dystopia is *anti-utopia*. This suggests that the obverse might also be possible: a story could invite us to imagine a dystopia-gone-right, or *anti-dystopia*. Some of Moylan's critical utopias illustrate that dynamic.

6.9 Ursula K. Le Guin, who wrote several variations on utopia and dystopia, theorized that the problem with most utopian thinking is that it is too absolute, too universalizing, too ambitious—in a word, too yang. Following up on this Taoist line of thought, she proposed a solution of creating or seeking out yin utopias: small, modest, yielding, and unfinished.

6.10 Le Guin and other pioneers of the critical utopia also demonstrated several ways of making utopian fiction interesting and dynamic. These can be sorted into a set of storytelling tropes: the Ambassador from Utopia, the Misfit in Utopia, the Would-Be Immigrant, the Threat to Utopia, Building Utopia, and the Neverending Revolution.

6.11 All of the utopian storytelling tropes potentially do different cultural work from that done by dystopia. The latter pinpoints problems in contemporary society—institutionalized injustices, the beginning of dangerous trends, seemingly innocent accommodations to evil—and extrapolates full-blown nightmares from them. Dystopia's work is to warn; it is a signpost saying "thin ice ahead." Eutopian fiction, though, asks the reader to consider what is worth keeping in the world as it is, and what might be thrown out with little loss. It invites us to see abuse as unnecessary; inequality as a relic of the bad old days (which include the present); repression as a bad bargain.

6.12 A truism about utopia is that you can't get there from here. Utopia can never be reached starting from a world of injustice and abuse. Yet even the worst society has moments of happiness and pockets of harmony: we can take off from those. More radically, we can say that those moments and niches *are* utopia, if utopias can be small, temporary, and partial; i.e., yin. They can be built up to be a little larger, a little longer-lasting, a little more complete, but only if we see certain changes as possibilities.

6.13 We need fiction to teach us to find the utopias already around us. Young people, especially, need encouragement to be radically hopeful. That means more eutopian texts but it also means learning to read differently, to see the yin utopia, or anti-dystopia in the darkest dystopia.

7.1 A general consensus within popular psychology is that fairy tales offer guidance for individual growth and healing. However, that guidance seems only to be available to women, and the tales invoked usually have female protagonists.

7.2 Likewise, the business of retelling and reframing tales is primarily considered a feminine enterprise, with the exception of the anti-feminist men's rights movement and its (mis)reading of folk tale.

7.3 In reality, a number of male writers have used fairy tales to explore alternatives to the dominant, or hegemonic model of masculinity. Many of those writers are also, at the same time, challenging heteronormativity, and a significant proportion of them are themselves queer—in the largest sense that includes any nonstandard sexuality or outsider gender identity.

7.4 Traditional tales themselves can be read as questioning hegemonic masculinity by representing it in the form of cruel or abusive authority figures: giants, ogres, and murderous husbands. Opposing these various male tyrants are small but clever tailors, neglected youngest sons, and helpful brothers of the heroine. These last are the figures that show up in many modern fantasies based on fairy tales.

7.5 The typical Disney prince, stiff and bland, represents a form of masculinity resulting from denial of any possible feminine traits such as grace and vulnerability. An alternative image of male desirability invokes fairy-tale figures such as beast bridegrooms and enchanted swans.

7.6 The swan as figure of male desirability marks a chain of transmission (or mitochondrial descent) from romantic folklore revivals to postmodern metafictions. Most of the artists in that chain have been queer men. By inviting audiences to see male figures as graceful and attractive—even dangerously seductive—these artists disrupt what cinematic theory calls the male gaze.

7.7 Fantasy's subversion of hegemonic masculinity is an outgrowth of its rediscovery of female autonomy. Both are achieved by recovering figures that had been edited out of scholarly and literary treatments of the folk tale.

7.8 The literary fairy tale and the fantasies that descend from it can do cultural work beyond individual healing. They can also reconfigure gender as a conceptual system and behavioral code, to the benefit of all.

8.1 Insofar as fantasy performs cultural work, it is informed by politics and immersed in political upheavals, even when it appears to be above such concerns. As the political landscape changes, fantasy's relation to it alters.

8.2 Fantasy stands alongside science fiction and utopian fiction as a way of conceiving of systems other than those that exist. Whereas realism often provides impetus for reform, fantasy can be liberating in a more radical if more elusive way; this power is related to its narrative strategies.

8.3 Representation of real-world power dynamics and political deals is not among fantasy's affordances: the things it is particularly suited to accomplish.

8.4 Rather fantasy best represents power symbolically and on a localized level through such plot elements as the suppression of speech (including magical speech like prophecy and spell-casting); potentially powerful characters' self-limitation as an internalized version of ideology; and the articulation of, resistance to, and replacement of, cultural master-narratives.

8.5 Fantasy's reliance on folklore can be, and has been, taken as authorization for political nostalgia or repression in the name of a return to a golden age that never actually existed.

8.6 The genre of fantasy has even been associated at times with fascist movements, while science fiction, with its connection to utopia, is seen as the more progressive option.

8.7   One reason for the above association is that the subgenre of fantasy that Maria Sachiko Cecire refers to as the Oxford school of fantasy reconstructs a legendary past from which certain groups and actions are excluded.

8.8   This imaginary past resembles the protected, innocent space of childhood within children's literature, which is based not on actual childhood experience but on the needs of adults to compensate for their own sense of a fallen nature.

8.9   The innocence of both childhood and the past is often defined by the non-innocence of outsiders, and especially the dark-skinned Other, who is the product of the binary thinking that equates light and darkness with good and evil respectively.

8.10 The prevalence of the Dark Other can function as a "keep-away" sign for readers of non-European ancestry, but it can also be read as an invitation to writers to shake up the categories. A symbol system that is already strongly in place can be repurposed.

8.11 The history of fantasy shows how its collective story-world can be opened up to new sorts of characters and events and new ways of representing those in language.

8.12 Silenced characters of one era of fantasy writing can become the powerful speakers of the next.

8.13 To combat the exclusionary power of a pure past, writers deliberately incorporate disruptive elements, mixing genres, languages, and locales to turn the story-space of fantasy into a Zone. A Zone is a story-space that is impossible, impure, heterotopic, and thus available to all.

8.14 A number of recent fantasies employ the trope of characters who should be able to perform magic but can't because they have absorbed society's lessons about who they are. When that trope is acted out within a Zone, the Zone's disruptive energy can shatter the coercive bonds of opinion.

8.15 The best way to subvert a cultural norm is to employ it against itself. An example is the retelling of old and powerful stories from new perspectives and with unexpected outcomes.

8.16 History is not the past but a story we tell ourselves about the past. So is fantasy. The difference is that fantasy never lets us forget that it is a story. Hence it is more easily reshaped—and can be used as a new metanarrative to reconfigure other stories.

9.1 One of the central concerns of fantasy is how to deal with the three great fears (which are variations of a single fear) of the unknown, the threatening outsider, and death.

9.2 Philosophers identify a particular form of fear that Kierkegaard calls *dread* or *angst* as being grounded in freedom. If there is no choice, then death and confrontation of difference are simply inevitable and thus may be feared but not dreaded.

9.3 The move from simple fear to angst involves narrative: the ability to tell ourselves the story of what might happen.

9.4 Many folk narratives center on this kind of narrated confrontation with the unknown. Modern fantasy picks up on this dynamic, as does horror fiction. The difference between the two genres is structural: horror stops short of the sort of integration or reconciliation that characterizes the fairy tale and its descendants. Tolkien's term for this reconciling move is *eucatastrophe*, the sudden and unexpected turn toward a positive outcome.

9.5 The structural difference between horror and fantasy means that the two genres perform very different kinds of cultural work. At the very least, fantasy's narrative arc encourages its audience to favor similar sorts of integration in other narratives, including personal stories and history.

9.6 Fantasy asks its heroes to do something about the three great fears mentioned at 9.1: to penetrate the mysteries of the unknown, to recognize the Other as potential ally rather than enemy, and to use the inevitability of death as a spur toward compassion and courage rather than despair.

9.7 As further cause to move away from the idea of conflict as the basis for narrative interest, the confrontation with fear is not a battle one can win. Nor are the things we fear evil in themselves, though they cause some people to do evil things.

9.8 The bodily basis for fear—the shivers and grues that mark its presence—allows it to function as a source for metaphors of all sorts. Through metaphor we impose our bodies on the universe; every abstraction masks a forgotten metaphor.

9.9 In order to keep from being overwhelmed by awareness of death and danger, fairy tales and fantasies advise us to face our fears and to name them.

9.10 The parallel constructions "face your fear" and "name your fear" are both misleading and revealing. They mislead in that the two operations involve very different actions. The latter is a kind of performative speech: a spell of sorts. The former sounds as if it only involves steeling oneself not to look away, but the wiser fantasies such as Le Guin's *A Wizard of Earthsea* and Lewis's *Till We Have Faces* offer a different interpretation: to face something it is necessary first to give it a face.

9.11   The more revealing aspect of the above parallelism is that facing and naming are thus both acts of providing something to that which is otherwise nameless and faceless (and thus truly terrifying).

9.12   Fantasy demonstrates that the only name that can be given to the unknown is one's own. Evil can only be tamed by acknowledging that it comes from oneself. Likewise, the only face that can be given to death is one's own.

9.13   Fear that has been named and faced (that is, given a face) no longer controls one's actions. The final outcome that fantasy promises is not triumph but freedom.

9.14   If fantasy could ever complete its cultural work, fear would lose its political clout. Propaganda and paranoia would no longer be effective tools for holding power. However, that work will never be complete, and fear will never go away completely. Therefore we will never stop needing stories of self-confrontation and transformation.

Works Cited

Introduction: Speaking of Fantasy

Ciardi, John. *How Does a Poem Mean?* Houghton Mifflin, 1959.
Tompkins, Jane. *Sensational Designs: The Cultural Work of American Fiction, 1790–1850*. Oxford University Press, 1986.

Chapter 1: How Fantasy Means: The Shape of Truth

Arnason, Eleanor. "Knapsack Poems." 2002. In *The James Tiptree Award Anthology 3*, edited by Karen Joy Fowler, Pat Murphy, Debbie Notkin, Jeffrey D. Smith. Tachyon, 2007, pp. 239–58.
Attebery, Brian. *Stories about Stories: Fantasy and the Remaking of Myth*. Oxford University Press, 2014.
Bujold, Lois McMaster. *Penric's Demon*. Kindle Edition. Spectrum Literary Agency, 2015.
Butler, Robert. "The Art of Darkness: An Interview with Philip Pullman." *Intelligent Life Magazine*, 3 December, 2007, *Internet Archive*. Available at: web.archive.org/web/20080305011900/http://www.moreintelligentlife.com/node/697. Accessed July 1, 2020.
Crowley, John. *Ka: Dar Oakley in the Ruin of Ymr*. Saga Press, 2017.
Crowley, John. *Little, Big*. Bantam Books, 1981.
Dickinson, Emily. Letter 459A to T.W. Higginson. In *Emily Dickinson Selected Letters*, ed. Thomas H. Johnson, Harvard University Press, 1971.
Dunsany, Lord (Edward John Moreton Drax Plunkett, 18th Baron of Dunsany). *The King of Elfland's Daughter*. Del Rey, 1969.
Egan, Greg. "Reasons to Be Cheerful." In *Luminous*. Gollancz, 1998, pp. 191–227.
Ekman, Stefan. *Here Be Dragons: Exploring Fantasy Maps and Settings*. Wesleyan University Press, 2013.
Fenton, Edward. *The Nine Questions*. Doubleday, 1959.
Hoban, Russell. *Riddley Walker*. Expanded edition. Indiana University Press, 1998.
Jones, Diana Wynne. *Fire and Hemlock*. Greenwillow, 1985.
Kushner, Ellen. *Thomas the Rhymer*. William Morrow, 1990.
Lakoff, George and Mark Johnson. *Metaphors We Live By*. With a new afterword. University of Chicago Press, 2003.
Le Guin, Ursula K. *The Beginning Place*. Harper & Row, 1980.

Le Guin, Ursula K. "Science Fiction and Mrs. Brown." In *The Language of the Night: Essays on Fantasy and Science Fiction*, edited by Susan Wood. Revised edition edited by Ursula K. Le Guin. HarperCollins, 1989, pp. 97–117.

Le Guin, Ursula K. "Why Are Americans Afraid of Dragons?" In *The Language of the Night*, pp. 34–40.

Lewis, C. S. *An Experiment in Criticism*. Cambridge University Press, 1961.

Lewis, C. S. *Till We Have Faces: A Myth Retold*. Harcourt, 1956.

MacDonald, George. "The Fantastic Imagination." In *A Dish of Orts*. Sampson Low, Marston and Company, 1893. Available at: Project Gutenberg, www.gutenberg.org/files/9393/9393-h/9393-h.htm. Accessed June 1, 2020.

MacDonald, George. "The Light Princess." In *The Light Princess and Other Fairy Stories*. Putnam's, 1893. Available at: Project Gutenberg, www.gutenberg.org/ebooks/18811. Accessed June 1, 2020.

MacDonald, George. *The Princess and the Goblin*. Strahan and Company, 1872. Available at: Project Gutenberg, www.gutenberg.org/ebooks/34339. Accessed June 1, 2020.

Nikolajeva, Maria. *The Magic Code: The Use of Magical Patterns in Fantasy for Children*. Almqvist & Wiksell International, 1988.

Poe, Edgar Allan. "The Fall of the House of Usher." In *Tales of the Grotesque and Arabesque*. The Edgar Allan Poe Society of Baltimore, 1840. Available at: www.eapoe.org/works/tales/usherb.htm. Accessed July 1, 2020.

Pullman, Philip. *The Golden Compass*. His Dark Materials, Book 1. Knopf, 1995.

Saler, Michael. *As If: Modern Enchantment and the Literary Prehistory of Virtual Reality*. Oxford University Press, 2012.

Saunders, George. *Lincoln in the Bardo*. Random House, 2017.

Stewart, Sean. *Cloud's End*. Ace, 1996.

Stewart, Sean. *Mockingbird*. Ace Books, 1998.

Tepper, Sheri S. *The End of the Game*. Book club edition combining *Jinian Footseer* (1985), *Dervish Daughter* (1986), and *Jinian Star-eye* (1986). Doubleday, 1987.

Thompson, Stith. *Motif-Index of Folk-Literature: A Classification of Narrative Elements in Folktales, Ballads, Myths, Fables, Mediaeval Romances, Exempla, Fabliaux, Jest-books, and Local Legends*. Revised and expanded edition. 6 vols. Indiana University Press, 1955–58.

Toelken, Barre. *Morning Dew and Roses*. University of Illinois Press, 1995.

Williams, Raymond. *Marxism and Literature*. Oxford University Press, 1977.

Wrightson, Patricia. *The Ice Is Coming*. Atheneum, 1977.

Chapter 2: Realism and the Structures of Fantasy: The Family Story

Alexander, Lloyd. "The Flat-Heeled Muse." *The Horn Book Magazine*, April 1, 1965. Available at: www.hbook.com/?detailStory=flat-heeled-muse. Accessed January 22, 2021.

Attebery, Brian. "Elizabeth Enright and the Family Story as Genre." *Children's Literature*, vol. 37, no. 1, 2009, pp. 114–36.

Barrish, Phillip. *American Literary Realism, Critical Theory, and Intellectual Prestige, 1880–1995*. Cambridge University Press, 2001.

Delany, Samuel R. "About 5,750 Words." In *The Jewel-Hinged Jaw: Notes on the Language of Science Fiction*. 1978. Reprinted Wesleyan University Press, 2009, pp. 1–15.

Eager, Edward. "Daily Magic." *The Horn Book Magazine*, October 1, 1958. www.hbook.com/?detailStory=daily-magic. Accessed January 21, 2021.

Eager, Edward. "A Father's Minority Report." *The Horn Book Magazine*. March 1948, pp. 74 and 104–09. Reprinted in *A Horn Book Sampler on Children's Books and Reading: Selected from Twenty-Five Years of the Horn Book Magazine, 1924–1948*, edited by Norma R. Fryatt. The Horn Book, 1959.

Eager, Edward. *Half Magic*. Harcourt Brace, 1954.

Eager, Edward. *Knight's Castle*. Harcourt Brace, 1956. Citations are to the Odyssey Classic paperback edition.

Eager, Edward. *Seven-Day Magic*. Harcourt Brace. 1954. Citations are to the Odyssey Classic Edition.

Eager, Edward. *The Time Garden*. Harcourt Brace, 1958. Citations are to the Odyssey Classic Edition.

Ellis, Anne W. *The Family Story in the 1960's*. Archon, 1970.

Enright, Elizabeth. The Caterpillar Summer." In *Doublefields: Memories and Stories*. Harcourt, Brace & World. 1966, pp. 67–75.

Enright, Elizabeth. Introduction. In *The Melendy Family*. (Omnibus volume of *The Saturdays*, *The Four-Story Mistake*, and *Then There Were Five*.) Holt, Rinehart and Winston, 1944, pp. vii–x.

Enright, Elizabeth. "The Hero's Changing Face." In *The Contents of the Basket: And Other Papers on Children's Books and Reading.*, edited by Frances Lander Spain. The New York Public Library, 1960, pp. 27–34.

Enright, Elizabeth. "Realism in Children's Literature." *The Horn Book Magazine* April 1967, pp. 165–70.

Enright, Elizabeth. *The Saturdays*. Cadmus Books edition. E. M. Hale. 1941.

Enright, Elizabeth. "The Shush Rush." In *Doublefields: Memories and Stories*. Harcourt, Brace & World. 1966, pp. 19–28.

Enright, Elizabeth. *Tatsinda*. Harcourt, Brace & World, 1963.

Enright, Elizabeth. *Then There Were Five*. Holt, Rinehart and Winston, 1944.

Hirsch, Corinne. "Perspectives on Literary Realism: A Review." *Children's Literature Association Quarterly* vol. 5, no. 3, 1980, pp. 9–15. DOI: 10.1353/chq.0.1370.

Jameson, Fredric. *The Antinomies of Realism*. Verso, 2013.

Kelso, Sylvia. "Re: Quoting You." Email received by Brian Attebery, February 22, 2020.

Lewis, C. S. *An Experiment in Criticism*. Cambridge University Press, 1961.

Lynch-Brown, Carol and Carl M. Tomlinson. *Essentials of Children's Literature*. Allyn, 1993.

Mastern, A. S. "Ordinary magic: Resilience process in development." *American Psychologist*, vol. 56, no. 3, 2001, pp. 227–38.

Pincus, Sarah. "Ordinary Magic: D. W. Winnicott and the E. Nesbit Tradition in Children's Literature." English Honors Papers, Connecticut College, 2014.

Rieder, John. "On defining SF, or Not: Genre Theory, SF, and History." *Science Fiction Studies*, vol. 37, no. 2, 2010, pp. 191–209.

Tolkien, J. R. R. "On Fairy-stories." In *Tree and Leaf*. Allen, 1964. Reprinted in *The Tolkien Reader*. Ballantine, 1966, pp. 3–84.

White, Hayden. "The Historical Text as Literary Artifact." In *Tropics of Discourse: Essays in Cultural Criticism*. Johns Hopkins, 1978, pp. 81–100.

Chapter 3: Neighbors, Myths, and Fantasy

Berger, Peter L. *A Rumor of Angels: Modern Society and the Rediscovery of the Supernatural*. Doubleday, 1970.

Crowley, John. *Aegypt*. Bantam, 1987.

de Bodard, Aliette. *The House of Binding Thorns*. Ace, 2017.

de Bodard, Aliette. *The House of Shattered Wings*. New American Library, 2015. Citations are to the Kindle edition.

de Bodard, Aliette. *The House of Sundering Flames*. Gollancz, 2019.

Dilthey, Wilhelm. *Wilhelm Dilthey: Selected Works, Volume VI: Ethical and World-View Philosophy*. Edited by Rudolf A. Makkreel and Frithjof Rodi, Princeton University Press, 2019.

Greenblatt, Stephen. *Shakespearean Negotiations: The Circulation of Social Energy in Renaissance England*. University of California Press, 1988.

Haraway, Donna. "Situated Knowledges: The Science Question in Feminism and the Privilege of Partial Perspective." In *Simians, Cyborgs, and Women: The Reinvention of Nature*. Routledge, 1991, pp. 183–201.

Hume, Kathryn. *Fantasy and Mimesis: Responses to Reality in Western Literature*. Methuen, 1984.

Le Guin, Ursula K. "Freedom." (A speech in acceptance of the National Book Foundation Medal for Distinguished Contributions to American Letters, November 2014). In *Words Are My Matter: Writings about Life and Books, 2000–2016*. Small Beer Press, 2016, pp. 113–14.

Mandelo, Lee. "Living in Hope is a Discipline: *Fire Logic* by Laurie J. Marks." Tor. com. 23 May 2019. Available at: www.tor.com/2019/05/23/living-in-hope-is-a-discipline-fire-logic-by-laurie-j-marks/. Accessed April 21, 2020.

Marks, Laurie J. *Air Logic*. Small Beer, 2019.

Marks, Laurie J. *Earth Logic*. Tor, 2004.

Marks, Laurie J. "Elemental Magics." Available at: *LaurieJMarks.com* (author's website), lauriejmarks.com/shaftal/elemental-magics.html. Accessed April 29, 2020.

Marks, Laurie J. *Fire Logic*. Tor, 2002.

Marks, Laurie J. *Water Logic*. Small Beer, 2007.

Miéville, China. *The City and the City*. Ballantine, 2009.

Moriarty, Chris. *The Inquisitor's Apprentice*. Harcourt Children's Books, 2011.

Stephens, John and Robyn McCallum. *Retelling Stories, Framing Culture: Traditional Story and Metanarratives in Children's Literature*. 1998.

Toelken, Barre. "Native American Myths Reconsidered." In *American Foundational Myths*, edited by Marin Heusser and Gudrun Grabher. Swiss Papers in English Language and Literature, Vol. 14. Gunter Narr Verlag, 2002, pp. 83–102.

van Sydow, Carl Wilhelm. *Selected Papers on Folklore*. Rosenkilde and Bagger, 1948. Reprinted Arno, 1977.

Wecker, Helene. *The Golem and the Jinni*. HarperCollins 2013.

Wecker, Helene. "Q and A with Helene." *Helene Wecker* (author's website; this Q and A no longer on the website). http://www.helenewecker.com/about-helene-wecker/q-a-with-helene/. Accessed April 16, 2020.

Chapter 4: If Not Conflict, Then What?
Metaphors for Narrative Interest

Aiken, Joan. *The Way to Write for Children: An Introduction to the Craft of Writing Children's Literature*. Revised and updated edition, Macmillan, 1999.

Atkin, Albert. "Peirce's Theory of Signs." October 13, 2006; revised November 15, 2010. *Stanford Encyclopedia of Philosophy*, available at: plato.stanford.edu/entries/peirce-semiotics/#Inter. Accessed April 3. 2020.

Carroll, Lewis (Dodgson, Charles). *Through the Looking-Glass*. 1871. The Millennium Fulcrum Edition 1.7. Available at: Project Gutenberg, www.gutenberg.org/files/12/12-h/12-h.htm, 2016. Accessed July 2, 2020.

Chatman, Seymour. *Reading Narrative Fiction*. Macmillan, 1993.

Chatman, Seymour. *Story and Discourse: Narrative Structure in Fiction and Film*. Cornell University Press, 1978.

Eager, Edward. *Half Magic*. Harcourt Brace, 1954.

Forster, E. M. *Aspects of the Novel*. Harcourt, 1927.

Hardinge, Frances. *Gullstruck Island*. Macmillan, 2009.

Hogan, Patrick Colm. *How Authors' Minds Make Stories*. Cambridge University Press, 2013.

Jones, Diana Wynne. *Witch Week*. Random House, 1988.

Lacan, Jacques. "Seminar on *The Purloined Letter*." Translated by Geoffrey Mehlman. *Yale French Studies* 48, 1972, pp. 39–72. DOI: 10.2307/2929623.

Lakoff, George and Mark Johnson. *Metaphors We Live By*. University of Chicago Press, 2008.

Le Guin, Ursula K. "Conflict." In *Dancing at the Edge of the World: Thoughts on Words, Women, Places*. Grove Press, 1989, pp. 190–1.

McKillip, Patricia. *The Bards of Bone Plain*. Ace, 2010. Citations are to the Kindle edition.

McKillip, Patricia. *The Riddle-Master of Hed*. Del Rey, 1976.

McNulty, Bridget, Brendan McNulty, et al. "6 story conflicts possible in your book." *Now Novel*. 2012–19. Available at: www.nownovel.com/blog/kind-conflicts-possible-story/. Accessed February 15, 2019.

Melnick, Daniel. "Fullness of Dissonance: Music and the Reader's Experience of Modern Fiction." *Modern Fiction Studies*, vol. 25, no. 2, 1979, pp. 209–22.

Merriam Webster Dictionary. Available at: https://www.merriam-webster.com/dictionary/occultation. Accessed January 22, 2021.

Miéville, China. "Editorial Introduction." *Historical Materialism*, vol. 10, no. 4, 2002, pp. 39–49.

Oziewicz, Marek. *Justice in Young Adult Speculative Fiction: A Cognitive Reading.* Children's Literature and Culture Book 33. Routledge, 2015.

Suede, Damon. "Fictional Friction." Available at: www.damonsuede.com/articles/FictionalFriction.html, 2010. Originally published in *The Pot of Gold* (#9, Q3, 2011), the newsletter of the Rainbow Romance Writers chapter of the Romance Writers of America. Accessed April 3, 2020.

Tolkien, J. R. R. "On Fairy-stories." In *Tree and Leaf*. Allen, 1964. Reprinted in *The Tolkien Reader*. Ballantine, 1966, pp. 3–84.

Wilson, G. Willow. *Alif the Unseen*. Grove Press, 2012. Citations are to the Kindle edition.

Chapter 5: A Mitochondrial Theory of Literature
Fantasy and Intertextuality

Atwood, Margaret. *The Penelopiad*. Canongate, 2005.

Bradley, Marion Zimmer. *The Firebrand*. Simon and Schuster, 1987.

Bradley, Mary Hastings. *On the Gorilla Trail*. Appleton, 1923.

Fowler, Karen Joy. *The Jane Austen Book Club*. Putnam, 2004.

Fowler, Karen Joy. *We Are All Completely Beside Ourselves*. Putnam, 2013.

Fowler, Karen Joy. "What I Didn't See." *Sci-Fiction* 2002. Reprinted in *What I Didn't See and Other Stories*. Small Beer Press, 2010, pp. 169–89.

Glyer, Diana Pavlac. *The Company They Keep: C. S. Lewis and J. R. R. Tolkien as Writers in Community*. The Kent State University Press, 2007.

Kessel, John. "Pride and Prometheus." In *The Baum Plan for Financial Independence and Other Stories*. Small Beer Press, 2008, pp. 279–315.

Kessel, John. "Stories for Men." In The Baum Plan for Financial Independence and Other Stories, pp. 85–163.

Lakoff, George and Mark Johnson. *Metaphors We Live By*. Revised edition. The University of Chicago Press, 2003.

Lawrence, Clinton. "Interview: Karen Joy Fowler." *Strange Horizons*, March 22, 2004. Available at: http://strangehorizons.com/non-fiction/articles/interview-karen-joy-fowler/. Accessed November 5, 2017.

Le Guin, Ursula K. *Always Coming Home*. Harper & Row, 1985.

Le Guin, Ursula K. "The Carrier-Bag Theory of Fiction." In *Dancing at the End of the World: Thoughts on Words, Women, Places*. Grove, 1989, pp. 149–54.

Le Guin, Ursula K. "Disappearing Grandmothers." In *Words Are My Matter: Writings About Life and Books, 2000-2016*. Small Beer Press, 2016, pp. 88–94.

Le Guin, Ursula K. *Lavinia*. Harcourt, 2008.

L'Engle, Madeleine. *A Wind in the Door*. Farrar, Straus and Giroux, 1973.

Miller, T. S. "Myth-Remaking in the Shadow of Vergil: The Captive(ated) Voice of Ursula K. Le Guin's *Lavinia.*" *Mythlore* 29: 1/ 2 (Fall/Winter 2010), pp. 29–51.

Moore, Alan. "By the Book." *The New York Times Book Review* September 8, 2016, p. 4.

Oyeyemi, Helen. *Boy, Snow, Bird.* Picador, 2014.

Phillips, Julie. James Tiptree, Jr. *The Double Life of Alice B. Sheldon.* St. Martin's Press, 2006.

Russ, Joanna. *How to Suppress Women's Writing.* University of Texas Press, 1983.

Sheldon, Alice (as James Tiptree, Jr.). "The Psychologist Who Wouldn't Do Awful Things to Rats." In *Star Songs of an Old Primate.* Ballantine, 1979, pp. 227–54.

Sheldon, Alice (as James Tiptree, Jr.). "The Women Men Don't See." 1973. In *The Norton Book of Science Fiction,* ed. Ursula K. Le Guin and Brian Attebery, with Karen Joy Fowler. Norton, 1999, pp. 255–79.

Sulway, Nike. "The Karen Joy Fowler Book Club." *Lightspeed Magazine,* October 2015. Accessed May 23, 2020.

Sulway, Nike. *Rupetta.* Tartarus Press, 2013.

Wood, Gaby. "The Invention of Angela Carter is an exemplary biography of a weird and wonderful writer—review." *The Telegraph,* October 16, 2016. www.telegraph.co.uk/books/what-to-read/the-invention-of-angela-carter-is-an-exemplary-biography-of-a-we/. Accessed November 5, 2017.

Chapter 6: Young Adult Dystopias and Yin Adult Utopias

Anderson, M. T. *Feed.* Candlewick Press, 2002.

Araújo, Carolina. "Philosopher-kings: A Communitarian Political Project." In *Philosopher Kings and Tragic Heroes: Essays on Images and Ideas from Western Greece,* edited by Heather L. Reid and Davide Tanasi. Parnassos Press, 2016, pp. 143–58. Available at: *JSTOR* https://doi.org/10.2307/j.ctvbj7gjn. Accessed September 8, 2021.

Attebery, Brian. *Decoding Gender in Science Fiction.* Routledge, 2002.

Atwood, Margaret. *The Handmaid's Tale.* McClelland and Stewart, 1985.

Bacon, Francis. *New Atlantis.* 1627. Republished in *Three Early Modern Utopias,* edited by Susan Bruce. Oxford University Press, 1999, pp. 149–86.

Baum, L. Frank. *The Emerald City of Oz.* Reilly & Britton, 1910.

Bellamy, Edward. *Looking Backward 2000–1887.* Ticknor, 1888.

Bradbury, Ray. "Coda." In *Fahrenheit 451.* Ballantine/Del Rey, 1979.

Burdekin, Katharine. *Swastika Night.* 1937 (as by Murray Constantine, pseudonym). Reprint, with an introduction by Daphne Patai. The Feminist Press, 1985.

Collins, Suzanne. *The Hunger Games.* Scholastic, 2008.

Delany, Samuel R. *Triton.* Bantam, 1976.Du Bois, William Pène. *The Twenty-One Balloons.* Viking, 1948.

Duncan, Andy. "An Agent of Utopia." In *An Agent of Utopia: New and Selected Stories.* Small Beer, 2018, pp. 1–32.

Gilman, Charlotte Perkins. *Herland*. Serialized in *The Forerunner*, 1915. First book publication The Women's Press and Pantheon, 1979.

Huxley, Aldous. *Brave New World*, Chatto & Windus, 1932.

Huxley, Aldous. *Island*. Chatto & Windus, 1962.

Jameson, Fredric. *Valences of the Dialectic*. Verso, 2009.

Jeffers, Robinson. "Shine, Perishing Republic." In *The Selected Poetry of Robinson Jeffers*, edited by Tim Hunt. Stanford University Press, 2001, p. 23.

Johnson, Alaya Dawn. *The Summer Prince*. Scholastic, 2013.Kotin, Joshua. *Utopias of One*. Princeton University Press, 2017.

Le Guin, Ursula K."All Happy Families." In *The Wave in the Mind: Talks and Essays on the Writer, the Reader, and the Imagination*. Shambhala, 2004, pp. 33–7.

Le Guin, Ursula K. *Always Coming Home*. Author's Expanded Edition, edited by Brian Attebery. Library of America, 2019.

Le Guin, Ursula K. "The Day Before the Revolution." *Galaxy*, 1974. Reprinted in *The Wind's Twelve Quarters: Short Stories*. Harper & Row, 1975, pp. 285–303.

Le Guin, Ursula K. *The Dispossessed: An Ambiguous Utopia*. Harper & Row, 1974.

Le Guin, Ursula K. "A Non-Euclidean View of California as a Cold Place to Be." *The Yale Review*, 1983. Reprinted in *Always Coming Home*, pp. 703–24.

Le Guin, Ursula K. "The Ones Who Walk Away from Omelas." *New Dimensions 3*, 1973; Reprinted in *The Wind's Twelve Quarters*, pp. 275–84.

Lensing, George S. *Making the Poem: Stevens' Approaches*. Louisiana State University Press, 2018.

Mannheim, Karl. *Ideology and Utopia: An Introduction to the Sociology of Knowledge*. Routledge, 1936.

Manuel, Frank and Fritzie P. Manuel, *Utopian Thought in the Western World*. Harvard University Press, 1979.

Mechling, Jay. "Solo Folklore." *Western Folklore*, vol. 65, no. 4, 2006, pp. 435–53.

Michel, Dee. *Friends of Dorothy: Why Gay Boys and Gay Men Love The Wizard of Oz*. Dark Ink Press, 2018.

Miéville, China. "Editorial Introduction." *Historical Materialism*, vol. 10, no. 4, 2002, pp. 39–49.

Moylan, Tom. *Demand the Impossible: Science Fiction and the Utopian Imagination*. Methuen, 1986.

Nesbit, E. *The Story of the Amulet*. Unwin, 1906.

Oring, Elliott. "Dyadic Traditions." *Journal of Folklore Research*, vol. 21, no. 1, 1984, pp. 19–28. Available at: *JSTOR*, www.jstor.org/stable/3814341. Accessed September 15, 2021.

Robinson, Kim Stanley. *Pacific Edge*. Tor, 1990.

Russ, Joanna. *The Female Man*. Bantam, 1975.

Sargent, Lyman Tower. *Utopian Literature in English: An Annotated Bibliography From 1516 to the Present*, 2016. Available at: https://doi.org/10.18113/P8WC77. Accessed June 15, 2020.

Shawl, Nisi. "Building Love, and the Future We Deserve: *The Summer Prince* by Alaya Dawn Johnson" Tor.com, Feb. 5, 2019. Available at: www.tor.com/2019/02/05/building-love-and-the-future-we-deserve-the-summer-prince-by-alaya-dawn-johnson/. Accessed July 6, 2020.

Sheldon, Raccoona (Alice Sheldon). "Your Faces, O My Sisters! Your Faces Filled of Light." In *Aurora: Beyond Equality*, edited by Vonda N. McIntyre and Susan Janice Anderson. Fawcett, 1976, pp. 16–35.

Stevens, Wallace. "The Man with the Blue Guitar. |In *The Palm at the End of the Mind: Selected Poems and a Play*, edited by Holly Stevens. Vintage, 1972, pp. 133–50.

Tiptree, James, Jr. (Alice Sheldon). "Houston, Houston, Do You Read?" In *Aurora: Beyond Equality*, edited by Vonda N. McIntyre and Susan Janice Anderson. Fawcett, 1976, pp. 36–98.

Walton, Jo. *The Just City*. Tor, 2015.

Walton, Jo. *Necessity*. Tor, 2016.

Walton, Jo. *The Philosopher Kings*. Tor, 2015.

Wells, H. G. *A Modern Utopia*. Unwin, 1905.

Wright, Austin Tappan. *Islandia*. Farrar & Rinehart, 1942.

Zamyatin, Yevgeny. *We*. First published (in English translation) in 1924. Translated by Mirra Ginsburg. Avon, 1972.

Chapter 7: Gender and Fantasy: Employing Fairy Tales

Andersen, Hans Christian. "The Ugly Duckling." In *Andersen's Fairy Tales*, translated by Mrs. E. V. Lucas and Mrs. H. B. Paull. Grossett, 1945, pp. 70–82.

Attebery, Brian. "Reinventing Masculinity in Fairy Tales by Men." *Marvels & Tales: Journal of Fairy-Tale Studies*, vol. 32, no. 2, 2018, pp. 314–37.

Bacchilega, Cristina. *Postmodern Fairy Tales: Gender and Narrative Strategies*. University of Pennsylvania Press, 1997.

Barzak, Christopher. "The Boy Who Went Forth." In *Brothers and Beasts: An Anthology of Men on Fairy Tales*, edited by Kate Bernheimer. Wayne State University Press, 2007, pp. 27–33.

Berman, Steve. *Red Caps: New Fairy Tales for Out of the Ordinary Readers*. Lethe, 2014.

Bernheimer, Kate, ed. *Brothers and Beasts: An Anthology of Men on Fairy Tales*, Wayne State University Press, 2007.

Bernheimer, Kate, ed. *Mirror, Mirror on the Wall: Women Writers Explore Their Favorite Fairy Tales*. Anchor Books, 1998.Bettelheim, Bruno. *The Uses of Enchantment: The Meaning and Importance of Fairy Tales*. Vintage, 1977.

Billy Elliot. Directed by Stephen Daldry, performances by Jamie Bell and Julie Walters. BBC Films, 2000.

Bly, Robert. *Iron John: A Book about Men*. Addison, 1990.

Brockmeier, Kevin. "A Day in the Life of Half of Rumpelstiltskin." In *My Mother She Killed Me, My Father He Ate Me: Forty New Fairy Tales*, edited by Kate Bernheimer, with Carmen Giménez Smith. Penguin, 2010, pp. 59–73.

Carter, Angela. *The Bloody Chamber*. Harper, 1979.

Carter, Angela. *The Virago Book of Fairy Tales*. Virago Press, 1990.

Cashorali, Peter. *Fairy Tales: Traditional Stories Retold for Gay Men.* HarperCollins, 1998.

Cunningham, Michael. *A Wild Swan and Other Tales.* Farrar, Straus & Giroux, 2015.

Cunningham, Michael. "Adult Fairy Tales: An Interview with Michael Cunningham." Interview with Michael Merriam. *Los Angeles Review of Books,* November 26, 2015. Available at: lareviewofbooks.org/article/adult-fairy-tales/. Accessed March 8, 2016.

Datlow, Ellen. "Re: Fairy Tales Series," Pers. comm. received by Brian Attebery, Mar. 20, 2016.

Datlow, Ellen and Terri Windling, eds. *Snow White, Blood Red.* AvoNova, 1993.

Dégh, Linda. *Folktales and Society: Story-telling in a Hungarian Peasant Community.* Translated by Emily M. Schossberger. Indiana University Press, 1969.

Frost, Gregory. *Fitcher's Brides.* Tor, 2002.

Gaiman, Neil. "Troll Bridge." In *Smoke and Mirrors: Short Fictions and Illusions.* HarperCollins, 2001, pp. 57–68.

Grahame, Kenneth. "The Reluctant Dragon." In *Dream Days.* John Lane, The Bodley Head, 1898.

Into the Woods. Directed by James Lapine, book by James Lapine, music and lyrics by Stephen Sondheim, American Playhouse,1991. DVD Image Entertainment, 1999.

Jacobs, Joseph. "A Dozen at One Blow." In *European Folk and Fairy Tales,* edited by Joseph Jacobs. G. P Putnam's Sons, 1916. Reprinted at *Surlalune Fairy Tales.* Available at: www.surlalunefairytales.com/a-g/brave-little-tailor/stories/dozenblow.html. Accessed June 5, 2020.

Jarrell, Randall. "The Black Swan." In *The Complete Poems.* Farrar, Strauss & Giroux, 1969.

Jorgensen, Jeana Sommer. *Gender and the Body in Classical European Fairy Tales.* Dissertation, Indiana University, 2012.

Lee, Tanith. *Red as Blood, or Tales from the Sisters Grimmer.* DAW, 1983.

Link, Kelly. "Travels with the Snow Queen." *Lady Churchill's Rosebud Wristlet,* Winter 1996–97. Reprinted in Kelly Link, *Stranger Things Happen.* Small Beer Press, 2001, pp. 99–120.

Lundell, Torberg. "Gender-Related Biases in the Type and Motif Indexes of Aarne and Thompson." In *Fairy Tales and Society: Illusion, Allusion, and Paradigm,* edited by Ruth B. Bottigheimer. University of Pennsylvania Press, 1986, pp. 149–63.

McCarthy, William Bernard, Cheryl Oxford, and Joseph Daniel Sobol, eds. *Jack in Two Worlds: Contemporary North American Tales and their Tellers.* UNC Press Books, 1994.

McKinley, Robin. *Beauty: A Retelling of the Story of Beauty and the Beast.* Harper & Row, 1978.

Mejia, Michael. "Nobeard." *Brothers and Beasts: An Anthology of Men on Fairy Tales,* edited by Kate Bernheimer, Wayne State University Press, 2007, pp. 123–33.

Munsch, Robert. *The Paper Bag Princess.* Annick Press, 1980.

Palwick, Susan. "Ever After." In *The Fate of Mice.* Tachyon, 2007, pp. 141–66.

Phelps, Ethel Johnston, ed. *Tatterhood and Other Tales: Stories of Magic and Adventure*. Feminist Press at CUNY, 1978.

Rowe, Karen. "Feminism and Fairy Tales," *Women's Studies: An Interdisciplinary Journal*, vol. 6, no.3, 1979, pp. 237–57.

Runberg, Marianne, Birgitte Brun, and Ernst W. Pedersen, eds. *Symbols of the Soul: Therapy and Guidance through Fairy Tales*. Jessica Kingsley Publishers, 1993.

Schimel, Lawrence. *The Drag Queen of Elfland and Other Stories*. Circlet, 1997.

Seifert, Lewis C. *Fairy Tales, Sexuality, and Gender in France, 1690–1715: Nostalgic Utopias*. Cambridge University Press, 1996.

Sherman, Delia. "Snow White to the Prince." In *The Armless Maiden and Other Tales for Childhood's Survivors*, edited by Terri Windling, Tor, 1995, pp. 40–1.

Silverman, Yehudit. "The Story Within—Myth and Fairy Tale in Therapy." *The Arts in Psychotherapy*, vol. 31, no. 3, June 2004, pp. 127–35.

Stone, Kay F. "Things Walt Disney Never Told Us," *The Journal of American Folklore*, vol. 88, no. 347, 1975, pp. 42–50. Available at: JSTOR, www.jstor.org/stable/539184. Accessed July 6, 2020.

Taggart, James M. *The Bear and His Sons: Masculinity in Spanish and Mexican Folktales*. University of Texas Press, 1997.

Tatar, Maria. *The Hard Facts of the Grimms' Fairy Tales*. Princeton University Press, 1987.

Thomas, Frank and Ollie Johnston. *Disney Animation: The Illusion of Life*. Abbeville, 1981.

Warner, Marina. *From the Beast to the Blonde: On Fairy Tales and Their Tellers*. Chatto & Windus, 1994.

Windling, Terri, ed. *The Armless Maiden And Other Tales for Childhood's Survivors*. Tor, 1995.

Wullschlager, Jackie. *Hans Christian Andersen: The Life of a Storyteller*. Knopf, 2000.

Yolen, Jane. *Sleeping Ugly*. Coward, McCann & Geoghegan, 1981.

Yolen, Jane. *Touch Magic: Fantasy, Faerie & Folklore in the Literature of Childhood*. Expanded edition. August House, 2000.

Zipes, Jack, ed. *Don't Bet on the Prince*. Routledge, 1987.

Zipes, Jack. *Fairy Tales and the Art of Subversion*. Heinemann, 1983.

Zipes, Jack. "Spreading Myths about Fairy Tales: A Critical Commentary on Robert Bly's Iron John." *New German Critique* no. 55 (Winter, 1992), pp. 3–19. Available at: JSTOR, https://doi-org.libpublic3.library.isu.edu/10.2307/488286. Accessed September 9, 2021.

Chapter 8: The Politics of Fantasy

Andersen, Hans Christian. "The Little Mermaid." Originally published in Danish, 1837, as "Den lille havfrue." In *Hans Andersen's Fairy Tales Second Series*, ed. J. H. Stickney, no translator listed. Ginn & Company, 1915. Electronic text, Project Gutenberg, 2010.

Anderson, M. T. *The Astonishing Life of Octavian Nothing Traitor to the Nation. Volume 1: The Pox Party*. Walker, 2007.

Attebery, Brian. *Decoding Gender in Science Fiction*. Routledge, 2002.

Attebery, Brian. "The Politics (If Any) of Fantasy." *Journal of the Fantastic in the Arts*, vol. 4, no.1, 1991, pp. 7–28.

Cecire, Maria Sachiko. *Re-Enchanted: The Rise of Children's Fantasy Literature in the Twentieth Century*. University of Minnesota Press, 2019.

Cho, Zen. *Sorcerer to the Crown*. Penguin, 2015.

Clute, John. "Taproot Texts." In *Encyclopedia of Fantasy*, edited by John Clute and John Grant. St. Martin's, 1997.

Delany, Samuel R. *Trouble on Triton*. Originally published as *Triton*. Bantam, 1976.

Delany, Samuel R. *Tales of Nevèrÿon*. Bantam, 1979.

Ellis, Bill. "'Fake News' in the Contemporary Legend Dynamic." *Journal of American Folklore*, vol 131, no. 522, Fall 2018, pp. 398–404.

Faucheux, Amandine H. "Race and Sexuality in Nalo Hopkinson's Oeuvre; or, Queer Afrofuturism." *Science Fiction Studies*, vol. 44, no. 3, November 2017, pp. 563–80. Available at: www.jstor.org/stable/10.5621/sciefictstud.44.3.0563. Accessed August 31, 2021.

Haraway, Donna. "A Cyborg Manifesto: Science, Technology and Socialist-Feminism in the 1980s." *Socialist Review*, 1985. Reprinted in *Simians, Cyborgs and Women: The Reinvention of Nature*. Routledge, 1991, pp. 203–30.

Hoffmann, E.T.A. "The Sandman." 1817. In *Weird Tales by E. T. A. Hoffmann, A new Translation from the German*. 2 vols. Translated by J. T. Bealby. Charles Scribner's, 1885. Electronic text, Project Gutenberg, 2010.

Hopkinson, Nalo. *The Chaos*. Margaret K. McElderry, 2012.

Hopkinson, Nalo. "*Code-sliding.*" Available at: http://blacknetart.com/Hopkinson.html. Accessed January 4, 2021. Originally published at www.sff.net/people/nalo/writing/slide.html.

Jackson, Rosemary. *Fantasy: The Literature of Subversion*. Methuen, 1981.

Le Guin, Ursula K. "From Elfland to Poughkeepsie." In *The Language of the Night: Essays on Fantasy and Science Fiction*, edited by Susan Wood, revised edition edited by Ursula K. Le Guin. HarperCollins, 1989, pp. 78–92.

Le Guin, Ursula K. *Gifts*. Harcourt, 2004.

Le Guin, Ursula K. *Tehanu*. Atheneum, 1990.

Le Guin, Ursula K. *Powers*. Harcourt, 2007.

Le Guin, Ursula K. *Voices*. Harcourt, 2006.

Luckhurst, Roger. "In the Zone: Topologies of Genre Weirdness." In *Gothic Science Fiction 1980–2010*, edited by Sara Wasson and Emily Alder. Liverpool University Press, 2011, pp. 21–35.

McBeth, Mark K. "Introduction: Political Science, Public Policy, and Narrative." In *Narrative, Identity, and Academic Commmunity in Higher Education*, edited by Brian Attebery, John Gribas, Mark K. McBeth, Paul Sivitz, and Kandi Turley-Ames. Routledge Research in Higher Education. Routledge, 2017, pp. 5–8.

McHale, Brian. *Postmodernist Fiction*. Methuen, 1987.

Monleón, José B. *A Specter is Haunting Europe: A Sociohistorical Approach to the Fantastic*. Princeton University Press, 1990.

Nodelman, Perry. "The Other: Orientalism, Colonialism, and Children's Literature," *Children's Literature Association Quarterly*, vol. 17, no. 1, Spring 1992, pp. 29–35.

Proietti, Salvator. Pers. comm. re: James Tiptree Book Club. Received by Brian Attebery, May 30, 2017.

Rose, Jacqueline. *The Case of Peter Pan, or, the Impossibility of Children's Literature*. Macmillan, 1989.

Shaw, Kristen. "'Sticky' Identities: Race, Gender, and Sexuality in Nalo Hopkinson's *The Chaos*." *Journal of the Fantastic in the Arts*, vol. 28, no. 3, 2017, pp. 425–50.

Shippey, T. A. *The Road to Middle-Earth*. Houghton Mifflin, 1983. Strugatsky, Arkady and Boris Strugatsky. *Roadside Picnic*. Translated by Antonina W. Bouis. Macmillan, 1977.

Stuart, Alasdair. "Interview: Kai Ashante Wilson, author of *The Sorcerer of the Wildeeps*." *The Man of Words* November 6, 2015 Available at: https://alasdairstuart.com/2015/11/06/interview-kai-ashante-wilson-author-of-the-sorcerer-of-the-wildeeps/. Accessed January 2, 2021.

Thomas, Ebony Elizabeth. *The Dark Fantastic: Race and the Imagination from Harry Potter to the Hunger Games*. New York University Press, 2019.

Thurber, James. *The 13 Clocks*. Simon and Schuster, 1950.

VanderMeer, Jeff. *Annihilation*. Fourth Estate, 2015.

Wilson, Kai Ashante. *The Sorcerer of the Wildeeps*. Tom Doherty Associates, 2015.

Wilson, Kai Ashante. *A Taste of Honey*. Tom Doherty Associates, 2016.

Wrede, Patricia C. and Caroline Stevermer. *Sorcery and Cecelia*. Ace, 1988.

Young, Helen. *Race and Popular Fantasy Literature: Habits of Whiteness*. Routledge, 2016.

Chapter 9: *Timor mortis conturbat me*: Fantasy and Fear

Baum, L. Frank. *The Wonderful Wizard of Oz*. 1900. Reprinted in *The Wizard of Oz*, Critical Heritage Series, edited by Michael Patrick Hearn. Schocken, 1983.

Clute, John. "Fantasy." In *The Encyclopedia of Fantasy*, edited by John Clute and John Grant. St. Martin's Press, 1997.

Clute, John. "Lose the Amnesia." Review of *The Butcher Bird* by Richard Kadrey and *Sides* by Peter Straub. In *Canary Fever: Reviews*. Beccon, 2009, pp. 320–23. Originally published in *Interzone* 212 (Sept–Oct 2007).

Eco, Umberto. *The Role of the Reader: Explorations in the Semiotics of Texts*. Indiana University Press, 1979.

Eddison, E. R. *The Worm Ouroboros*. 1922. Ballantine, 1967.

Eliot, T. S. "Marina." In *The Complete Poems and Plays: 1909–1950*. Harcourt, 1971, p. 72.

Garner, Alan. *The Weirdstone of Brisingamen*. William Collins, 1960.

James, Marlon. *Black Leopard Red Wolf*. Riverhead Books, 2019.

Johnson, Mark. *The Body in the Mind: The Bodily Basis of Meaning, Imagination, and Reason*. The University of Chicago Press, 1987.

Kierkegaard, Søren. *The Concept of Anxiety: A Simple Psychologically Orienting Deliberation on the Dogmatic Issue of Hereditary Sin*. Edited and translated by Reidar Thomte in collaboration with Albert B. Anderson. Princeton University Press, 1980.

Kierkegaard, Søren. *Fear and Trembling: A Dialectical Lyric*. Published 1843 as *Frygt og baeven: dialektisk lyrik*. Translated by Robert Payne. Oxford University Press, 1939.

King, Stephen. *Danse Macabre*. Berkley, 1983.

Le Guin, Ursula K. "The Child and the Shadow." In *The Language of the Night: Essays on Fantasy and Science Fiction*, edited by Susan Wood. Revised edition edited by Ursula K. Le Guin. HarperCollins, 1989, pp. 54–67.

Le Guin, Ursula K. *The Farthest Shore*. Atheneum, 1973.

Le Guin, Ursula K. "A Response to the Le Guin Issue." *Science-Fiction Studies* vol. 3, no. 1, 1976, pp. 43–46.

Le Guin, Ursula K. *A Wizard of Earthsea*. Parnassus, 1968. Lewis, C. S. *Till We Have Faces: A Myth Retold*. Harcourt, 1956.

Lovecraft, H. P. "Supernatural Horror in Literature." *The H. P. Lovecraft Archive*. Donovan K. Loucks, 2009. www.hplovecraft.com/writings/texts/essays/shil.aspx. Accessed June 16, 2020.

MacDonald, George. *The Princess and Curdie*. 1883. David McKay, n.d.

Moher, Aidan. "Art of SFF: Charles Vess on Working with Ursula K. Le Guin on *The Books of Earthsea*." Tor.com November 9, 2018. Available at: www.tor.com/2018/11/09/art-of-sff-charles-vess-on-working-with-ursula-le-guin-on-the-books-of-earthsea/. Accessed June 18, 2020.

Nesbit. E. *The Enchanted Castle*. 1907. Ernest Benn, 1956.

Okorafor, Nnedi. *Who Fears Death*. Daw Books, 2010.

Poe, Edgar Allan. "The Philosophy of Composition." *Graham's Magazine*, vol. XXVIII, no. 4, April 1846, 28: 163–7. *The Writings of Edgar Allan Poe*. The Edgar Allan Poe Society of Baltimore, 2011. Available at: https://www.eapoe.org/works/essays/philcomp.htm. Accessed June 16, 2020.

Propp, V[ladimir]. *Morphology of the Folktale*. Translated by Laurence Scott. Second edition revised and edited by Louis A. Wagner. University of Texas Press, 1968.

Roberts, Leonard W. *South from Hell-fer-Sartin: Kentucky Mountain Folk Tales*. The University Press of Kentucky, 1988.

Tolkien, J. R. R. "On Fairy-stories." In *The Tolkien Reader*. Ballantine, 1966, pp. 3–84.

Wrightson, Patricia. *A Little Fear*. New York: Atheneum, 1983,

Index

For the benefit of digital users, table terms that span two pages (e.g., 52–53) may, on occasion, appear on only one of those pages.